GLOBALIZATION
AND MONEY

GLOBALIZATION

Series Editors

Manfred B. Steger

*Royal Melbourne Institute of Technology
and University of Hawai'i–Mānoa*

and

Terrell Carver

University of Bristol

"Globalization" has become *the* buzzword of our time. But what does it mean? Rather than forcing a complicated social phenomenon into a single analytical framework, this series seeks to present globalization as a multidimensional process constituted by complex, often contradictory interactions of global, regional, and local aspects of social life. Since conventional disciplinary borders and lines of demarcation are losing their old rationales in a globalizing world, authors in this series apply an interdisciplinary framework to the study of globalization. In short, the main purpose and objective of this series is to support subject-specific inquiries into the dynamics and effects of contemporary globalization and its varying impacts across, between, and within societies.

Globalization and Sovereignty
John Agnew

Globalization and War
Tarak Barkawi

Globalization and Human Security
Paul Battersby and Joseph M. Siracusa

Globalization and the Environment
Peter Christoff and Robyn Eckersley

Globalization and American Popular Culture, 3rd ed.
Lane Crothers

Globalization and Militarism
Cynthia Enloe

Globalization and Law
Adam Gearey

Globalization and Feminist Activism
Mary E. Hawkesworth

Globalization and Postcolonialism
Sankaran Krishna

Globalization and Media
Jack Lule

Globalization and Social Movements, 2nd ed.
Valentine Moghadam

Globalization and Terrorism, 2nd ed.
Jamal R. Nassar

Globalization and Culture, 2nd ed.
Jan Nederveen Pieterse

Globalization and International Political Economy
Mark Rupert and M. Scott Solomon

Globalization and Citizenship
Hans Schattle

Globalization and Islamism
Nevzat Soguk

Globalisms, 3rd ed.
Manfred B. Steger

Rethinking Globalism
Edited by Manfred B. Steger

Globalization and Labor
Dimitris Stevis and Terry Boswell

Globaloney 2.0
Michael Veseth

 Supported by the Globalization Research Center at the University of Hawai'i, Mānoa

GLOBALIZATION AND MONEY
A GLOBAL SOUTH PERSPECTIVE

SUPRIYA SINGH

ROWMAN & LITTLEFIELD
Lanham • Boulder • New York • Toronto • Plymouth, UK

Published by Rowman & Littlefield
4501 Forbes Boulevard, Suite 200, Lanham, Maryland 20706
www.rowman.com

10 Thornbury Road, Plymouth PL6 7PP, United Kingdom

British Library Cataloguing in Publication Information Available

Library of Congress Cataloging-in-Publication Data
Singh, Supriya, author.
  Globalization and money : a global South perspective / Supriya Singh.
    pages cm — (Globalization)
  Includes bibliographical references and index.
  ISBN 978-1-4422-1355-5 (cloth : alk. paper) — ISBN 978-1-4422-1356-2 (pbk. : alk. paper) — ISBN 978-1-4422-1357-9 (electronic) 1. Globalization—Economic aspects—Developing countries. 2. Money—Social aspects—Developing countries. 3. Banks and banking—Developing countries. 4. Banks and banking, Mobile—Developing countries. 5. Mobile commerce—Developing countries. 6. Electronic funds transfers—Developing countries. 7. Women—Developing countries—Finance, Personal. 8. Households—Economic aspects—Developing countries. 9. Migrant remittances—Developing countries. I. Title. II. Series: Globalization (Lanham, Md.)
  HG1496.S56 2013
  332.491724—dc23

2013030895

Printed in the United States of America

CONTENTS

PREFACE

The full moon shines over the Mara River in Kenya just before dawn. People have come from the United States, Italy, Portugal, China, Mexico, and Australia to a safari lodge on the grasslands of Maasai Mara to see wildebeests, giraffes, zebras, topis, impalas, and Thomson's gazelles grazing side by side. People waiting in the early dawn have paid by credit card (which attracts a surcharge), bank transfer (through a correspondent bank), or cash. The market, the wilderness, and personal dreams come together as people wonder if they will see cheetahs sitting on a rock, lions hidden in the grass, hippos in the river, crocodiles sunning themselves satiated on dead wildebeest, or perhaps even a few elephants, though most have moved away to escape the sound made by the hundreds of thousands of wildebeests who have migrated to the Maasai Mara.

Later in the day my guide goes to the dusty and nearly deserted market town of Talek to deposit his tips in euros and US dollars into his mobile money M-PESA account in Kenya shillings. "KSh 21,000," he says, showing me his M-PESA balance—worth about $250—on his mobile phone. He transfers some of this to his daughter in Nairobi, who has just been appointed to her first teaching job. The rest goes to his wife two hours away so that she can put it toward the new house they are building in town.

This book is about how men and women, particularly the poor and the unbanked in the global South, use money in ways that empower them. It tells how women and men use technologies backed by enabling regulation to improve their lives and those of their families. Some of the most exciting changes in harnessing people's savings, widening credit and insurance, and lowering the cost of technologies, payments, and money transfers are taking place in Africa, Asia, and Latin America. Half the world

remains unbanked. However, financial inclusion has become a key plank for the regulation of banking and payments. Women are half the world's population, do most of the work, produce half of the food in the world, earn 10 percent of the income, and own 1 percent of the property. But legislative barriers preventing women from getting a job, opening a bank account, working in all industries, setting up businesses, and owning and inheriting property are coming down in many parts of the world. It gives hope for a more inclusive, fair, and equitable economic globalization. Half the world that is unbanked and half the world of women can become an important part of the story of globalization.

Strategies to help the poor and marginalized have gone global in South–South conversations. These conversations are about policies that enable financial inclusion, gender equity, and the innovative use of technologies. National regulators share innovations such as M-PESA in Kenya, GCash in the Philippines, the Bolsa Familia conditional cash transfer scheme in Brazil, and banking agents worldwide to increase financial inclusion and try to alleviate poverty. These conversations draw attention to continued pockets of poverty and disadvantage in high-income countries. The unbanked and underbanked, which in the United States comprise more than one in four households (28.3 percent), pay more in fees and interest rates for informal financial services to cash checks and get small flexible loans. Countries often face common problems, but solutions have to suit cultural values and historical patterns in the development and regulation of markets.

This broader view of economic globalization has money as a social phenomenon at the center. Money is a social and cultural concept, as well as belonging to the markets. Connecting money in markets and money in personal lives means considering financial markets and their regulation as well as the way women and men manage and control money in households across cultures. These households are banked and unbanked. They have been affected in different measure by financial markets and global finance, the global financial crisis, global supply chains, fluctuating exchange rates, and international trade.

The connected worlds of money in the market and personal lives link banking in the market with the way women and men manage money and negotiate commitment, power, and sharing in households. Migrants send money home to show they care for their families and communities left behind. These remittances also make up one of the largest international flows of funds, worth more than three times official development assistance.

The personal and market dimensions of globalization and money are intertwined. In a global world, Western values coexist with Asian, African, and Latin American values around money. Globalization increases the awareness of cross-cultural differences relating to money and how it connects with families, households, banking, regulation, migration, and the use of information and communication technologies (ICTs).

Just as the social concept of money broadens the reach of economic globalization, placing money in a global context also transforms its use and meanings. When money crosses borders, transnational families have to deal with exchange rates and currency conversion. At the same time, the value of money changes across borders according to the way people perceive the connection between work, money earned and sent, and physical caring for families. Often the dollar sent is not the dollar received.

In this book, I also focus on the ways in which ICTs change money and economic globalization. A common picture of globalization is electronic information about money whizzing instantaneously around the globe, making possible global markets of greater scale and interconnectedness than before. This is what gives globalization its current form. The use of new ICTs like the mobile phone and the Internet underlies the current phase of global interconnectedness and electronic forms of money. At the same time, financial hubs of global markets are co-located in global cities. The regulation of currencies and banking remains national, with an overarching international harmonization of standards and safety nets. The use of electronic and mobile money is shaped by this national regulation of telecommunications and banking on the one hand and the cultural and historical meanings ascribed to technologies and financial activities on the other. Our use of ICTs and their applications shapes their further development.

I bring to this study insights shaped by my research on money, banking, and ICTs in Australia, India, Malaysia, Papua New Guinea, and Kenya. (When writing about the participants in my qualitative research, all the names are pseudonyms.) These perspectives have become increasingly central as South–South discussions increase about money, regulation, globalization, equity, and development. I bring a sociological imagination linking the broad patterns of globalization to personal experience and issues as a woman and a migrant twice over—first from India to Malaysia and then to Australia. I also bring to this study an immersion in the user-centered design of ICTs, focusing on how the new ICTs change people's lives and are themselves shaped by their use in different social and cultural contexts.

In the first two chapters I write of the conceptual frameworks I have found useful in understanding the history and sociology of money, economic globalization, and the use of ICTs, particularly in the global South. In the succeeding chapters, I examine how a consideration of the unbanked, women, banking, electronic money, mobile money, and migration lead to a rethinking of economic globalization, the use of ICTs, and global money.

Acknowledgments

This book is like money in a global world. It reflects my personal and intellectual relationships and the debts I owe across the world.

It was Manfred Steger who suggested I write this book for the Rowman & Littlefield Globalization series. I would like to thank him for connecting my world of money with his world of globalization. He was the first to recognize that this book had become one of money, technology, and empowerment. Terrell Carver, also a commissioning editor for the series, engaged with the second draft to insist I speak in my own voice. As the book took shape, I connected more and more with Susan McEachern, my editor at Rowman & Littlefield, and her team.

Lyn Richards was with me as I worked through the connections between money and globalization. She came with roses and rhubarb and zucchini from her garden and brought home-baked scones for coffee. The conversation always ended up on money, and she went home with yet another draft. She helped me connect the strands as if I was doing macramé. Hearing me talk of gender in all aspects of money, our conversations led to it becoming a major theme.

In the United States, I would like to thank Karen Leonard. She is a friend who goes back to our time together in Delhi at Miranda House. She was my host in Los Angeles and facilitated my connection with Bill Maurer. I knew his work and went to discuss mobile money with him. We spent the morning discussing shared lives, money, and relationships. He has been generous in his comments on the second draft of the manuscript, leading me to a more nuanced understanding of new methods of payment and the importance of infrastructure as a public good. He also used his global contacts in mobile money to connect me to people in Kenya.

In Washington, D.C., Deepak Bhattasali from the World Bank, and a friend from the Malaysian period of my life, introduced me to Dilip Ratha. It was a privilege to spend time with Dilip, who helped the World Bank recognize that personal family and community remittances are part of one of the largest international flows of money.

In Nairobi I would like to thank my hosts Puni and Ajay Patel for their gracious hospitality. Professor Njuguna Ndung'u, governor of the Central Bank of Kenya, made time to see me and directed me to Stephen M. Nduati, head of the National Payments System of the Central Bank of Kenya. Both of us found money and payments so engrossing that we spent the whole day together. Thank you also to Chris Gacicio for ensuring that the governor had time for me. I would also like to thank Philip Machoka from the United States International University who molded his schedule to suit mine as my day at the Central Bank of Kenya kept getting longer and longer.

I was also privileged to meet with Tonny Omwansa through Christoph Stork. Tonny had written of M-PESA. Bill Maurer led me to Ben Lyon of Kopo Kopo and Angela Crandall and Lillian Nduati of iHub. David Lemayian worked next door and came to talk about M-PESA. Ben Lyon and Stephen Nduati led me to a conversation with John Staley of Equity Bank.

Angela and I kept talking as I began to delve into the relationship between gender and access to technologies. Rohan Samarajiva from LIRNEasia and Alison Gillwald from Research ICT Africa spoke of the importance of income, education, and cultural values for ensuring equal access to technologies. I also benefitted from my conversations with Kammy Naidu and Nadia Bulbilia at the joint conference of CPRafrica and CPRsouth in Mauritius.

I would also like to acknowledge Charles Klingman who manages the unbanked list, a continuous source of news about the unbanked and mobile money.

Perle Besserman and I are connected by a love of writing. I would like to thank her for seeing that the book read well. Viviana Zelizer and Bob Holton read the manuscript. This was a great privilege for me. Bob Holton, Sandra Holton, and I have spent memorable times in Melbourne, Dublin, and Somerset talking of global networks, global finance, and Quaker women, usually over Bob's dishes of Indian curry.

Viviana and I came together on money, but our conversations over the years have been about our mothers, our children, and the way money has been woven into all facets of our relationships. We share the intimacy of ideas though our lives have been lived in different ways across continents. I am particularly grateful for her additional references from Latin America and women and money.

I would also like to thank my colleagues at RMIT University. Heather Horst read the first draft of the mobile money chapter. Jonathan O'Donnell shared with me his world of new ways of borrowing and lending. Anuja Cabraal went through the parts on microfinance. I benefitted from Yaso Nadarajah's readings on gender and our work together in Papua New Guinea.

I am particularly grateful to my colleagues in the Smart Internet Co-operative Research Centre and the Global Cities Research Centre at RMIT University for their research collaboration and friendship. I would also like to thank the College of Business and the Graduate School of Business and Law for research leave to engross myself in the world of money and globalization while I was writing this book.

CHAPTER 1

MONEY

HISTORICAL, SOCIAL, AND CULTURAL DIMENSIONS

I stood in the Australian Museum in Sydney looking at shell money from Kiribati in the Pacific. It was a necklace of spherical shells held together by a tightly woven braid. For no particular reason, I had expected a string of shells, a bit like a beaded curtain. This encounter with traditional money exchanged face to face and gifted ceremonially took me back to history and also to the present in the Pacific.

The history of money highlights the importance of its social aspects. Money has taken multiple forms across regions and times. The role of money in ceremonial and religious presentations pre-dates its use as a means for funding war and for enabling finance, trade, and investment. The spread of coinage across countries reflects the global aspects of empire and trade. In the postcolonial period, money within a country has become more uniform and centralized. Currency has become one of the important symbols of national identity.

The sociology of money, as with the history of money, also centers on the social and cultural aspects of multiple monies. Money is part of the market. At the same time, "one of money's chief functions is remembering."[1] Money is involved in the give-and-take among families, for negotiating power, commitment, and sharing in intimate relationships. Money is a medium of relationship and part of the social fabric of life.

THE HISTORICAL DEVELOPMENT OF MONEY

The shell money of Kiribati highlights the continuing use of traditional money. Among the isolated Kwaio of the Solomon Islands, strings of red, pink, white, and black shell money called "kofu" continue to be used for purchase, bride-price, and mortuary payments. It is particularly important for buying pigs, which are essential for ceremonies.[2] "The manufacture of shell money in the Solomon Islands is barely keeping pace with demand."[3] Pigs, shell strings, and pandanus mats in Vanuatu enable ceremonial presentations and symbolize traditional wealth.[4] A few years ago in Vanuatu, "the Pentecost Council of Chiefs (supported by the director of the Vanuatu Cultural Centre, Marcellin Abong) imposed the maximum traditional fine in tusker pigs on Digicel for encroaching on a sacred site."[5]

It is not unusual for new and traditional monies to coexist. Money in the form of cowries, cloth, grain, cattle, salt, bullion, jewelry, stone, and shells have coexisted with coins and paper money in many societies. Cowries "remained the chief currency of the poor in many parts of India until recent times,"[6] though the first silver coins in India go back to 400 BC. In 1780 the value of the coins issued by the East India Company were given as 5,120 cowries to the rupee.[7] Silk, coins, and grain were used as money in China during the Tang dynasty (618–907). In Japan, rice was used to pay taxes up to 1868, the time of the Meiji restoration. In Nigeria, cowries could still be used for small purchases in the twentieth century.[8] Even thirty years ago, old people in Cameroon could remember how the *bikie*, iron rods used primarily for marriage payments and also for regional trade, were manufactured, controlled, and used in transactions.[9]

What remains constant across history and the different forms of money, like cowries, coins, Ithaca HOURS, and the digital bitcoin, is the faith and belief that money has the value it says it has and that this value will be honored. Its value does not lie in the value of metal or cloth or shell. Money is "trust inscribed."[10]

THE SOCIAL IMPORTANCE OF MONEY

The history of money emphasizes its social importance. Evidence from Mesopotamia, China, India, and the Mediterranean world shows that the role of money in ceremonial and religious presentations, blood price, bride-price, tributes, ornamentation, and gifts at times pre-dates its use for payments, trade, and exchange. The earliest gold and silver coins were primarily used for ceremonial presentations and religious dedication. They were too valuable for trade.[11]

By most accounts, the earliest coins date back to the seventh century BC. These are ninety-three roughly oval-shaped Lydian coins made of electrum, a naturally occurring alloy of gold and silver. They were found buried under the temple of Artemis at Ephesus (now in Turkey) together with seven unstamped silver nuggets. This suggested they were used as a religious dedication. Later mentions of these coins were in the context of ceremonial presentations.[12]

A hoard of one hundred Frankish and Anglo-Saxon gold *tremisses* was found buried with a few ornaments from 645 at Crondall, Hampshire. It is thought that the "round sum of 100 gold shillings . . . represent a *wergild* (compensation payment for a killing)."[13] It has been suggested that one of the main reasons for the golden dinar in the fourth to sixth centuries in India in the Gupta period was to enable the king to perform religious rituals to establish his identity as a world ruler. Brahmin priests conducting rituals such as the horse sacrifice had to be paid in gold.[14]

The social use of money went together with the use of multiple kinds of money. A specific kind of money was "earmarked" for activities with particular social meanings. In many Pacific countries, some of the important rituals and prestigious transactions can only be conducted with pigs and shell money. Among the precolonial Tiv of central Nigeria, there were three spheres of exchange. The first dealt with everyday subsistence. Locally produced foodstuff, chickens, goats, household utensils, handicrafts, and some tools were exchanged for each other by barter or gift giving. The second category related to prestige. It included slaves, cattle, metal bars, ritual offices, medicines and magic, and a type of large white cloth called *tugudu*. The third and highest category involved rights over human beings other than slaves, especially rights over women and dependent children. These rights could not be traded. Many of its values were articulated through marriage and kinship. To get a woman, a person needed to exchange another. But in the interim, payment of cattle and brass rods could be an "earnest" payment until the exchange could be completed.[15]

These three categories were hierarchical in that it was desirable to trade up from the subsistence category to the prestige category and then on to kinship. Brass rods, cattle, and cloth could be exchanged within the prestige category. But brass rods would not ordinarily be used to buy food. This was seen as an inappropriate use of that particular kind of money.[16] Sometimes the move from one sphere to another could be done by taking side steps in small increments in the regional economy of Atlantic Africa. *Tugudu* cloth could be traded for cattle and brass rods from the northwest. Cattle in the prestige sphere could then be converted into wealth in people to pay for bride wealth for marriages to the northeast.[17]

This social use of money went together with the need to pay for everyday purchases, the salaries of large armies for empire, and regional trade. Low-value bronze coins and often cowrie shells were used for everyday purchases. But the prolific gold and silver coinage of the early Greeks and the Romans of the third and fourth centuries was mostly used to pay for military expenditure.[18]

THE GLOBAL SPREAD OF MONEY

Currency today is one of the defining symbols of a nation, and sometimes of a region. It tells a distinctive story of the people of a country, its heroes, its distinctive flora and fauna, and its social institutions. It is often the first indicator of having crossed borders. But money in its different forms used to be more global, following the routes of empire and trade. Cowrie shells circulated as money across Asia, the Middle East, Oceania, and Africa. Coins from Greece, Rome, and the Islamic empires spread across many countries. They were often imitated so that the design of the coins, the images used, and the positioning of the inscriptions followed foreign patterns. Unlike the Islamic, British, and Chinese traditions, coins did not always represent state authority. This was true for the Romans, who allowed local currency to circulate in parts of their empire. "The concept of legal tender never seems to have taken root in Hindu India."[19]

Collections of coins from India in the British Museum illustrate the Persian, Greek, Roman, Islamic, and British influence of empire and trade. The first punch-marked silver coins in India in the fifth and fourth centuries BC were from the Achaemenid Empire of Persia. It is thought that their coins came from Lydia and the other Greek cities of Asia Minor.[20] Alexander the Great's conquests in northwestern India (329–325 BC) and the successive Greek kings brought Greek coins to the region. Coins made in the Greek tradition were copied locally and subsequently modified with inscriptions made around the image in the Indian script. Greek-style coins continued circulating in India even after Greek rule. Roman coinage followed traders from Roman Egypt and Syria. This was reflected in the gold coin called "dinar" issued during the Gupta period of the fourth to sixth centuries. It was named after the Roman equivalent *denarius aureus*. The coins followed Greek design, with a standing king on one side and inscriptions around the image in the Indian Brahmi script. The images were modified to reflect Indian emblems from earlier Indian coins in the first century BC. During the eighth to tenth centuries in northern India, the dominant coinage was the *dramma*. The designs were copied from Iranian silver drachms of an earlier Sasanian king (AD 459–84). There was no indication as to who issued the coins and no image of the ruler.[21]

There was no felt need in India to associate coins with the issuing authority until the long period of Islamic rule in India from the twelfth to the nineteenth centuries. Arabic designs and the Persian script were grafted onto indigenous designs. Gold and silver coins came back to the region, but cowrie shells continued to be used as small change. The Portuguese, the first Europeans to issue coins in India in the late sixteenth century, adopted the Mughal system of the silver rupee and the copper paisa, but with more European imagery. The East India Company also found that for wider acceptance they had to issue the Mughal-style coins. The coins struck in 1780/81 were in the name of the Mughal emperor Shah Alam. This gave the coins legitimacy but not a standard value. The value of the three hundred different rupees circulating in India was not controlled by the emperor but by the shroffs, the local money changers. The Indian rupee introduced by the Mughals in the sixteenth century was standardized by the British East India Company in 1835.[22]

Trade carried Indian coins to Central Asia, Iran, Iraq, and Ethiopia. Indian coins entered Tibet from Nepal in the sixteenth century. The British Indian rupee became so popular in Tibet during the late nineteenth and twentieth centuries that imitation rupees were minted in western China for the Tibet trade. With the spread of Indian culture and religion, Indian coinage was dominant in Southeast Asia till the eleventh century. The standardization of the rupee by the British East India Company further spread the coin to Indonesia, the Persian Gulf, and southern Arabia. The rupee was also used in British East Africa, South Africa, Italian Somalia, German East Africa, and Portuguese Mozambique. The rupee in different variants continues to be used in Pakistan, Nepal, and Sri Lanka. It is also the standard currency in Mauritius and Seychelles. In Indonesia it is called the "rupiah."[23]

China's story is of the independent development of money that had a global influence. Proto-coinage in bronze arrow-shaped objects was discovered in China from around 600 BC as well as the area of the Black Sea. There is a dispute over the dates of the round bronze Chinese coins with a square hole in the middle. They originated anywhere between the twelfth and fourth century BC.[24] The design linked the domed heaven and the square earth according to Chinese belief. There was no pictorial image. The inscription in valued calligraphy was the design. The Qin state (221 BC), the Han (118 BC), and the Tang Empire (618–907) issued their own coins that became the dominant coinage during their rule, replacing previous coins. The bronze round coin with the square hole in the middle remained the same, though the inscriptions and weight changed. Unlike the silver and gold coins of the Mediterranean, bronze coins were of low denomination used mainly for payment.[25]

Chinese coinage and Chinese culture spread with the influence of the Tang dynasty. Between AD 708 and 1097, the *kaiyuan* coins of the Tang Empire spread to Japan, Central Asia, Korea, and Vietnam and Southeast Asia. Trading links took these coins to the Middle East, South Asia, Australia, and Africa. The *kaiyuan* became the model for all East Asian coins for two thousand years.[26]

Paper money was introduced in China in the tenth century during the Song dynasty (960–1279) to enable regional trade within China and supplement official expenditure. During the period of the Mongol Yuan dynasty (1206–1367), only paper money was allowed. Paper money spread slowly beyond China. Paper money had some halting starts in Europe until the end of the seventeenth century.[27]

In the nineteenth century, the influence of foreign monetary systems increased in China as foreign domination increased. After the First Opium War (1840–42), foreign commercial banks such as the Hongkong and Shanghai Banking Corporation issued silver dollar and silver ounce banknotes. Eventually the Chinese government and provincial offices issued their own silver ounce and silver dollar exchange notes. There was a multiplicity of paper monies, as pawnshops, larger mercantile institutions, and government institutions also issued their own notes.[28]

In a postcolonial world, what went on a currency note or coin became a matter of national importance. In countries like Malaysia, where the colonial dollar had been used since 1939, a colonial currency nearly became a common currency for Singapore and Malaysia. At the last minute, differences over seemingly small details opened up wider issues of identity and control. On June 12, 1967, nearly ten years after independence, Malaysia issued its own currency. In light of the tribulations of the euro, the story of the Malaysian currency is one where the divorce happened before the marriage.

THE STORY OF MALAYSIAN CURRENCY

Malaya, Singapore, British North Borneo, Sarawak, and Brunei shared the same currency when they were under the British. They were part of a Currency Board from 1939. A dollar was equal to two shillings and four pence and was automatically convertible to sterling. When Malaysia was formed in September 1963, Brunei opted out. In August 1965, the separation of Malaysia and Singapore was announced. Yet it was hoped the two countries could continue with the common currency and banking system that they had shared since the beginning of the twentieth century.[29]

Between November 1965 and May 1966, Malaysia and Singapore reached an agreement about the broad issues related to a common currency. In June 1966, the details began to be negotiated. There was a sense of urgency about the negotiations, for Malaysia had already given notice to the Currency Board that it would issue its own currency. Orders for the currency had to be given by mid-August 1966 if the deadline was to be met.

The two sides were already discussing the design of the currency and the mechanics of printing when "presentation problems" came up. What do you call the new currency? What should the joint central bank be called? Meetings went on past midnight. In the end, the negotiations faltered around the question, will Bank Negara Malaysia hold legal title to Singapore's currency reserves? On August 17, 1966, the two governments said in diplomatic language that Malaysia and Singapore would issue their own currency.

Both Malaysia and Singapore had been considering designs of separate currencies before and during the negotiations. In Malaysia in 1962, the prime minister, Tunku Abdul Rahman, had approved having the portrait of the first king, the Yang di-Pertuan Agong, on the notes. The tiger was the watermark. The *kijang*, the barking deer, was on the obverse of the notes issued from 1967 to 1982. The *kijang* was the motif of seventeenth-century Malaysian gold coins.

The design of the coins was more difficult. Tun Ismail Ali, the governor of Bank Negara Malaysia, showed the winning five designs from a national competition to the prime minister in 1966. These featured a proboscis monkey, the Malayan tapir, the pangolin, the *kijang*, and the Argus pheasant. The prime minister said, "No, this won't do. People will think we eat them. Why not have the picture of the Parliament building on the coins, since we're a parliamentary democracy?"[30] He also suggested that there was a good picture of the Parliament on the packet of Parliament cigarettes. This is how the coins came to have the picture of the Parliament. A crescent moon and a star filled the empty spaces.

THE SOCIAL AND CULTURAL CONCEPT OF MONEY

The social history of money highlights some of the themes that have been at the center of the sociology of money. In the last three decades, Western sociologists of money have shown that money is a social phenomenon that belongs to the market and personal lives. The social concept of money differs from the market concept of money, which is at the center of most economics literature. Seeing money as a social phenomenon brings to the fore multiple monies, cross-cultural differences in the meanings, as well as the management and control, of money. As the household becomes an important site for the use of money, the role of women becomes crucially important. Financial inclusion agendas that miss the social uses of cash also miss the familial and gender dynamics at work. Promoting financial inclusion may have the contrary effect of increasing gender inequality.

MONEY, MARKETS, AND INTIMATE LIVES

The market concept of money has dominated economic thought and policy. It has also been central to classical sociology. Karl Marx, Max Weber, and Georg Simmel, the three most influential classical sociologists in the fields of production, markets, money, and social life, saw money mainly in terms of the market. They emphasized different effects of money on society and culture, but did not consider the influence of social patterns and cultural values on money. They saw money as qualitatively the same, differing only in quantity. This characteristic made it perfect for economic calculation and thus made it central to the market. It also made for a sharp dichotomy between money on the one hand and personal, social, moral, and sacred values on the other. Karl Marx wrote that money transformed quality into quantity and so debased and perverted social values and relationships.[31] Georg Simmel also saw money as being distinguished by quantity.[32] Max Weber, building on Simmel's account of money, saw it as a rationalizing force. He identified money only with the market situation, saying, "Where money calculations are highly developed, this will be called the 'market situation.'"[33] He argued that the abstractness and impersonality of money made it "the most 'perfect' means of economic calculation."[34]

Seeing money as homogenous and synonymous with the market changed in the 1980s. Viviana Zelizer, a social historian, arrived at a broader understanding of the scope of money and economic activity through her historical study of life insurance, the market for children, domestic money in the United States from 1870 to 1930,[35] and the legal disputes arising from the coming together of intimate relationships and economic activity.[36] I build on her work to argue that seeing money as a social phenomenon is central to an inclusive and empowering framework of economic globalization. I show how the frameworks of globalization help define the characteristics of global money as a "special money." I use her "connected worlds" approach that links money in personal lives and the market to connect economic globalization to the unbanked, gender, money management and control in households, cross-cultural differences in banking, and migrant remittances.

Zelizer describes how money shapes and is shaped by social relationships and cultural values. She argues that markets and money have to be understood within "dense webs of meaningful relationships."[37] We have to go beyond "standard thinking about economic structures"[38] to capture the multiple ways in which people organize their economic lives. We cannot treat firms, corporations, currencies, and financial markets as central market activities while trivializing economic activities of households, remittances, the rotating savings and credit associations (RoSCAs), microcredit groups, and other "circuits of commerce" working through trusted relationships. We need to go beyond activities relating to production to consumption.

The "hostile worlds" approach that pitches the market against intimate lives needs to be replaced by a perspective that connects markets and personal lives. The "connected worlds" approach goes beyond seeing market institutions as being socially embedded, illustrating the relationship between the economic and noneconomic aspects of social life. Her emphasis has been to widen the reach of money and economic life so that their study would embrace both markets and personal lives. Focusing on connected lives, she emphasizes how "all of us use economic activity to create, maintain, and renegotiate important ties—especially intimate ties—to other people."[39]

Money not only transforms social patterns and cultural values but is itself shaped by cultural and structural factors. People feared that insurance would commercialize the personal and sacred value of life. It was not anticipated that money itself would be "transformed in the process, as it became part of the structure of social relations and the meaning system of the family."[40]

Her historical data about domestic money shows that there are multiple monies, each one being qualitatively distinct. She argues that there is no "single general-purpose type of money." She says that "not all dollars are equal."[41] One kind of money cannot always substitute for another kind of money, because some monies have meanings that are particular to them. People "earmark" different kinds of monies so that their use and meanings are appropriate to the particular set of social relationships. Gender becomes important to the meanings of money in the household. Money has different meanings and uses in the household if it is an allowance, a "wage," or money earned by women in the household, such as "egg money" or "butter money." A working-class woman had more control than a middle-class woman over household money.

CROSS-CULTURAL MEANINGS OF MONEY

While Zelizer's work has been rooted in the United States, though informed by difference because of her own experience as a migrant from Argentina, it is the anthropology of money that emphasizes the importance of cross-cultural meanings and patterns of the use of money in families. This approach becomes particularly important in the study of money and globalization as a corrective to taking Western experience as a norm. Cultural differences in the flow of money across generations in households and families shape the way people bank and the flow of remittances. The use of cash as a gift in many countries in Asia and Africa also places limits on the replacement of cash with electronic money.

Western frameworks do not necessarily fit understandings of money in the household and the family in Africa and Asia. In middle-income Anglo-Celtic families in Australia, money and information about money flow one way between parents and children or between grandparents and grand-children. Domestic money is bounded by the couple. In many Asian and African families, money flows two ways between parents and children. The family, nuclear or extended, is the boundary of domestic money.[42]

From cross-cultural studies, we know that domestic money flows within wider boundaries in Asia, Africa, and the Pacific than in the West. In the Indian patrilineal joint family, money management and control has to be studied in the broader context of the family and across generations. The importance of the family rather than the couple is seen in that information about money is exchanged at times between father and son, rather than husband and wife. Parents commonly have joint accounts with their adult children and with each other.[43]

In the Aboriginal Ngukurr community in southeast Arnhem Land, money is distributed within the fluid household cluster rather than the household. Gifts, mainly of money, comprised an average of 16 percent of the income of the household cluster.[44] Vinita Godinho, studying money among two remote indigenous communities in Arnhem Land in North Australia, found that most of her participants agreed, though one young man quipped, "I reckon it's 20 percent you actually keep."[45]

Maori money also shows the importance of a wider boundary for domestic money. It is important to study the money that goes from households to the *whānau*, a group of kin descended from a common ancestor or an extended family group. Money is gifted up and down generations so that younger people also give to parents, grandparents, and other kin in their parents' generation. They also give to brothers, sisters, and cousins. Money is gifted to the *whānau* for ritual gatherings to mark crises in the lives of *whānau* members. The obligation to gift money for the funeral meeting at the *whānau* takes priority over every-day household expenses.[46]

There is such a strong moral imperative to share money with extended kin and clan networks that migrants from many countries in Africa are subject to intense pressure. As we will see in chapter 8, Somali refugees in London remit money to extended kin as well as parents and siblings.[47] Dinka male migrants in the United States are expected to contribute to bride-prices for three immediate generations on their father's side. They also have obligations to the wife's kin. Not meeting these obligations means a Dinka man is not a "good moral person."[48]

In *Economic Lives* (2011), Viviana Zelizer asks, when are "gifts of cash appropriate and when are they tacky? When does offering a gift certificate offend the recipient?"[49] My sister who lives in New York and I in Melbourne found ourselves facing a very different question. Our aunt's grandson was getting married, and we were going to be in Delhi to attend the wedding. We wanted to give a handsome gift, because this aunt was especially close to our late mother. We finally decided on an intricately carved dressing table. We checked it with our cousin—the groom's father. He said, "Don't become so Western. Why don't you just give *shagun*?" This is the ritual gift of cash at weddings and births. So my sister and I decided on a handsome sum of cash for the *shagun*. We gave it to our aunt, as it was for her to decide how to use it. We succeeded in respectfully marking the relationship between us, for she walked from the wedding *shamiana*, the decorated large tent, to her house nearby. She wanted to give each of us *salwar kameez* suits to show that we were close family members and our mother's daughters. It didn't work out, for the suits were locked away in trunks. My aunt died soon after.

In New Delhi, it is possible to buy gift envelopes with a rupee coin stuck on the outside so that the *shagun* can be made in auspicious denominations, such as Rs 51, 101, or 501. It is also not possible to think of Chinese New Year without the red *ang-pow* gift packet for children and younger unmarried men and women. In Malaysia, banks not only distribute the traditional red envelopes for the *ang-pow* but also ensure they have a supply of crisp new notes during Chinese New Year. In Japan, the preference for clean notes as gifts has also migrated to the electronic world where some ATMs deodorize and clean the notes before delivering them. These notes are particularly used for wedding gifts.[50]

Among the Simunul Bajaus of Sabah, Malaysia, cash is the most appropriate gift from most of the guests at a wedding or funeral. Gifts of cash are taken into account when planning the expenditure. This cash is most often presented in envelopes with the giver's name on the outside for purposes of record. Sometimes the cash is elaborately transformed, as used to happen with the payment of bride-price. At one particularly ostentatious wedding in the late 1970s, in a Simunul Bajau village in Sabah, the MR 3,000 was arranged in the shape of the National Mosque. At another wedding, the money was arranged in floral designs, with the red of the ten-ringgit and the green of the fifty-ringgit notes carefully matched.[51] But three years ago, when I returned to the village, the cash was only wrapped in a handkerchief. I was told it is illegal to use currency for decoration. The imams of the village counted the bride-price in public to document that it had been paid in full.

In many European communities, cash also used to be the preferred gift for weddings. Ukrainian farming communities in western Canada have retained the "presentation," that is, the giving of money at weddings.[52] Italian and East European Jewish migrants to New York at the turn of the twentieth century customarily gave money as wedding gifts. At times, this money would help to pay for the wedding itself.[53]

Cash is becoming a preferred gift in Australia when couples who have lived together in de facto relationships get married, and for couples who have been married before. It is recognized that cash gifts are practical. At times the couple or the parents suggest that these cash gifts will be used for the honeymoon, or to build a carport. There is still a lingering sense of discomfort about these cash gifts because in Anglo-Celtic society in Australia, there is a deep-rooted opposition between cash and gifts. Gifts of cash are accepted from grandparents and sometimes from parents. But in other cases, cash is only acceptable if it is transformed into gift certificates. And even then there is a question lurking in the background that perhaps you had taken the easy, impersonal way of giving a gift.[54]

Indians, Chinese, Malaysians, Ukrainians, Italians, East European Jewish migrants, and Australian de facto couples, however, would be surprised that men among the rural Merina of Madagascar present lovers with money or goods after sexual intercourse. These gifts are given for premarital or extramarital sex. They are also given to wives, but on a less regular basis. It is the casualness of the relationship rather than cash that converts sex into prostitution.[55]

MONEY MANAGEMENT AND CONTROL

Despite these cultural differences, there are some generalities about how women and men manage and control money in the home. Women spend more of their money than men on the children and the household. Women approach money as a collective good, targeting more of their resources to the family's needs, especially the children's nutrition. This perception and use of money is found among women across the world. It is found among women who control the money in the household and those who do not.

In the United Kingdom, a body of work has developed around the management and control of money in marriage and intimate relationships.[56] I have found this literature useful for studying how women and men negotiate commitment, power, and togetherness in intimate relationships. At the same time, it has made me conscious that the frameworks that explain money management and control in Western couple relationships need to be broadened to explain the two-way flow of money and information between parents and children in extended families in Asia, Africa, and the Pacific.

An important contribution of the literature on money management and control is to go beyond the household as a "black box" to study the allocation of money between the marital couple. I remember Jan Pahl telling me that studying women in a refuge made her realize how much women, even in those straitened circumstances, valued their ability to manage and control their own money. This literature also presented a typology that has been used to explain money management and control in Western marriage. It distinguished between the whole-wage system where the husband gave most of his wages to his wife to manage, and the housekeeping-allowance system, where the man gave his wife an agreed amount to cover household expenses. Sometimes it included a margin for personal spending money. About half the couples used pooled systems, sharing overall management and control. There was also independent management and control.[57]

Recently the focus has moved to charting the more individualistic management and control of money in intimate relationships, particularly among younger and more affluent couples, cohabiting couples, and those who have remarried. This has raised issues about continuing commitment in intimate relationships in the West and the conflict between equality and equity in the context of differences between male and female earnings.

This work presents a starting point for a more detailed consideration of the way men and women manage and control money in families in Asia, the Pacific, Latin America, and Africa. We know there are important cultural differences relating to the boundaries of domestic money, the flow of money across generations in households and families, the privacy attached to information about money, and issues around gender, generation, and money management and control. There are also important differences in the structure of households and families, with extended families often seen as the norm, particularly in Asia. So in considering money management and control, generation becomes an additional factor to be considered. This is because there are differences in money management and control among the constituent couples in the extended family.

Money management also has a different meaning when the ideology is one of male dominance, as in many parts of India. A woman may manage the kitchen, but it is the man who buys the groceries and provisions the house, does the banking, pays the bills, and manages the money.[58]

At present, there are individual studies in different cultural contexts but few comparative studies of money management and control in the household and family in a global framework. Without such studies it is difficult to design effective financial services and policies for financial inclusion. This is why some policies designed to address financial exclusion—as in India—continue to aim at having at least one bank account per household or family. This is an important benchmark when nearly half the population is unbanked. However, with the focus on the household, women's access to money and financial services will become opaque. It is even more worrying that governments, particularly in South Asia, will appear to be supporting the male control of money as the desired norm. I discuss this further in chapter 4 when I write of women, money, and globalization.

NOTES

1. Keith Hart, "Money Is Always Personal and Impersonal," *Anthropology Today* 23, no. 5 (October 2007): 15.

2. David Akin, "Cash and Shell Money in Kwaio, Solomon Islands," in *Money and Modernity: State and Local Currencies in Melanesia*, ed. David Akin and Joel Robbins (Pittsburgh: University of Pittsburgh Press, 1999), 103–30.

3. Kirk Huffman, "Making Real Money in the Solomons," *Explore* 32, no. 2 (2010): 2.

4. Kirk Huffman, "Pigs, Prestige and Copyright in the Western Pacific," *Explore* 29, no. 6 (2007): 22–25.

5. Personal communication, Kirk Huffman, January 22, 2013.

6. A. L. Basham, *The Wonder That Was India* (New York: Grove Press, 1954), 21.

7. Catherine Eagleton and Jonathan Williams, *Money: A History* (London: British Museum Press, 2007).

8. Glyn Davies, *A History of Money: From Ancient Times to the Present Day* (Cardiff: University of Wales Press, 1994); Eagleton and Williams, *Money: A History*.

9. Jane I. Guyer, "Soft Currencies, Cash Economies, New Monies: Past and Present," *Proceedings of the National Academy of Sciences of the United States of America* 109, no. 7 (2012).

10. Niall Ferguson, *The Ascent of Money: A Financial History of the World* (Camberwell, Victoria: Allen Lane, 2008), 30.

11. Eagleton and Williams, *Money: A History*; Davies, *A History of Money*.

12. Eagleton and Williams, *Money: A History*; Ferguson, *The Ascent of Money*.

13. Eagleton and Williams, *Money: A History*, 67.

14. Eagleton and Williams, *Money: A History*, 67.

15. Paul Bohannan, "The Impact of Money on an African Subsistence Economy," *Journal of Economic History* 19, no. 4 (1959).

16. Bohannan, "The Impact of Money."

17. Guyer, "Soft Currencies."

18. Eagleton and Williams, *Money: A History*.

19. Basham, *The Wonder That Was India*, 221.

20. Basham, *The Wonder That Was India*.

21. Eagleton and Williams, *Money: A History*.

22. Eagleton and Williams, *Money: A History*.

23. Eagleton and Williams, *Money: A History*.

24. Eagleton and Williams, *Money: A History*; Davies, *A History of Money*.

25. Eagleton and Williams, *Money: A History*.

26. Eagleton and Williams, *Money: A History*.

27. Eagleton and Williams, *Money: A History*.

28. Eagleton and Williams, *Money: A History*.

29. Supriya Singh, *Bank Negara Malaysia: The First 25 Years, 1959–1984* (Kuala Lumpur: Bank Negara Malaysia, 1984).

30. Singh, *Bank Negara Malaysia*, 140.

31. K. Marx, "Economic and Philosophical Manuscripts," in *Karl Marx: Early Texts*, ed. D. McLellan (Oxford: Basil Blackwell, 1971).

32. Georg Simmel, *The Philosophy of Money* (London: Routledge & Kegan Paul, 1990).

33. Max Weber, *The Theory of Social and Economic Organization* (New York: Free Press, 1947), 180.

34. Max Weber, *Economy and Society* (Berkeley: University of California Press, 1978), 86.

35. Viviana A. Zelizer, *Economic Lives: How Culture Shapes the Economy* (Princeton, NJ: Princeton University Press, 2011); *Morals and Markets: The Development of Life Insurance in the United States* (New York: Columbia University Press, 1979); *Pricing the Priceless Child: The Changing Social Value of Children* (New York: Basic Books, 1985); "The Social Meaning of Money: 'Special Monies,'" *American Journal of Sociology* 95, no. 2 (1989); *The Social Meaning of Money* (New York: Basic Books, 1994).

36. Viviana A. Zelizer, *The Purchase of Intimacy* (Princeton, NJ: Princeton University Press, 2005).

37. Zelizer, *Economic Lives*, x.

38. Zelizer, *Economic Lives*, 303.

39. Zelizer, *The Purchase of Intimacy*, 3.

40. Zelizer, *Pricing the Priceless Child*, 370.

41. Zelizer, "The Social Meaning of Money," 343.

42. Supriya Singh, *Marriage Money: The Social Shaping of Money in Marriage and Banking* (St. Leonards, NSW: Allen & Unwin, 1997).

43. Supriya Singh and Mala Bhandari, "Money Management and Control in the Indian Joint Family across Generations," *Sociological Review* 60, no. 1 (2012).

44. Kate Senior, David Perkins, and John Bern, "Variation in Material Wellbeing in a Welfare Based Economy" (Wollongong: South East Arnhem Land Collaborative Research Project, University of Wollongong, 2002).

45. Vinita Godinho and Supriya Singh, "Indigenous Money Is a 'Special Money'" (Unpublished, 2012).

46. Julia TeUrikore Turupa Taiapa, *"Ta Te Whanau Ohanga": The Economics of the Whanau—The Maori Component of the Intra Family Income Study* (Palmerston North: Department of Maori Studies, Massey University, 1994), 52.

47. Anna Lindley, "The Early-Morning Phonecall: Remittances from a Refugee Diaspora Perspective," *Journal of Ethnic and Migration Studies* 35, no. 8 (2009).

48. Stephanie Riak Akuei, "Remittances as Unforeseen Burdens: The Livelihoods and Social Obligations of Sudanese Refugees," in *Global Migration Perspectives* (Geneva: Global Commission on International Migration, 2005), 4.

49. Zelizer, *Economic Lives*, ix.

50. "High-Tech Cleaning in Japan," http://factsanddetails.com/japan.php?itemid=66 6&catid=19&subcatid=126#03.

51. Supriya Singh, *On the Sulu Sea* (Kuala Lumpur: Angsana Publications, 1984).

52. David Cheal, *The Gift Economy* (London: Routledge, 1988).

53. E. Ewen, *Immigrant Women in the Land of Dollars: Life and Culture on the Lower East Side, 1890–1925* (New York: Monthly Review Press, 1985).

54. Supriya Singh, "The Digital Packaging of Electronic Money," in *Usability and Internationalization: Global and Local User Interfaces*, ed. Nuray Aykin (Berlin: Springer, 2007).

55. Maurice Bloch, "The Symbolism of Money in Imerina," in *Money and the Morality of Exchange*, ed. J. Parry and M. Bloch (Cambridge: Cambridge University Press, 1989).

56. Jan Pahl, *Money and Marriage* (London: Macmillan, 1989); Carolyn Vogler, Clare Lyonette, and Richard D. Wiggins, "Money, Power and Spending Decisions in Intimate Relationships," *Sociological Review* 56, no. 1 (2008); C. Vogler and J. Pahl, "Social and Economic Change and the Organisation of Money within Marriage," *Work, Employment and Society* 7, no. 1 (1993); S. Lukes, *Power: A Radical View* (London: Macmillan, 1974); Carolyn Vogler, "Money in the Household: Some Underlying Issues of Power," *Sociological Review* 46, no. 4 (1998).

57. Pahl, *Money and Marriage*.

58. Singh and Bhandari, "Money Management."

CHAPTER 2

GLOBALIZATION AND TECHNOLOGIES

Placing the social concept of money at the center changes the story of globalization and the use of information and communication technologies (ICTs). The action moves to the global South, where policy makers are fashioning policies for greater financial inclusion using mobile technologies. People are using new channels and forms of money to take greater charge of how they pay and how they connect with family and friends through the transfer or gifting of money.

In this chapter I broaden the frameworks for the study of globalization and elucidate how "global money" is developing its own defining characteristics that go beyond exchange rates in the market. I focus on the user-centered design of ICTs to show how technologies and globalization shape each other.

FRAMEWORKS FOR THE STUDY OF GLOBALIZATION

Globalization is neither new nor wholly Western. The history of money makes this clear. Globalization also does not involve nested concepts of place where the local fits into the national and then into the global. Global cities and nation-states remain important at the same time as international organizations deal with global issues. Globalization is an imaginary rather than a geographical distinction between the local, national, and the global, as the global is often powerfully seen in the local. The interpenetration of local, transnational, and cosmopolitan experiences is not only an issue of definition and conceptual clarity but is central to describing how the global imaginary is transforming money as it moves across borders.

Globalization has changed all aspects of the way we live—the television programs and films we see, the music we listen to, global news stories, the food we eat, being part of religious services across the world, the clothes we wear, the global spread of ideas, the ease of communication across distance, and the ability to live and function in different national and cultural worlds. Globalization has led us to ask what the contours of a just world would look like and how we can best achieve it. With globalization comes a greater awareness of cultural difference. At the same time there is greater communication that could lead to a deeper understanding of different ways people make meaning of their lives.

The distinctiveness of the present experience of globalization is that the new ICTs have enabled the instantaneous and simultaneous transmission of money across the globe, leading to a greater interconnectedness of markets and global supply chains across the world. Financial markets that trade money have outstripped manufacturing and trade, with finance becoming a greater proportion of the economy than before. The global financial crisis (GFC) revealed the contagion inherent in this increased interconnectedness.

These understandings of globalization draw on the work of Manfred Steger, Robert Holton, and Saskia Sassen and form the building blocks for my story of money and globalization.[1]

In this section, I first focus on the GFC because it has become the reference point for what can go wrong with economic globalization. I consider how far the GFC led to a questioning of the neoliberal underpinnings of economic globalization. I then move to the social concept of money to describe how this approach broadens the frameworks of globalization to include economic activity in the market and outside it. Globalization thus also includes the unbanked and households and directs attention to markets as social institutions. Gender as well becomes a crucial dimension of globalization.

THE GLOBAL FINANCIAL CRISIS

The global financial crisis that began in the United States in 2007 with the fall of the subprime mortgage market spread globally. Banks in the United States, the United Kingdom, and Iceland had to be recapitalized. World trade faltered, and the supply of credit was reduced, impacting Latin America, Asia, and Africa. Currency, equity, and capital markets declined. Australian councils which placed their trust in the judgment of ratings agencies lost millions of dollars. People lost their homes, their jobs, their retirement incomes, and their sense of who they were. Six years on, people are still recovering from the loss of jobs and homes, a lower US dollar, a euro crisis, and doubts about their sense of place.

One of the contributing factors to the GFC was the strong belief that house prices do not fall. In the US there was a push to increase home ownership, linking it to democracy. People with below-median incomes, mainly Hispanics, blacks, and those under the age of thirty-five, were offered mortgages. The interest rate was fixed for the first two years, and then the interest rate rose markedly.[2]

The subprime lenders took their commissions on the loan contracts and resold the loans in bulk to Wall Street banks. The banks then performed "financial alchemy."[3] They bundled the loans into residential mortgage-backed securities (RMBS) and sold them around the world to investors as high-yielding securities. The RMBS were repackaged as collateralized debt obligations (CDOs). The packages containing subprime mortgages were certified by the two dominant rating agencies, Moody's or Standard & Poor's, as securities that were unlikely to go into default.

The original lenders who knew that some of these were "NINJA" loans (to someone with "no income, no job or assets") kept none of the risk. This risk through the CDOs spread "across the globe from American state pension funds to public health networks in Australia and even to town councils beyond the Arctic Circle."[4]

At the same time the interest rate went up by roughly a quarter (from 5.34 percent to 6.66 percent). By March 2007 this was having a devastating effect. By July 2007 the ratings agencies began to downgrade RMBS and CDOs, leading to all kinds of financial institutions facing huge losses. Lehman Brothers, an investment bank, went bankrupt and was allowed to fail. Liquidity froze. The first reactions were to deny that there was a crisis. Then the United States began to bail out the banks, fearing a systemic breakdown in the banking system. By May 2008, one in ten single-family homes in the United States had negative equity. It could mean that in subsequent years 12.7 percent of American homeowners with mortgages would lose their homes.[5]

Explanations for the GFC range from growing inequality in the United States, untrammeled greed, mispricing of risk, incomprehensible derivatives, and failed regulation.[6] The trade in derivatives like the RMBS and CDOs grew fast in an unregulated market. The GFC revealed that few people in the market understood derivatives, though for a while they traded them profitably.

Anthropological and historical accounts of derivatives give the organizational and personal context of the creation of derivatives, the calculation of risk, and the diffusion and lack of regulation.[7] Derivatives were designed to disperse risk and insure against it. Derivatives went wrong when people used them without the safeguards that the innovators had put around them. They went wrong also because banks, investment funds, and ratings agencies had flawed incentives. The mathematical models behind the derivatives could not account for fear and emotion. The regulators did not understand them enough to give these new financial instruments the required oversight. The 2008 crash was not just about bankers being greedy. It was about compartmentalized silos in banks, banks forgetting they are a social institution, and regulators too focused on narrow indicators they did not understand rather than the social good.[8]

One form of credit derivatives was launched in 1997 by a small group of bankers at J. P. Morgan. They securitized corporate loans, packaging them into three different bundles of risk, each with its own rating. J. P. Morgan's confidence was based on the availability of good data on the risk of defaults in corporate loans. This packaging of credit default risk took the loans off the bank's books, enabling it to lend more. At the same time it offered a financial instrument where the profits rose with the accepted risk. The derivative was marketed as a BISTRO (broad index secured trust offering). This structure underlay a variety of collateralized debt obligations. The Morgan team did not follow the market in packaging mortgages, because they did not have sufficient data on the risk of mortgages defaulting to inform a credible model. They wondered where the others were getting the information.[9]

The GFC was also about a betrayal of trust. At the very least, it was about silos in the bank, with one division of the bank not knowing what the other is doing. Goldman Sachs, once a hallowed banking institution, was accused of selling mortgage securities to its clients while betting that this market would drop. The bank has not admitted or denied guilt, but it settled the *SEC v. Goldman Sachs* case by agreeing to pay a record fine of $550 million.[10]

This betrayal of trust also happened when ratings agencies guaranteed securities as crash proof, bowing to the pressure of banks and because of incompetence. Sydney Federal Court justice Jayne Jagot ruled on a case in 2012 involving ABN Amro's derivatives that were rated as AAA by Standard & Poor. Australian local councils lost millions invested in these derivatives because of this rating. Justice Jagot ruled that Standard & Poor had been incompetent in using the bank's model and code for testing the securities. The ratings agency also did not check the derivatives for the required level of volatility, accepting the bank's analysis. S&P has rejected the findings and is appealing.[11]

ECONOMIC GLOBALIZATION AND THE NEOLIBERAL FAITH IN MARKETS

Economic globalization is the dominant strand in studies of globalization. Economic globalization is identified with a neoliberal faith in free and self-regulating markets, the liberalization of trade, and the privatization of state-owned enterprises. This faith in open markets is seen as universally applicable, across nations and cultural differences.[12]

The coming together of economic globalization and neoliberalism made market globalism the dominant ideology of globalization. It outstrips justice globalism, which deals with distributive justice; global solidarity; and "jihadist globalism," which defends allegedly Islamic values that are seen to be under attack.[13]

The enthusiasm for market globalism has been dulled by the global financial crisis.[14] The Occupy Wall Street protest that began on September 17, 2011, in Zuccotti Park in New York's Wall Street Financial District spread to nine hundred cities across the world within a month.[15] It expressed global outrage against growing inequality and the greed and inequity of a financial system that offered bankers bonuses while people lost their homes.

The GFC has led to a limited questioning of the neoliberal ideology of free markets, though it is unclear if a new and wider social approach to money and markets is in place. One of the results of the GFC is that the need for appropriate regulation is now accepted. Financial institutions have always been regulated to some extent so that the players can trust that the system will work and that transactions will be honored according to accepted rules. This trust is also based on the assumption that financial institutions will have enough funds to cope with the risks they take in their financial intermediation. It has become obvious that there is a need for an effective mix of public and private regulation. The challenge remains to harmonize national systems of regulation and global markets.

Some regulatory stiffening has already happened at the Bank for International Settlements, the United States, and the United Kingdom. Banks have to keep a greater proportion of their funds as a buffer against which they lend. Off-balance-sheet items like derivatives come under greater regulatory scrutiny. The need for consumer protection is more openly acknowledged in institutional structures. But as yet there is little move to see markets as social institutions influenced by history and cultural differences. The GFC has yet to lead to a holistic market and social approach to markets. Regulators are talking to bankers and the market mainly in the language of law and economics, rather than addressing public anger at banks and bankers placing profit over the social good.

The disjuncture between the national and the global that is central to banking regulation is also dramatically seen in currency markets. This is particularly important for the imaginary of global money. Most currencies can be bought and sold globally. But currencies remain national and subject to national economic policies. National currencies continue to express national and cultural identity. They mimic the paradox of national financial regulation influenced by a country's history and values about the role of government versus the global "contagion" of interconnected markets during the GFC.

The experiment with a regional currency like the euro is being closely watched. The troubles of the euro in the aftermath of the GFC are leading to questions about currencies, history, and economic policy. Can a common currency survive differences of history, regulation, and monetary policies? Can there be a euro without a federation of European states? When countries differ in their economic performance, do fixed exchange rates of the euro become problematic?[16]

One of the most fervent stands of neoliberalism focused on currency exchange rates. The neoliberal approach supported by international financial institutions such as the International Monetary Fund (IMF) and the

World Bank until recently was that currencies should be allowed to freely oscillate according to market forces. The experience in Asia is that some currency controls bolster the economy in times of global financial crises. Jagdish Bhagwati, an avid supporter of the positive effects of free trade, argued against the IMF and the World Bank, saying there is a clear and powerful case for not liberalizing capital controls.[17]

China and India with their strong economies continue to have controls in place on their currency exchange and the flow of foreign capital for equity and investment. They were not as badly affected by the GFC as other countries with freely floating currencies. One of the reference points to this debate in Asia is the Asian financial crisis that swept through Indonesia, Malaysia, Thailand, the Philippines, and South Korea in 1997.

The crisis started in Thailand in 1997. In the summer of 1996, stock markets and property prices were at record highs. East Asia had had a decade of high growth and low inflation. Capital had flowed to East Asia from Japan. After bouts of currency speculation, Thailand floated the baht on July 2, 1997. By the end of the day the baht lost about 14 percent of its value in onshore trading and 19 percent in offshore trading. On the same day the Philippine peso was attacked. Malaysia and Indonesia were next. By October, the crisis had also engulfed Hong Kong, and in December, South Korea had to call on the IMF. By the end of December 1997, the won, rupiah, baht, and ringgit had lost 15 to 55 percent of their value, and stock markets had plunged between 10 and 50 percent since July 1997. Inflows of over $65 billion in 1996 in the five countries became annual outflows of nearly $20 billion in 1997 and 1998. Per capita incomes declined from a quarter to nearly half the levels of 1996.[18]

In the region, this was seen as a battle between "rogue speculators" and the economies of ASEAN (Association of Southeast Asian Nations) countries. On July 24, 1997, Dr. Mahathir Mohamad, then prime minister of Malaysia, lashed out against the call for open economies. He saw it as leaving the door open for "rogue speculators" and "anarchists wanting to destroy weak countries in their crusade for open societies."[19]

On September 1, 1998, Malaysia introduced selective exchange controls, which lasted until 2003. The response from the West was one of almost complete condemnation. IMF economists saw currency controls as an example of national controls trumping the ideology of free markets. The IMF stood behind their belief that successful financial openness promotes a stronger domestic financial sector and greater economic efficiency. It blamed "inappropriately rigid exchange rate regimes" as "the root problem behind most developing country financial crises of the past two decades."[20]

In 2010, after the GFC, the IMF reversed its opposition to capital controls. It agreed that emerging economies with capital controls in place had fared better in the global financial crisis. The IMF said that under some conditions, "(the) use of capital controls—in addition to both prudential and macroeconomic policy—is justified as part of the policy tool kit to manage inflows."[21]

THE SOCIAL CONCEPT OF MONEY BROADENS THE SCOPE OF ECONOMIC GLOBALIZATION

Economic globalization focuses on international trade, direct foreign investment and capital flows, the mobility of labor and people, and the use of technologies.[22] It also includes financial and banking globalization, trade liberalization and currency capital controls, the proliferation of derivatives and other forms of money aiming at risk minimization in the market, and the role of international institutions such as the World Bank, the IMF, and the Bank for International Settlements.

Money sits behind trade as a medium of exchange. It is present in flows of money in foreign direct investment. Money is traded as a commodity in financial markets. There is little discussion about the social characteristics of money because economists see money as synonymous with markets. There is also no discussion of the ways in which social relationships and cultural values shape market norms and interactions.

Discussions of the GFC dwelled on the human misery that resulted from the crash in terms of loss of homes and jobs. The Occupy Wall Street movement displayed people's anger and lack of faith in banks and the government. But the government and market response focused on the capitalization of banks and on ensuring the continued flow of credit and economic growth. The courts dealt with cases where the behavior of banks and ratings agencies toward their corporate clients and homeowners resulted in compensation. These are necessary and important policy moves. But other than isolated bankers talking about social responsibility and the social contract, there was silence. It was as if society needs banks and thus banks must not be allowed to suffer the financial consequences of their actions. But bankers can continue to feel entitled to high wages and bonuses, and banks can continue to flourish without understanding their social responsibilities.

Bankers' bonuses depend on their contributions to bank profits rather than their impact on clients' well-being and their contributions to social and human development. This is why most banks continue to ignore the poor, the unbanked, and the underbanked even when they suspect profits can be made in this space. Though some banks in the West have tried to fashion products to address the needs of the underbanked, most bank systems are not designed to offer immediate, small, and frequent loans that can be profitable. In Australia, the United States, and the United Kingdom, the annual percentage rates of payday loans can vary from 400 percent to more than 3,000 percent. Legislation has been patchy to cap interest rates charged by payday lenders and the practice of giving multiple loans.

Because money has been seen as belonging solely to the market, discussions of economic globalization have excluded half the world of the unbanked and women. I consider this in greater detail in chapters 3 and 4. In the last decade, financial inclusion and issues of gender equity in work, money, and access to technologies have become important for central banks in the global South and international institutions. The unbanked and women deal with money every day. They pay for goods and services, exchange gifts, and give and receive loans. They save and borrow frequently, sometimes with the help of savings clubs, kin, and neighbors. In chapter 3, I discuss the importance of understanding how the poor manage their money in order to design reliable and effective financial instruments to empower them and address global poverty.

The emphasis on national and global financial markets has also meant that discussions about economic globalization have not focused on the way women and men manage and control money in the household. The world of economic globalization is symbolized by trillions of dollars of fast-moving money across global financial markets rather than the smaller money transactions of families. This is why it was only in 2003 that it was realized that the small amounts migrants send to their families can add up to one of the largest international flows of money that is now more than three times official foreign aid.

GENDER AND ECONOMIC GLOBALIZATION

For a long time, discussions of globalization have been gender neutral, as if globalization affected men and women in the same ways. The faith in free and open markets does not lead to an awareness of gender discrimination. In much of the writing on economic globalization, questions about gender are not asked. But once the question is asked, gender becomes one of the most important dimensions of economic globalization. Women are 49.6 percent of the global population. How is it that they do 66 percent of the work (only 40.8 percent of the workforce in the formal sector), produce 50 percent of the food, but earn only 10 percent of the income and own only 1 percent of the property?[23] Why has globalization not led to women enjoying "decent work"?

National economic growth and economic globalization are weakened by not drawing on the potential of half the population. Women work more than men but have less money. Women have less access than men to financial services and ICTs. I examine this in more detail in chapter 4. This inequality seeps into every aspect of a woman's life. She is less able to choose the kind of life she wants, to resist domestic and sexual abuse, and to become a strong role model for gender equality for her sons and daughters. Patriarchy becomes normalized when men dominate the control of economic resources at home and at work. This male bias seeps across borders, for when families migrate together, remittances are overwhelmingly male. Diaspora philanthropy also has a male face, even when women may be behind the vision of a better future for the community. I detail this in chapter 8.

International organizations have recently begun to recognize gender issues in the legal frameworks, conditions of paid work, and access to technologies. The World Bank has measured legal gender parity in 141 economies from June 2009 to March 2011, focusing on the expansion of women's formal economic opportunities. Though women's financial empowerment depends on a variety of economic, social, and cultural factors, the legal framework around gender and economic opportunity is an important dimension. There are differences between law and practice, but identifying gender disparity in law is a first step.[24]

The most competitive economies also have the least legal discrimination against women. Legal gender disparity is most common in the Middle East and North Africa, South Asia, and sub-Saharan Africa. The discrimination is found in the areas of accessing institutions and using property. Sri Lanka is an exception in South Asia. In sub-Saharan Africa, the exceptions are Angola, Burkina Faso, Ethiopia, Kenya, Liberia, Mauritius, Namibia, South Africa, Zambia, and Zimbabwe. Kenya stands out globally as having made the most progress in the world in increasing women's legal equality. Its new constitution grants women equal rights in inheritance. It has a fast-track court procedure for small claims. Customary law is void if it is not consistent with the constitution.[25]

The International Labour Organization (ILO) has highlighted gender as one of the issues that needs to be addressed to achieve "decent work." The ILO introduced this concept in 2000 to take into account people's universal and basic aspirations. It is an essential component of a fair and just form of globalization.[26] Increased cross-border production, with a greater emphasis on outsourcing and offshoring work has led to more paid work opportunities for women in developing countries. Women, however, are clustered in the low-skilled roles in banking, telecommunications, and insurance. They are often involved in simple tasks like data entry and call-center work. These roles do not provide opportunities for career development and are at risk with further developments in technology.

Women are also the overwhelming majority of those who do the labor-intensive work for export industries in developing countries. Increased competition has led to poorer conditions of work. The conditions for "decent work" are not achieved, particularly at the bottom of global supply chains where work is contracted out and workers are employed on a temporary, casual basis or are home workers.

ILO conventions and international codes of conduct are also hard to monitor across different nation-states. The expected protections are particularly difficult to implement in the international care services dominated by women migrants. Working as domestic workers, women are vulnerable to exploitation and abuse. "The allocation of low-wage care work to migrant women reinforces the lower valuation of unpaid care within families, and of women's labour."[27]

GLOBAL DIMENSIONS OF MONEY

Just as the social concept of money changes the way we look at globalization, money also changes meaning and value when seen in a global context. The concept of "global money" draws attention to the way money crosses borders and changes characteristics and value when it moves across national boundaries.

Sending money across borders is not new for market transactions. Migrants have also long sent money overseas to families left behind in the source country. This was most often done through postal orders or via the remittance office in banks. It could take a month or more.[28] Bank drafts took equally long, particularly if they involved correspondent banks in the country of destination. It is the greater ease and speed of global transfers of personal money that has made remittances a powerful medium of family relationships.

Even now there are limits to this capacity for sending personal money across borders. Remittance transfer prices remain high. The average cost of sending remittances is 8.96 percent of the amount sent. To send $200, the average costs vary between 2.5 percent for the lowest-priced transfer between United Arab Emirates and Pakistan to 22.9 percent between South Africa and Zambia. The lack of transparency and the steep prices charged by banks means that a person sending money from Australia to Samoa can pay 29.52 percent via a bank rather than 0.88 percent through a money transfer organization.[29]

Transnational money—that is, money sent by migrants to family and community in the source country—can be local and global at the same time. As Sassen, Holton, and Steger say, the local, national, and global are not spatial categories that get progressively greater in scale. There are global aspects of the local, and the national is often the setting for the global.[30] So the setting of global money can also be local and national. Diaspora philanthropy as seen in chapter 8 is an apt example because it often involves giving to a local organization in one country for global causes in another.

Globalization at its present scale and interconnectedness is a new social and cultural context for money. Neither the sociology of money nor studies of globalization have focused on this transformation of money. Global money is wider than global finance, which relates to credit across borders. Global money takes into account trade in money as a commodity, payments, transfers like remittances, compensation, and gifts. It includes money in the markets and money in personal lives that are being lived locally and across countries. For migrants and their transnational families, global money is money that flows between different members of the family across countries. In the process, "transnational money" is valued differently from money earned in the source country. This is partly because of the different values of currencies in which the money is earned and spent. It is also the perceived relationship between work and income. Transnational money is also valued against physical care in the source country. It is often found wanting. A dollar sent is not the dollar received. I examine this in greater detail in chapter 8.

The change in the value of money sent and received connects with questions about the calculability of money in the market that was stressed by the classical sociologists. It brings to the fore anthropologists of money who have noted that the focus needs to move from the calculation of number to the interpretation of number in different social and cultural contexts. In questioning the calculability of number, they also question Weber's assertion that it is calculability that makes money "perfect" for markets. This questioning is important for global money as it moves between local, national, and global approximations of value.

The anthropology of money shows that number can be ambiguous and has to be interpreted in social and cultural contexts. Multiple monies are used as a means of ordering social relationships in different spheres of activity. Number can be used for approximation, for dealing with asymmetry, and for moving from one scale of valuation to another.[31] The approximation of number is particularly important when we see money as a social payment rather than focusing all our attention on money as market exchange.[32]

Exchange and calculation are not necessarily the defining characteristics of money in market situations. A study of security traders shows that numbers are interpreted in these market situations in the context of a social narrative.[33] I consider this work in more detail in chapter 5. Another study of the South African "gray money" amnesty illustrates the role of interpretation rather than calculation in markets. The government allowed a one-time payment to forgive offshore tax evaders. This measure "reconfigured 'tax minimizers' as law-abiding and rational economic actors hedging against risk."[34]

Globalization generates images of money traversing the globe instantaneously. Money is imagined globally but used locally. The local, national, and global "rub up against each other in myriad settings and on multiple levels."[35] The global imaginary of money struggles to express itself in lived experience. "The transformation of the national imaginary is a slow and messy business."[36] This is particularly true for money because a person has to slowly learn to approximate and interpret the value of money in local, national, and regional contexts.

PEOPLE AT THE CENTER OF ICTs, GLOBALIZATION, AND MONEY

The new information and communication technologies have changed both globalization and money. It is also important to ask how the global spread of money has changed the use of ICTs. In order to answer this question I combine perspectives from computer science, sociology, and media studies to place people at the center of the study of money, globalization, and new technologies.

The transformations of money and globalization brought about by the new ICTs have happened differently in personal life and in the market since the 1970s. The popular images of globalization are computer screens constantly flashing and moving money around the world. Financial markets have increased vastly in terms of scale, interconnectivity, and proportion to the aggregate gross domestic product. Financial markets are a greater percentage of the economy. Complicated software has multiplied the number of participants and transactions and has made longer transaction chains possible. It has enabled decentralized access, simultaneity, and interconnectivity. This has increased the amount of money in circulation that is many multiples—and growing—of long-term capital flows, direct foreign investment, and trade.[37]

Equally important is households' increasing use of electronic money within a country. I use the term "electronic money" to include all noncash and nonpaper payment instruments such as plastic cards, direct transfer and electronic wallets, and all money transactions via electronic channels such as automated teller machines (ATMs), electronic funds transfers at point of sale (EFTPOS), fixed and mobile telephones, and the Internet. Electronic money has become virtual, abstract, multiple in form and channel, mobile, and impersonal. Multiple forms and channels of money coexist.

People no longer talk of the distinction between "real money" and "plastic money" in everyday life in high-income countries. Automated teller machines, direct online transfers, and the credit card are everyday channels of money. Going to the branch or writing a check has become unusual for the younger generations. I write more about this in chapters 5 and 6. Mobile money, which uses the mobile phone as a channel of payment, gift, and transfer, is becoming increasingly important for the unbanked. M-PESA in Kenya, described further in chapter 7, is the success story where the banked and the unbanked use mobile money to send money home to their families, pay wages, and buy goods and services. By making payment and transfer instantaneous, mobile money makes money more immediate and empowering.

USER-CENTERED DESIGN

As a sociologist and anthropologist, it makes immediate sense to put people and their activities at the center of a consideration of money and technology. However, at general sociology conferences in Australia in the 1990s and early 2000s, the combination of money and technology was shunted to the edge. In international telecommunications and computer science conversations, the focus was more often on providers' perspectives and technical specifications. Though providers are intensely interested in the way people use their products and services, much of their research starts from the products and services they offer, rather than the world of the customer.

Bringing people to the center involves four major shifts. The changes have to do with the key questions, the conceptual frameworks, the methodological approach, and the language of discussion.[38]

Placing the user at the center of the study of the use of the new ICTs, globalization, and money shifts the questions from issues of supply to those of understanding the way a person uses the technologies in his or her money activities. Instead of asking how many people use the Internet for banking, I ask, how has the Internet changed the management and control of money? Placing the user at the center leads to a different set of questions, which probes how a person chooses a particular communication channel over another and the nature of the mix of channels. The issue, then, is to discover the changed nature and use of money as a result of the use of the new media.

Let me illustrate the importance of this shift from my early study *The Use of Electronic Money*.[39] This study began with questions taken from the current banking and information discourse. A central question was, how do you use plastic cards? When the plastic card was at the center of the question, the responses showed the plastic card was being used in all the important activities of a person's life (see figure 2.1). It is the kind of question the head of a debit and credit card department in the bank would ask. If this picture is taken as the whole picture, it can lead us to conclude that we are on the threshold of a cashless society.

The question was changed by placing the user and his or her payment activities at the center. The question became, how do you pay for shopping, education, films, and theater? Unpacking only some of the activities referred to in figure 2.1, it became clear that although plastic cards are being used in varied ways, cash, checks, EFTPOS and direct entry remain important. People said they paid for incidentals wholly by cash. Travel was paid by a mix of payments instruments, that is, check, cash and the credit card (see figure 2.2).

The conceptual frameworks shift with the social and cultural concept of money at the center of globalization. The preferred methodological

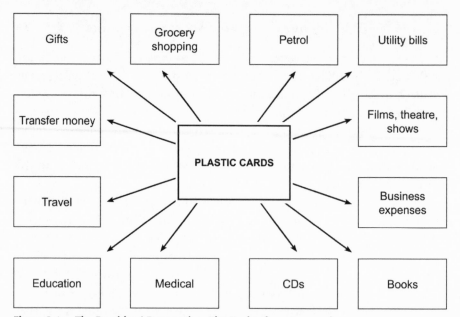

Figure 2.1. The Providers' Perspective: The Technology Approach
Source: Supriya Singh, *The Use of Electronic Money in the Home* (Melbourne: Centre for International Research on Communication and Information Technologies, 1996).

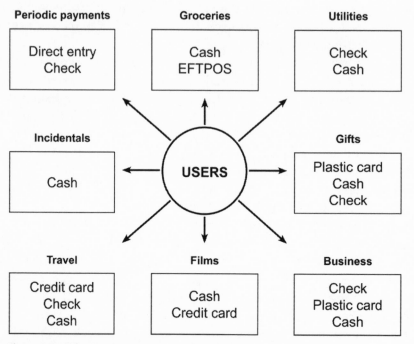

Figure 2.2. The Consumers' Perspective: The Activity Approach
Source: Supriya Singh, *The Use of Electronic Money in the Home* (Melbourne: Centre for International Research on Communication and Information Technologies, 1996).

approach is a blend of qualitative and quantitative studies of people's use of technologies in their social and cultural contexts. The mixed-method approach can cope with ambiguity and the need to discover questions as well as the policy need for numbers. With globalization, cross-cultural studies become essential to prevent universalizing one culturally appropriate way of use.

Some of the most far-reaching advances in "user-centered" or "human-centered" design have come from computer scientists who recognized the importance of the sociological perspective. Sociologists and anthropologists have been responsible for the broad concept of money connecting markets and personal lives. They have also directed attention to the use of new technologies, though not always connected with money. Media studies have focused on the use of new media and the "domestication" of ICTs. This combined body of work has influenced my approach to money, globalization, and technologies.

Michael Dertouzos, director of the MIT Laboratory for Computer Science (LCS) from 1974 until his death in 2001, was one of the passionate advocates of human-centered design. He argued that the information technology revolution remained unfinished as long as people were not at the center of design. He went beyond a focus on user-friendly computers to say that human-centric computing is the new approach whereby "computer systems should focus on our needs and capabilities."[40] He said, "We must pay attention to both the human and the computer side of the relationship."[41] His critique of machine-centered ways of designing was powerful because it was coming from a leading computer scientist.

John Seely Brown went further and addressed the social and cultural context of the use of technologies. He was head of Xerox PARC (Palo Alto Research Center) for a decade until June 2000 and is now a senior fellow at the Annenberg Center for Communication at the University of Southern California. He wrote an influential book with Paul Duguid called *The Social Life of Information* in which they argued that a concentrated focus only on technologies leads to tunnel vision. It overlooks the social context of the meaning and significance of information. Hence even enthusiasts of technologies have to focus on social practices and institutions.[42] Brown saw one of his biggest innovations at PARC as "getting the social-life perspective understood—looking at the dynamics of information and how it takes on meaning in social contexts."[43]

Sociologists emphasized that technologies shape and are shaped by social relations and cultural values. After a large body of literature on the social shaping of technologies,[44] it is no longer appropriate to ask only how the new technologies change globalization and money. We also need to ask how the social and cultural meanings of money and globalization shape the use of the new technologies.

Finding a common language is necessary for connecting the users' and providers' perspectives. "The way of saying is the what of saying."[45] Providers who speak in terms of the "rollout" of technologies and of "convergence" are also telling a story where technology provides the solutions to modern problems. Many of the metaphors of the public debate around ICTs are from engineering and economics. Hence the talk of "tool kits," "drivers," and "applications" on the one hand, and "demand," "price," "determinants," and "take-up" on the other. The relationship is linear and is depicted by value chains. It is measurable. New technology is better technology. It is presented as the idiom of the future. "The influence of metaphors is . . . often more powerful when they are so deeply embedded in a discourse that even the participants are not aware of it."[46] These metaphors often dictate the way the story is told or not told.

A different shaping of the story is seen with the user's perspective. The emphasis is on "use," "access," "constructing meaning," the "mix and match," and the "fit." These metaphors are influenced by anthropology and sociology. Bridge concepts like "trust" and "customer relationship" allow us to begin the conversation connecting the users' and providers' perspectives.

There is a body of work on the domestication of technologies which becomes pertinent to the study of electronic money in the household. This approach focuses on the fine grain of the use of ICTs in the household in the context of structural changes to the family. The design of ICTs anticipates and is shaped by use in domestic contexts.[47]

Media studies have also made valuable contributions to our knowledge of the use of new media. What is new in a social sense of domestic use may not be technologically new. New media differs from the old in that there is the multiplication of personally owned media—multiple televisions, telephones, and radios. The newness here is the social context of use rather than the technologies themselves. Both old and new media are diversifying in form and content and are encouraging a Western trend toward individualization. The convergence of media such as cable television and the personal computer—and now the mobile phone—is also new. The most radical change is the move from one-way mass communication to the user generating the content.[48]

Studying young people and new media takes some of these themes further. The new media are examined within the context of other leisure activities of the young person within the home, family, and everyday life. This shows how media shapes and is shaped by leisure. The new media coexists with the old, adding to the available options of use and preexisting practices and priorities.[49]

This coming together of new and old media, sometimes in different ways, is particularly pertinent to what is happening to banking and to domestic remittances. People may stop going to the branch in order to transact, but the branch can take on new meanings in framing the relationship between the bank and its customer. I also write in chapter 7 how mobile money has transformed the way people send money to their family and friends over distance. But they still send money with friends, or with bus or taxi drivers. They may use a bank or a mobile phone to save money. But at the same time, many continue to save money under the mattress.

In this chapter I have made transparent the conceptual underpinnings of the story of globalization and ICTs. I have shown how the social and cultural concept of money enlarges the reach of globalization. Money itself gets transformed when it crosses borders to become "global money." Placing people at the center helps to reveal how the new ICTs shape both money and globalization and are themselves changed in the process. In the following chapter I examine money in the lives of half the world that is unbanked.

NOTES

1. Saskia Sassen, *A Sociology of Globalization* (New York: Norton, 2007); "The Embeddedness of Electronic Markets: The Case of Global Capital Markets," in *The Sociology of Financial Markets*, ed. Karin Knorr Cetina and Alex Preda (Oxford: Oxford University Press, 2005); Manfred B. Steger and Ravi K. Roy, *Neoliberalism: A Very Short Introduction* (Oxford: Oxford University Press, 2010); Manfred B. Steger, *Globalization: A Very Short Introduction* (Oxford: Oxford University Press, 2009); *The Rise of the Global Imaginary: Political Ideologies from the French Revolution to the Global War on Terror* (Oxford: Oxford University Press, 2008); Robert J. Holton, *Global Finance* (New York: Routledge, 2012); *Making Globalization* (New York: Palgrave Macmillan, 2005); *Globalization and the Nation-State* (New York: St. Martin's, 1998).

2. Robert J. Shiller, *The Subprime Solution: How Today's Financial Crisis Happened, and What to Do about It* (Princeton, NJ: Princeton University Press, 2008).

3. Niall Ferguson, *The Ascent of Money: A Financial History of the World* (Camberwell, Victoria: Allen Lane, 2008), 269.

4. Ferguson, *The Ascent of Money*, 269.

5. Ferguson, *The Ascent of Money*, 269.

6. Raghuram Rajan, *Fault Lines: How Hidden Fractures Still Threaten the World Economy* (Princeton, NJ: Princeton University Press, 2010); Shiller, *The Subprime Solution*; Holton, *Global Finance*.

7. See Gillian Tett, *Fool's Gold: How the Bold Dream of a Small Tribe at J. P. Morgan Was Corrupted by Wall Street Greed and Unleashed a Catastrophe* (New York: Free Press, 2009); Edward LiPuma and Benjamin Lee, *Financial Derivatives and the Globalization of Risk* (Durham, NC: Duke University Press, 2004).

8. Tett, *Fool's Gold*.

9. Tett, *Fool's Gold*.

10. William D. Cohan, *Money and Power: How Goldman Sachs Came to Rule the World* (London: Allen Lane, 2011).

11. Bernard Lagan, "The Smartest Girls in the Room," *Global Mail*, December 3, 2012.

12. Steger and Roy, *Neoliberalism: A Very Short Introduction*.

13. Steger, *Globalization: A Very Short Introduction*.

14. Joseph Stiglitz, *Freefall: Free Markets and the Sinking of the Global Economy* (London: Penguin, 2010).

15. Karla Adam, "Occupy Wall Street Protests Go Global," *Washington Post*, October 15, 2011.

16. Amartya Sen, "Ruinous Policy Stymies Europe's Grand Vision," *The Age*, July 5, 2012.

17. Jagdish Bhagwati, *In Defense of Globalization* (Oxford: Oxford University Press, 2004, 2007).

18. Andrew Sheng, *From Asian to Global Financial Crisis: An Asian Regulator's View of Unfettered Finance in the 1990s and 2000s* (Cambridge: Cambridge University Press, 2009).

19. Cited in Sheng, *From Asian to Global Financial Crisis*, 25.

20. M. A. Kose et al., "Financial Globalization: A Reappraisal," *IMF Staff Papers* 56, no. 1 (2009): 10.

21. Jonathan D. Ostry et al., "Capital Inflows: The Role of Controls," in *IMF Staff Position Note* (International Monetary Fund, 2010), 5.

22. Bhagwati, *In Defense of Globalization*.

23. World Bank, *Removing Barriers to Economic Inclusion: Measuring Gender Parity in 141 Economies* (Washington, DC: World Bank, 2012).

24. World Bank, *Removing Barriers*.

25. World Bank, *Removing Barriers*.

26. "ILO Declaration on Social Justice for a Fair Globalization," http://www.ilo.org/public/english/bureau/dgo/download/dg_announce_en.pdf (accessed November 4, 2012).

27. Amelita King Dejardin, *Gender Dimensions of Globalization* (International Labour Organization, 2008), 19.

28. See Nancy Foner, "Transnationalism Then and Now: New York Immigrants Today and at the Turn of the Twentieth Century," in *Migration, Transnationalization, and Race in a Changing New York*, ed. Héctor R. Cordero-Guzmán, Robert C. Smith, and Ramón Grosfoguel (Philadelphia: Temple University Press, 2001); Supriya Singh, *Bank Negara Malaysia: The First 25 Years, 1959–1984* (Kuala Lumpur: Bank Negara Malaysia, 1984); Karen Isaksen Leonard, *Making Ethnic Choices: California's Punjabi Mexican Americans* (Philadelphia: Temple University Press, 1992).

29. World Bank, *Remittance Prices Worldwide: Making Markets More Transparent* (Washington, DC: World Bank, 2012).

30. Steger, *Globalization: A Very Short Introduction*; Holton, *Making Globalization*; Sassen, *A Sociology of Globalization*.

31. Jane I. Guyer, *Marginal Gains: Monetary Transactions in Atlantic Africa* (2004).

32. Bill Maurer, "Incalculable Payments: Money, Scale, and the South African Off-shore Grey Money Amnesty," *African Studies Review* 50, no. 2 (2007).

33. Caitlin Zaloom, "Ambiguous Numbers: Trading Technologies and Interpretation in Financial Markets," *American Ethnologist* 30 (2003).

34. Maurer, "Incalculable Payments," 125.

35. Steger, *The Rise of the Global Imaginary*, 15.

36. Steger, *The Rise of the Global Imaginary*, 194.

37. Sassen, "The Embeddedness of Electronic Markets."

38. Supriya Singh, "Studying the User: A Matter of Perspective," *Media International Australia* 98 (February 2001).

39. Supriya Singh, *The Use of Electronic Money in the Home* (Melbourne: Centre for International Research on Communication and Information Technologies, 1996).

40. Michael L. Dertouzos, *The Unfinished Revolution: Human-Centered Computers and What They Can Do for Us* (New York: HarperCollins, 2001), xii.

41. Dertouzos, *The Unfinished Revolution*, 6.

42. John Seely Brown and Paul Duguid, *The Social Life of Information* (Boston: Harvard Business School Press, 2000).

43. Michael Schrage, "The Debriefing: John Seely Brown," *Wired*, http://www.wired.com/wired/archive/8.08/brown.html?pg=2&topic=&topic_set= (accessed October 6, 2005).

44. Judy Wajcman, "Addressing Technological Change: The Challenge to Social Theory," *Current Sociology* 50, no. 3 (2002); Maria Bakardjieva and Richard Smith, "The Internet in Everyday Life," *New Media and Society* 3, no. 1 (2001); Wiebe E. Bijker and John Law, "General Introduction," in *Shaping Technology/Building Society: Studies in Sociotechnical Change*, ed. Wiebe E. Bijker and John Law (Cambridge, MA: MIT Press, 1992); Annegrethe Hansen and Christian Clausen, "Social Shaping Perspectives in Danish Technology Assessment," *Technology in Society* 25, no. 3 (2003); Donald MacKenzie and Judy Wajcman, eds., *The Social Shaping of Technology* (Buckingham: Open University Press, 1999); William H. Dutton, ed., *Information and Communication Technologies: Visions and Realities* (Oxford: Oxford University Press, 1996).

45. Clifford Geertz, *Works and Lives: The Anthropologist as Author* (Stanford, CA: Stanford University Press, 1988), 68.

46. H. Sawhney and K. Jayakar, "Universal Service: Migration of Metaphors" (paper presented at the Telecommunications Policy Research Conference, Solomons Island, Maryland, 1996), 20.

47. Roger Silverstone and Leslie Haddon, "Design and Domestication of Information and Communication Technologies: Technical Change and Everyday Life," in *Communication by Design: The Politics of Information and Communication Technologies*, ed. Robin Mansell and Roger Silverstone (Oxford: Oxford University Press, 1996).

48. Sonia Livingstone, "New Media, New Audiences?," *New Media & Society* 1, no. 1 (1999).

49. Sonia Livingstone, *Young People and New Media* (London: Sage, 2002).

CHAPTER 3

HALF THE WORLD IS UNBANKED

Irene, thirty, sits in a pandanus hut fringed by mountains in the Morobe province of Papua New Guinea and tells how her family of six lives on $2.79 a day. They grow 150 kilograms of betel nut that brings them about 1,000 kina (roughly $430) a year. This is money from her husband's land, so it is money she does not control. She sells taro, fruit, and greens every fortnight at the market, a half an hour's walk from her village. From the 40 kina she gets, she buys oil and salt. Sixteen kina go for her husband's mobile phone top-up every fortnight, paying for twenty minutes' talk time. "I buy rice if there is money. If not, we eat taro every day, every month."

Irene saves her money in the walls of the pandanus hut or in a hole in the ground. Irene's dream is to educate her four boys. There is no bank branch within easy reach. She uses whatever mechanisms she can to save money. But most of the time, it is a difficult subsistence because there isn't enough money.

The annual school fees for her three who are in school are nearly 100 kina. The government has been talking of making the first few years of primary schooling free. Holding her youngest close to her, she says she went to the clinic at the market and paid 50 toya (half a kina) to have him seen. She gives two to three kina a week to her husband who has gambling debts.

There are weddings and funerals where each family gifts two or three kina plus food. Her two brothers send her money when they can. Her father, who lives in a village farther north, gives her money toward the school fees. He sends her a message on her husband's mobile phone, and she meets him at the public motor vehicle stop when he is on his way to Lae.

She wants a secure place for her savings. Irene needs to be able to manage small, irregular, and unpredictable amounts of money for the family's daily needs. She saves in order to spend later and borrows if she can. She wants to separate money that is immediately available for everyday needs and some that can be sequestered away from herself and her husband so that it slowly builds up to pay school fees. And as with all of us, money is a medium of relationship. She says she will open a mobile bank account in Lae, a six-hour ride one way, when she has 100 kina to spare for the return trip. She is most likely also budgeting for a mobile phone.

Irene is one of the unbanked. Nearly half the people in the world aged fifteen and above do not have an account with a bank, credit union, cooperative, post office, or microfinance institution. When the social concept of money, rather than markets, is at the center of globalization, the story includes Irene. The challenge for developing countries is to see how, with the help of technology and the effective design of money management services, this half of the population can be brought into the formal payment and banking systems. The savings available to the country would increase. Irene's life would be easier if she had a secure and private place to save near her home. Access to flexible and sustainable credit would help with emergencies and help her cope with a shortage in the school fees. It would also help Irene if her father could send her money via the mobile phone, as is happening in Kenya and many other countries in Africa and Asia.

Financial inclusion will work only if it fits with the way Irene manages her money. It will be important for Irene to be able to keep the social and cultural context of the give-and-take that is part of her life now. She most likely will continue to use a mix of formal and informal money management tools. Some of the most interesting innovations around the management of money are happening among the unbanked. These are a mirror image of new ways of dealing with money in the developed world and will remain part of the future of money.

The literatures and players in the world of the unbanked differ from those involved in discussions of globalization. In the world of the unbanked, at the center are international organizations like the World Bank, the Consultative Group to Assist the Poor (CGAP), and the Alliance for Financial Inclusion. The United Kingdom's Department for International Development (DFID) is a prominent player, as is the Bill and Melinda Gates Foundation. Relevant research is about poverty, financial and social exclusion, and the ways technology can help. The regulation of banking and payments revolves around these issues. Global financial markets, the global financial crisis, the role of derivatives, and even banking money seem distant. Money as a medium of relationship remains a constant.

There are five stories told in this space. The first story is about bringing people from informal financial services to the world of formal financial services, adding to transparency and economic growth. We have to find out how many people are unbanked, who are the unbanked, and why they are unbanked. A global picture is just emerging. The second story introduces the way regulators are addressing this issue with the help of new technologies. The third story is how the poor manage money. The fourth revolves around broad theoretical approaches to development, freedom, and capabilities. This story, articulated by Amartya Sen and Martha Nussbaum, says that development and financial inclusion mean the freedom for people to live the kind of life they choose. This is done by giving people the capability to choose and act in their preferred ways, while putting in place the institutional structures and values that are supportive.[1]

The fifth story moves the focus to the reduction of poverty at the ground level. One part of the story is about social justice and inspirational programs, like Muhammad Yunus's Grameen Bank, while advocating a greater participation in market economies. Another is the approach advocated by the late C. K. Prahalad.[2] He introduced the concept of the "bottom of the pyramid" to describe the bottom two-thirds of the global population who live on less than $2 a day. He argued that we must see the poor as value-conscious and entrepreneurial customers who need to be served, and as customers who will be profitable.

Gender in relation to financial inclusion is such an important subject that I will consider it at length in the next chapter. It takes us to the marketplace and inside the family and the household to ensure that women are well served by the policies and programs of financial inclusion.

COUNTING THE UNBANKED

The figures are stark, they vary across continents, and they are changing fast in some countries, given the impact of financial inclusion initiatives. It is important to grasp the extent of the problem. What is clear from the most recent data is that 2.5 billion people—that is, half the world fifteen years of age and above—are unbanked. In developing countries, the percentage rises to 59 percent. More than three-fourths (77 percent) of those who live on less than $2 a day do not have an account, with women being even more excluded. Financial exclusion, poverty, and gender and intertwined.[3]

The Global Financial Inclusion (Findex) database includes data collected in 2011 on more than 150,000 adults in 148 economies. This represents about 97 percent of the world's population. They asked more than seventy thousand people why they did not have an account in a formal financial institution. The most common answer (65 percent) was that they did not have enough money to use one. Other reasons were that banks or accounts were too expensive and that another family member already had an account. Banks were also too far away and/or customers did not have the necessary papers to open an account. Others did not trust banks, and yet others had religious reasons for not having a formal account.

Approaches to accounting for the financially excluded differ according to the perceived importance of different gradations of exclusion. The latest data from Africa separates those who are formally included—that is, those who have accounts in banks and other formal financial institutions—from those who are informally served and those who are financially excluded from formal and informal financial services. With this approach, those who are financially excluded even from the informal sphere vary from 27 percent in South Africa in 2011 to 78 percent in Mozambique in 2009. If we include those who are only informally served among the financially excluded, the figures go up to 32 percent for South Africa and 87 percent for Mozambique. If we take being banked as the marker for financial inclusion, the figures for the unbanked are 37 percent in South Africa and 88 percent in Mozambique and Tanzania (personal communication, Kammy Naidoo, September 6, 2012). In all the countries surveyed, women are more financially excluded.[4]

There are also significant percentages of people who are financially excluded to varying degrees in high-income countries. These pockets of inequality and marginalization have been difficult to address, as financial inclusion is not the central plank of government or regulatory policies. A

Federal Deposit Insurance Corporation survey done in 2011 found that in the United States 8.2 percent of households are unbanked. This translates to one in twelve US households. This is a 0.6 percent increase since the first survey in 2009—that is, an additional 821,000 households. The figures would most likely be higher if measured according to individuals.

In addition, one in five households (20.1 percent) is underbanked. The underbanked belong to households that have a checking and/or a savings account and had used alternative financial services such as nonbank money orders, nonbank check-cashing services, nonbank remittances, payday loans, rent-to-own services, pawnshops, or refund anticipation loans (RALs) in the previous twelve months.[5]

The Australian picture is minimally better than the United States in that 17.2 percent of the adult population is financially excluded. Only 1.1 percent of Australians do not have a transaction account with a formal financial institution, as all government benefits have to be paid into such an account. But another 16.1 percent are financially excluded because they only had one financial services product. The factors leading to financial exclusion include the high costs of using these services, distance from a bank branch, language and literacy difficulties, and problems related to providing identity documents. Low income, low education, being born overseas, living in a large rural or remote area or the inner-city areas of major capital cities, being eighteen to twenty-four years of age, plus unemployment increase the chances of being financially excluded. Thirty-nine percent of the population does not have any mainstream credit products. Indigenous consumers are overrepresented among consumers who are unbanked and underbanked. The percentage could be as high as 43.1 percent.[6] They face additional barriers with difficulties in obtaining birth certificates because of cost and lack of awareness. Without this basic identity document, it is difficult to access government and financial services.[7]

TECHNOLOGY, REGULATION, AND FINANCIAL INCLUSION

The social, economic, and regulatory challenge is to ensure that people have access to formal financial services. Financial inclusion for most policy makers has meant that people have bank accounts where they can save and access credit. The major push is economic, but the passion behind financial inclusion is to encourage people to develop their capabilities and live a life where they have the freedom of choice.

There is a strong push by governments in the global South to address financial exclusion. The coming together of international institutions, philanthropic bodies, national governments, telecommunications operators, and financial institutions has made for some success in increasing financial inclusion.

In order to increase financial inclusion, a balance has to be struck between regulation that is flexible enough to allow for innovation, while at the same time providing trust in the system and maintaining consumer protection. Regulators have to be conscious of "enablement."[8] They need to strike the balance between enabling new models and markets to emerge and protecting customers who must entrust their money to new providers. Technology is an important component for solutions, for it is not feasible to extend the branch and ATM network to every part of the country. This has led to the search for branchless solutions, whether it be mobile money services, banking correspondents, or mobile ATMs.

The issue often discussed between regulators in the South is whether the regulatory strategy should be payments led or bank led. Should we see financial inclusion as being banked, or should the emphasis be on providing the poor with formal payment services and safe storage of savings? These formal payments may in turn become a bridge to being banked.

Stephen Mwaura Nduati, head of the National Payment System of the Central Bank of Kenya, says the Central Bank sees access to formal payment services as being part of a broader push toward financial inclusion (personal communication, August 29, 2012). The Central Bank of Kenya sees its role in relation to payments as one of monitoring existing payment systems and, "where necessary, inducing change."[9] This approach has contributed to the resounding success of M-PESA, Kenya's mobile money service, which has enabled the poor to move to formal payment services. A 2012 survey of Kenyans at the base of the pyramid showed that more than four-fifths (84.4 percent) now use M-PESA.[10]

For the Central Bank of Kenya, M-PESA has become a central plank in what Maurer calls the "empowerment story."[11] M-PESA allows the transfer of money via mobile phone without the need for a bank account. Mobile money has extended the reach of formal payments, leading in time to people becoming banked and using credit for economic growth. The Central Bank of Kenya's focus is on financial inclusion while balancing it with the need for security, safety, and efficiency. It argues that banking and payments need to be regulated for different kinds of threats. The focus is on banks and mobile network operators

(MNOs) "integrating," rather than allowing for interoperability of different MNO networks.

Some of the regulatory challenges for mobile money were summarized well after a meeting in Malaysia between regulators from Asia Pacific countries, providers, and international organizations.[12] Issues of consumer protection, privacy, and fraud needed to be addressed. Policies needed to be in place to fulfill "Know Your Customer" (KYC) guidelines, which identify the customer and guard against money laundering and financing terrorism. But perhaps the greatest challenge was to allow "an appropriate balance of competition and cooperation in retail payment systems in order to promote a certain degree of interoperability."[13] This meant preventing monopolies that would be against the customer's interests while providing incentives for new players to invest in branchless banking.

Everybody agrees that the future of financial services in Kenya and perhaps elsewhere is mobile. There has been a significant increase in formal access to payments in Kenya since M-PESA. The Global Findex database (2012) shows that 43 percent of those who used M-PESA in the last twelve months have no bank accounts. The banks have also expanded their network and customer reach in terms of bank branches, particularly in rural areas, and their ATM network. But according to the Global Findex database (2012), only 42 percent of adult Kenyans aged fifteen years and above have an account with a formal financial institution. This compares with 26.47 percent in 2006 according to the FinAccess survey. It is still short of the 60 percent needed to achieve the targets of Kenya's vision to become a developed country by 2030.[14]

Despite M-PESA's success, questions continue to be asked of the Central Bank of Kenya. Have they enabled a level playing field for the operation of mobile money and mobile banking? In pushing "integration" of the banks and mobile operators, are they forgetting the importance of the interoperability of mobile networks? Has the Central Bank put M-PESA on such a pedestal that they have allowed it to become uncompetitive, unregulated, and unsustainable? Does M-PESA provide the poor with the financial intermediation that is needed? Why do banks have to pay M-PESA's monopoly rates to use its network even when the bank partners with M-PESA? Are banks partners or competitors? The question that at least some banks may be asking themselves is, will we become the backroom boys for the storage of money while payments come to center stage? Behind these questions lies a potential conflict of interests, for Safaricom is owned partly by the government of Kenya.

The accusation that the Central Bank's policies are uncompetitive strikes a nerve, especially when they are seemingly supported by the World Bank. A 2012 World Bank report notes that there needs to be greater regulatory attention to issues of competition and interoperability. Safaricom, which has 68 percent of the mobile subscribers market, is in a position to dictate the terms of M-PESA, which can only be used by Safaricom customers. The Central Bank needs to avoid introducing premature competition that may suppress the growth of mobile money services. At the same time, if anticompetitive practices are not curtailed in a timely manner, there will be financial and social costs.[15]

The report cites the example of Nigeria where interoperability between MNOs, between banks, and between banks and MNOs is mandated to prevent one player from dominating the market. But it has to be noted that mobile money services in Nigeria have hardly taken off.

The World Bank report led to a limited debate in Kenya and among mobile money intellectuals. The report was interpreted as criticizing the Central Bank for being uncompetitive. Kevin Donovan reiterated in his blog that the World Bank recognizes that "the appropriate form of regulation is still emerging" and that the benefits of mobile money should be sustainable and have a broad reach.[16] Monopoly concerns have heightened with M-PESA using its agents to service its M-Shwari savings and microloans service exclusively with the Commercial Bank of Africa.[17]

The Central Bank of Kenya has followed Brazil and Colombia's banking agents model and in May 2010 permitted banks to expand through banking agents. The tension between the MNOs and the banks lies in the fact that M-PESA's agent network is exclusive in practice, while banking agents, by regulation, cannot be exclusive. Banking agents are required to have an eighteen-month business track record compared to the six months for mobile money agents. Banking agents also are not allowed to sign clients to bank accounts, though M-PESA agents can open bank accounts for their customers, admittedly with lower transaction and deposit limits. Banks are liable for agents' actions. The liability of telecommunications companies for payment agents is not explicit.

The nonexclusivity of banking agents has given later players an advantage, for they have a free ride on Equity Bank's initial investment in the network in order to identify and train agents with enough liquidity. Almost every Equity Bank outlet is co-branded with five or six other commercial banks, Airtel Money, Orange Money, and co-op banking agents.

The banks are being heard. Matu Mugo, assistant director of bank supervision at the Central Bank of Kenya has recommended that banks be permitted to have payment agents—that is, "cash merchants"—as well as full-fledged banking agents. As cash agents would incur less risk in that they would provide basic payment services only, there needs to be a review of the guidelines covering exclusivity and institutional liability.[18]

Nduati acknowledges that developing appropriate regulations to safeguard consumers and the banking system is "tricky."[19] But the main task before the Central Bank is to raise the level of the banked to 60 percent by 2030. This means getting an additional twenty-one million people in the banking system between 2010 and 2030, particularly from rural areas. This will be possible only with lower costs for banks and consumers. And that translates to mobile. There also needs to be a wide range of locations and channels for customers to "deposit and withdraw cash in exchange for electronic value."[20]

It also remains to be seen how far the Central Bank of Kenya will go toward reducing the effects of the dominance of Safaricom. In May 2012, Safaricom's share of Kenya's total mobile money market of 19.7 million customers was 77 percent, and in June 2012 it had 67 percent of the mobile money agents in Kenya. This dominance has been one of the factors in M-PESA's stellar success in increasing one aspect of financial inclusion in Kenya. Moreover, most people in Kenya are besotted by M-PESA. I did not hear anyone say they wanted to return to the pre-M-PESA days. Ignacio Mas relates in a blog how the perception that he was not giving sufficient weight to the success of M-PESA was enough to get him a hostile reception.[21]

Brazil has taken a different route and succeeded in introducing business correspondents to extend the reach of banks. They were first introduced in the 1970s. Their number has grown. Business correspondents are used by governments for the payment of social benefits. For consumers they are the most-used channel for the payment of utility and other bills and for credit transfers. As a result, access to financial services has improved in every region and municipality.

This success has come through gradually expanding the services of business correspondents. In 1999, business correspondents were allowed to receive and refer applications to open demand, fixed-term, and savings deposit accounts. They could also take receipts and payment for these accounts, as well as investment funds. At first business correspondents could only operate in areas where there was no bank branch. But in 2000, this restriction was removed. It led to an increase in access and greater competition for banking services. In February 2011, business correspondents were also allowed to engage in foreign exchange business. This was up to a limit of $3,000 per transaction or the equivalent in other currencies. The principal bank remains solely responsible and liable for these services provided by its affiliated business correspondents.[22]

Getting the right balance around mobile money and financial inclusion troubles many central banks in the global South. Bank Indonesia is reflecting whether its bank-led regulation has prevented mobile money from taking off. T-Cash, the first mobile money scheme in Indonesia, was launched in 2007, the same year as M-PESA. Telkomsel, like Safaricom, is the country's biggest MNO. But only 3.8 percent of its mobile phone subscribers use mobile money. Siti Hidayati, senior payment system overseer at Bank Indonesia, said the Central Bank was concerned that "Know Your Customer" requirements were fulfilled, as they were essential for anti–money laundering (AML) efforts and combating the financing of terrorism (CFT). So it asked for each agent to individually apply to be a money remitter. This has resulted in there being only five thousand outlets for T-Cash in the big cities compared with Telkomsel's five hundred thousand airtime dealers. She recommended that "cash-out activities should not be considered money remittance activities because they only exchange electronic value to cash, in real time."[23] Mobile money providers should, however, be required to train their agents regarding AML/CFT and be responsible for their agents' misconduct.

India is moving toward mobile money, mobile banking, and financial inclusion. Progress has been slow, with India experimenting with mobile money services, banking correspondents, and mobile ATMs. As Ignacio Mas, formerly of the Bill and Melinda Gates Foundation, told David Wolman in Seattle, "Because it's so massive, and the need so pronounced, India is the ultimate proof of principle for mobile money."[24] India has a large unbanked population of 65 percent, near universal telephone coverage with low costs, and a culture of remittances. Sending money home is a feature of family life, both for urban–rural and international remittances.

Senior officials of the Reserve Bank of India (RBI) speak often and passionately about financial inclusion. Since 2006, the Reserve Bank has permitted and liberalized banks' use of third-party business correspondents. It has relaxed its "Know Your Customer" guidelines for small-value accounts. RBI, however, allows mobile money to be offered only in partnership with banks.[25] There is a growing recognition that banks have not been chasing the unbanked market. Even when the number of accounts opened is impressive, a large percentage of the accounts have no transactions. The RBI is offering new banking licenses expected by March 2014, with one of the conditions being that the banks open 25 percent of their branches in rural areas.[26]

Ensuring that the population can be identified for the opening of bank accounts is itself a massive operation. An ambitious national identity scheme being implemented by the Unique Identification Authority of India (UIDAI) has been under way since 2009. By the end of April 2013, UIDAI had issued over 320 million Aadhaar (identity) cards. A million Aadhaar cards are issued every day. But this still leaves many of India's 1.2 billion people without an identity card.[27]

New mobile money initiatives are continually being announced in India. Some of them seem to have a lot of potential, though none of them have reached the proportions of M-PESA in Kenya. Progress is slow and difficult to measure. The State Bank of India (SBI) has been in partnership with Eko since 2009. Some accounts of this partnership are glowing, with the focus on the increasing number of customers, the volume and value of transactions, and the profitability for business correspondents and their customer service point (CSP) agents.[28] A survey of 814 Eko customers showed that the Eko partnership with SBI is reaching the unbanked. Thirty-nine percent "had not used any form of financial services before and only 48 percent had previously had a bank account."[29]

SBI and Eko's most popular "Tatkal" (instant) service offers a simple way of sending money in real time to an SBI bank account anywhere in India. The sender gives the cash, the mobile numbers of the sender and receiver, plus the receiver's bank account to the agent. The agent dials a short sequence of numbers for the money to be deposited into the account. An SMS (instant message) is sent to both the sender and the recipient verifying the transaction, the time, and the fees levied. The recipient can go to any ATM and withdraw the money with no fee payable. Each of Eko's three hundred most active agents in Delhi complete 150 to 200 transactions per day. Most transactions are around $80, though they are capped at $200. These transactions yield some $20 in fees for the agents. This is higher than the usual $1 to $5 earned by agents in India.[30]

Other more localized accounts reveal that the model of agent banking in India has yet to become sustainable. In Canning, a small town about two hours away from Kolkata, a local bank agent enrolled one hundred people for the State Bank of India. Six months later, their accounts still have not been activated. This is similar to the findings of a national survey by CGAP and the College of Agricultural Banking, which shows that approximately a quarter of the bank agents are either "unavailable or unable to transact."[31] The survey also shows that being a bank agent brings with it an elevated status within the community. But in most cases, bank agents' income is low. Agents are dissatisfied by the lack of support from the business correspondent who hires the agents. But overall, 51 percent of the customers are satisfied with their experience.[32]

The latest push is coming from the Indian government's decision to begin transferring some subsidies, benefits, and scholarships in cash directly to bank accounts. Brazil's Bolsa Familia, a conditional cash transfer scheme that was launched in 2003, is quoted as the inspiration behind India's scheme. Bolsa Familia is credited with a positive impact on the alleviation of poverty, an increase in education and health welfare for the poorest families, and greater financial inclusion.[33]

The scope of India's cash transfer scheme has been shifting in terms of the number of districts to be covered, the kinds of subsidies, and the expected date of completion. It is hoped the move toward cash transfers will block leakage of government funds, ensure that the money is with the recipients, increase financial inclusion, and lead to more votes for the present United Progressive Alliance (UPA) government in the elections most likely to be held in 2014.

The first reactions to the announcement have been mixed. There are fears its failure may lead to people being worse off. If this initiative works, and banks and post offices work with the government, it will mean that financial inclusion will be fast-tracked. The real payoff will be that most of the people will then have a place to securely place their savings, as well as access to credit and insurance. Banks and the economy as a whole will benefit from the savings coming into the banking market and from some cash transactions becoming electronic. This will become especially true when another suggestion is implemented, that is that information in bank accounts can be accessed via mobile phones by dialing *99# at no charge.[34]

There have been a few muddles since the announcement of the scheme and its beginning in January 2013. At present, most people in India do not have an Aadhaar card or a bank account. The bridging mechanisms are unclear between banks and the Aadhaar numbers. It is feared that people may be excluded from this cash transfer scheme. Though the subsidies originate from the center, it is the states that hold the databases which will need to be digitized. The politics behind this move will no doubt play a part in the scheme's success or failure.[35]

The use of technology and enabling regulation together with adequate consumer safeguards is part of the mix for a successful assault on financial exclusion. There are different roads to this success, and many countries are still finding their way. Success, however, will come when the solutions address customers' needs. And for that it is essential to know how the poor manage their money.

HOW THE POOR MANAGE THEIR MONEY

The traditional notion has been that the poor have too little money to have a financial life. It is only recently that this approach has been overturned by an empirical focus on how the poor manage their money. The star turn in this literature is *Portfolios of the Poor* by Collins, Morduch, Rutherford, and Ruthven in 2009.[36] The book focuses on the complicated ways in which the poor actively manage money, how they manage the peaks and troughs of their income and expenditure by frequently saving and borrowing small amounts of money, and how they do this in a way that connects them to their family, kin, and neighborhood. This book succeeded in bringing these insights to the consciousness of the development and philanthropic community. Though anthropologists have focused on money, livelihood, and family through more intensive engagement, Collins et al.'s comparative study, covering India, Bangladesh, and South Africa, succeeded in connecting the perspectives of the poor to the language and frameworks of the communities trying to address financial exclusion.

Collins et al.'s insights are based on fortnightly interviews over a year, written up as financial diaries. Their data improved after the sixth diary visit, partly because they were trusted more, and partly because they were able to note the informal saving, lending, and borrowing they had missed earlier. It is this detailed picture built up over a year of continued interaction that makes their study insightful.

Their study shows that because of the uncertainty, irregularity, and smallness of incomes, the poor have to actively save to spend later, and borrow to spend before money is earned. They found that even the poorest households living on less than a dollar a day divert a large proportion of income into savings or use it to pay down loans. They save in multiple ways by storing savings at home, keeping them with others, or depositing them with banking institutions. They join different kinds of savings clubs, sometimes savings and loans clubs. They also borrow from neighbors, employers, moneylenders, relatives, or financial institutions. They say, "At any one time, the average poor household has a fistful of financial relationships on the go."[37]

At the beginning of the book we meet Hamid and Khadeja who live in a one-room home in a Dhaka slum. Hamid is a reserve driver of a motorized rickshaw, while Khadeja stays at home to look after their child and run the household. She earns a little from taking in sewing. In all, in an average month they make $70. It is unpredictable, depending on whether Hamid has work or not. After paying a fifth for rent and much of the rest for food, they have $76 in a life insurance savings policy, $30 sent for safe keeping to his parents, $40 lent to a relative, $16.80 in a microfinance savings account, $8 saved with a money guard, $2 kept at home in case money is needed, and $2 in Hamid's pocket so that he has money on the road.

They manage their money by borrowing interest free from family, neighbors, and Hamid's employer. This comes to $24. In addition they have a loan of $153 from a microfinance institution and owe money to their grocery store and landlord. Khadeja holds $20 as a money guard for two neighbors who are trying to keep their money safe from their husbands and sons, and Hamid also stores $8 with his employer while waiting to send money to his parents in the village.

They are able to manage their debts, which were $48.54 more than their financial assets, though negative net worth was fairly rare in their sample of 250 households across urban slums and villages in Bangladesh, India, and South Africa between 1999 and 2004. It is cash flow and the "push" and "pull" of savings and loans, rather than their balance sheet, which reveals how Hamid and Khadeja managed their money every day. Over a year, the couple "pushed" $451 into savings, insurance, or loan repayments and "pulled" $514 out of savings by taking loans or agreeing to act as a money guard for others.

Nomsa's story in South Africa shows much the same push and pull of money as that of Khadeja and Hamid in Bangladesh. In South Africa, though, for the accumulation of larger amounts, saving-up clubs and RoSCAs, the rotating savings and credit associations, are important. Nomsa is seventy-seven years old and lives with her four grandchildren in the village of Lugangeni in South Africa. Nomsa's daughter died of AIDS, and Nomsa's two youngest grandchildren arrived just before the research year.

She has a government old-age grant of $114 a month that is deposited into her bank account. She takes out all the money and keeps some spare cash in her home. She supplements this grant by selling produce from her garden, which brings in an average of $6 a month. Even then she had to borrow from moneylenders. Her daughter's funeral came after she had already borrowed to rebuild her traditional round hut. She has been able to keep the repayments current.

Food, home maintenance, and the purchase of household products take up $55 of her $120 monthly income. She also pays $4 in church fees and $10 to pay back her loans. But $40, a third of her monthly budget, is saved in the savings clubs. One saving-up club consists of a group of women in the neighborhood. Each deposits $9 at the monthly meeting. The secretary keeps the money in her home. In the twelfth month, each woman takes back $99. Nomsa prefers to save here rather than in the bank because she feels compelled to contribute her monthly payment so that she does not let down her friends.

Nomsa's second savings club is a RoSCA with three close friends as members. Each of them puts in $31 every month. When it is Nomsa's turn to take the money, she takes away $93. Both her savings clubs require regular payments within a social context and predictable savings amounts at the end of a stipulated period. Collins et al. note that this "slow and steady" schedule is similar to Khadeja's microcredit loan. They say that "a key difference between saving and borrowing is *when* the large sum is received; at the very start with a loan, or at the very end through saving."[38]

As Collins et al. studied the poor, their perspective changed on world poverty and market responses to the needs of poor households. They came to understand that money management is important for the poor. If the poor had reliable access to better financial tools, they could most likely improve their lives. But "at almost every turn poor households are frustrated by the poor quality—above all the low reliability—of the instruments that they use to manage their meager incomes."[39] Collins et al. argue that the poor need but seldom receive three key services required for managing their money. The first is to help them "manage money on a day-to-day basis." The second is to help them "build savings over the long term." And the third is to help them "borrow for all uses."[40]

In this effort to help the poor, the focus needs to be not only on some of the big issues—making banks more accessible and designing suitable bank and payment services—but also on the small marketing interventions that make the management of money through banking more amenable. These include thinking of using default measures for direct deposits of benefits and savings. Simpler forms, giving information in small discussion groups emphasizing the losses from not opening a bank account rather than the benefits, also make a difference. It is also important to frame banking by focusing on a person's identity as a family member and money manager rather than as somebody who is poor.[41]

FREEDOM, CAPABILITIES, AND DEVELOPMENT

The fourth story in the unbanked space is that of freedom, capabilities, and development articulated by Amartya Sen and Martha Nussbaum. Sen's perspectives on development combine human agency with society's institutional structures and value systems. He says the "expansion of freedom is viewed . . . both as the primary end and as the principal means of development."[42] The key is to increase people's capabilities and remove the institutional obstacles that hinder such an expansion of freedom and take away people's opportunity to exercise choice.

Development seen as a matter of freedom and capabilities shifts the emphasis in poverty analysis from the means to the ends that people pursue. By focusing on the freedoms needed to satisfy these ends, the focus shifts to people's capabilities to do things and the freedom to live in ways they value. This approach to development is central to financial inclusion and the empowerment of the poor and the marginalized. Providing suitable financial tools that answer the needs of the poor will give them freedom and help them develop the ability to manage money as a means to better lives.

Sen's concept of development in terms of freedoms and capabilities goes beyond seeing development only in terms of a rise in the gross domestic product (GDP). He says income is one indicator, but ensuring that people have the freedoms of health and education does more for their well-being than a general indicator of income. A story did the rounds in India when he visited after he was awarded the Nobel Prize for Economics. Ministry of Finance officials and economists hovered, hoping for a mathematical mantra for economic growth. He told them to invest more in health and education.

Martha Nussbaum[43] develops this framework of freedom and development in a narrative context. She gives greater detail to capabilities and the cultural values and institutional frameworks that enable people to exercise these capabilities. The capabilities approach begins with the questions, what are people actually able to do and to be? and what real opportunities are available to them?

Nussbaum tells the story of Vasanti, thirty, in Ahmedabad, India. Vasanti left her abusive husband and went back to live with her brothers and their families. They welcomed her back, though Vasanti could not have taken this for granted. In time, her brothers gave her a loan to get a sewing machine that rolls the edges of a sari so that it does not unravel. She was grateful though insecure, because her brothers had growing families and could ask for the money back when they needed it. Through the Self-Employed Women's Association (SEWA), she got a loan. SEWA helps develop "the ability of women to control and plan their own lives."[44]

Vasanti was able to pay her brothers back. Several years later, she has repaid most of the loan. She has a friend with whom she is combating domestic violence in her community and is planning to learn to read and write.

Nussbaum examines the cultural values and institutional structures that led to Vasanti's poor quality of life and the lack of basic social justice. Gender is an important focus for this approach to development via freedoms and capabilities. Poor nutrition, unequal access to family resources, illiteracy, and few choices for an independent and rich connected life led her to be unable to live the kind of life she might have chosen. In going beyond national income to a study of the freedoms and capabilities that individuals can enjoy and use, the focus moves to people who constitute the family and household. This is when it becomes apparent—as in Vasanti's story—how gender bias reduces the freedoms of women.

POVERTY-REDUCING MECHANISMS GO GLOBAL

When globalization includes the unbanked and the poor, the focus moves to successful global strategies to help the poor. Microfinance has overturned the long-held belief that lending to women is risky, and lending to poor women is impossible. It uses the social and community context of money management by lending to groups of women. Nomsa spoke of not wanting to let her friends down in relation to her saving-up club and RoSCA. The same sentiment also comes into play with credit.

Microcredit programs are seen as friendly to women in a way that banks are not. When Muhammad Yunus tells the story of the success of Grameen Bank lending to women in Bangladesh, it is inspirational because it is unusual. Microfinance brings together lending small amounts of money to groups of women for setting up a microenterprise. Women together get trained to use and manage the loan and are responsible for paying it back. Yunus found that the social context of borrowing and repaying meant there was a lower percentage of nonperforming loans. The stories most often told are of women who had bettered the fortunes of their household and were empowered as a result.

Microfinance loans are small, and interest rates can be high. Random control trials of microfinance show that it is possible to lend to the poor. It is difficult to say whether and to what extent microfinance loans have transformed the lives of the poor. But it is a remarkable achievement that microfinance loans have achieved their present scale. However, the factors that make the program succeed with the poor are also those that prevent it from being used to finance larger businesses that may develop.[45]

The microfinance model has been followed in many parts of the world. Niall Ferguson writes of stopping at a coffee shop in a street market in El Alto in Bolivia and discovering that the indigenous woman owner had taken a microfinance loan from Pro Mujer to enlarge her coffee stall. Her coffee shop was now helping put her daughters through school.

The Association of Cambodian Local Economic Development Agencies (ACLEDA), set up in 1992 as a microfinance nongovernmental organization, has now become a bank in Cambodia and will begin operations in Myanmar in 2013.[46] Women's World Banking, the world's largest network of microfinance institutions and banks, provides technical services and strategic support to thirty-nine leading microfinance institutions and banks in twenty-seven countries in Africa, Asia, Eastern Europe, Latin America, and the Middle East.

This "public transcript" of microfinance has been challenged by anthropological studies that show that the majority of women handed over the loans to their husbands to control. These studies also found increased instances of male violence against women. Yet when women themselves were asked to evaluate the impact of the loans, they said the loans have increased their ability to negotiate management and control over some sections of household money.[47] Participation in microfinance groups in West Bengal has led to women taking action against domestic violence and sexual transgressions by men and to organizing festivals and the repair of roads. Women's increased agency and social capital resulted from participating in a group focused on economic ties, the structure of the groups, participation in regular group meetings, and exposure to new perspectives through training and information.[48]

Self-help groups that use some of the principles of microfinance and work within a network of social ties have also empowered women. The popularity of RoSCAs in South Africa rests on many of the same factors. Anuja Cabraal's study of microfinance in Australia found the empowerment of women to be one of the most positive effects of low or no-interest financial programs.[49]

The Grameen Bank has remade itself based on lessons learned. The key messages from the first version of microfinance were that the success of the program depended on the group solidarity of women. Money was lent to set up microenterprises. However, responding to the needs of the poor for more flexible loans linked to savings, Collins et al. (2009) say the second version of microfinance concentrates on providing broad banking services, including savings. Its loans are less tied to microenterprises and are more flexibly aligned to the use of credit as a way of evening out cash flows and responding to emergencies. It offers the Grameen Pension Savings, with good long-term interest. The program is moving from lending money to groups of women for microenterprises to positioning itself to provide comprehensive money management services to poor households.

Microfinance straddles the mission of the not-for-profit organizations but has to exist in a commercial world. Any suspicion that microfinance is seen as a profit-making device, as happened in India, hurts the brand. Where different microfinance lenders compete for business, leading to multiple loans and overcommitment, the nightmare scenario is the one that unraveled in Andhra Pradesh in India. It was alleged that farmers indebted to multiple microfinance institutions (MFIs) committed suicide. The state government reacted by retroactively waiving loans and tightening up repayment conditions and the registration of MFIs. It sparked massive defaults in the state accompanied by a loss of MFI capital. This led a group of intellectuals working with the poor to remonstrate that the state's attempts at destroying microfinance would leave the poor with little recourse but to go back to informal sources of credit at higher interest rates and no regulation. They agreed that microfinance had its problems, particularly stemming from rapid growth. But the poor borrow mainly from informal sources and moneylenders. Only 11 percent had a loan from an MFI. They suggested that regulators should address the problem of high interest rates by focusing on institutional reform that enables MFIs to lower the cost of their products. This in turn will encourage MFIs to charge reasonable rates.[50]

Microfinance in India is turning around. In 2012, $144 million of equity was injected into microfinance groups. Microlenders' loan books outside Andhra Pradesh rose by 33 percent in value in the third quarter of 2012 when calculated year on year. This renewed confidence is due to India's central bank releasing national guidelines at the end of 2011. It set up a national licensing system. Microlenders are not allowed to lend to anyone with more than one outstanding loan. Microlenders' annual interest rates were capped at 10 to 12 percentage points above their borrowing costs. Most microlenders now charge 23 to 27 percent compared to the 40 percent some charged during the boom.[51]

Another approach that specifically addresses Muslim poverty and financial exclusion is Islamic microfinance. The primary characteristics of Sharia-compliant banking are that no interest should be given or received and that money should be used for productive purposes. Combining this approach with the principles of microfinance can be empowering particularly for the Muslim poor.[52] About 72 percent of people living in Muslim-majority countries do not use formal financial services. A number of surveys of low-income respondents in Syria, Jordan, Yemen, and Algeria show that 20 to 40 percent of respondents say they do not take conventional micro-loans for religious reasons. Microfinance practitioners say that in Afghanistan, Indonesia, Syria, and Yemen, borrowers who have taken conventional microfinance loans switch when Islamic products become available.

Despite the empowering potential of Islamic microfinance, a global survey in 2007 revealed that Islamic microfinance accounts for only one-half of 1 percent of the total microfinance outreach. This is despite government support and regulatory structures. Islamic microfinance is concentrated in Bangladesh, Pakistan, and Afghanistan. Bangladesh is the largest market with over one hundred thousand Islamic microfinance clients and two active institutions. But in comparison, Bangladesh has nearly eight million who use conventional microfinance products.[53]

What has gone wrong? Part of the answer is that Islamic microfinance has not come up with a new business model that can reach millions of poor and unbanked Muslims. Religious leaders who have influence over their poor Muslim congregations see that Islamic microfinance has just been "rebranded." It has copied and pasted from conventional microfinance, adding a few products.[54] The inclusion of the Muslim unbanked via Islamic microfinance is still waiting to happen.

The late C. K. Prahalad went the market route to show multinational corporations that the poor can be profitable customers. Prahalad's *The*

Fortune at the Bottom of the Pyramid (2005) has an evangelical tone, citing the success stories of firms that succeeded by selling to the poor.[55] He argues that we must see the poor as value-conscious and entrepreneurial customers who need to be served. But business practice has to change in order to serve the bottom of the pyramid (BOP). Of the nearly seven billion people on earth, there are four billion who earn less than US$2 a day. There are profits to be made, for the combined spending power of the BOP is immense, if the products and services suit their needs and ability to pay. Prahalad says BOP markets are brand conscious and connected. BOP consumers readily accept advanced technology. But the marketing has to create their capacity to consume by making unit packages small and affordable. The low margin per unit and high volume delivers a high return on capital.

Prahalad writes of Casas Bahia in Brazil. It was founded in 1952 and is now one of the largest retailers in the country. It has been able to give consumers with low and unpredictable income streams access to high-quality appliances and furniture. This is done through a sophisticated credit-rating system coupled with counseling to ensure that consumers are not overstretched. There is also a culture of serving the poor as valued consumers who aspire to a better life. Once the customer has paid off 50 percent of the loan, cross-selling becomes possible. Having to repay the loan installments brings the customers back to the store. The default rate is low at 8.5 percent, compared to over 15 percent for competitor firms. Giving BOP customers choice and dignity and building up trust ensures that the firm has a pool of repeat customers.

The story of CEMEX in Mexico, which sells housing solutions rather than cement to the poor, is equally inspiring. CEMEX works with groups of three women with a record of saving for five weeks and then advances them materials worth another five weeks of savings toward building a room in the house. With it goes architectural expertise and training in building methods, if desired. ICICI Bank in India also works with groups of women from the same village—twenty in this case—to encourage monthly savings of INR 50. They are then encouraged to lend to each other—short-term loans at 24 percent per annum. One year later, the group can submit a proposal to the bank manager who then lends them Rs 12,500 at 18 percent each to invest in a business, home or land, or livestock.

Prahalad's approach has been much admired and criticized. It is seductive to make profits while doing good. He is admired for his recognition of the BOP as an important market and his challenge to corporations to be in-novative in order to serve and profit from this market. Prahalad is criticized for connecting profit from consumption by the BOP while also arguing that this reduces poverty.[56] Others have questioned Prahalad's definition of pov-erty, the size of the BOP market, and the relevance of the examples cited. An exclusive emphasis on increasing the consumption of the poor devalues the role of the state in trying to enhance people's freedoms and capacities by investment in education, health, and infrastructure.

The average customers of Casas Bahia earn twice the minimum wage and thus are not part of the BOP. It is difficult to find examples where a decrease in unit cost has been achieved without loss of quality, unless technological innovations are involved. The examples cited by Prahalad are more often of small enterprises and nonprofit organizations rather than multinational corporations (MNCs).[57]

Prahalad's achievements may be more modest than his examples sug-gest. But his lasting contribution is that he pointed to the BOP as a large possible market. Organizations need to understand the needs of the poor to be able to service them. In the process, there is the possibility of provid-ing better education, health care, and financial services to help increase poor people's choices and capacities. But this approach is more attuned to developing an MNC's corporate responsibility agenda, which may indi-rectly build brand rather than be a direct path to greater profits.

Placing the broader social concept of money at the center of globaliza-tion recognizes that half the world is unbanked and poverty is a global problem. Enabling regulation and technology will be part of increasing financial inclusion. But any solution has to accept that the poor have spe-cific and challenging needs for managing their money. They use irregular flows of income to save for future emergencies and life-stage events while paying for everyday subsistence needs. Microfinance offers solutions to the global problem of poverty and financial exclusion. But as Sen says, development is a matter of increasing people's freedoms and their capaci-ties to live the kind of lives they would like to choose. In the next chapter, we see how these issues connect with women, money, and globalization.

NOTES

1. Martha C. Nussbaum, *Creating Capabilities: The Human Development Approach* (Cambridge, MA: Belknap Press of Harvard University Press, 2011); Amartya Sen, *Development as Freedom* (Oxford: Oxford University Press, 1999).

2. C. K. Prahalad, *The Fortune at the Bottom of the Pyramid* (Delhi: Pearson Education [Singapore], 2005).

3. Asli Demirguc-Kunt and Leora Klapper, *Measuring Financial Inclusion: The Global Findex Database* (Washington, DC: World Bank, 2012).

4. Maya Makanjee, "Access to Financial Services in Africa: Gender Analysis" (paper presented at the African Women's Economic Summit, Nairobi, 2010); Demirguc-Kunt and Klapper, *Measuring Financial Inclusion.*

5. Federal Deposit Insurance Corporation, *2011 FDIC National Survey of Unbanked and Underbanked Households: Executive Summary* (Federal Deposit Insurance Corporation, 2012).

6. Chris Connolly et al., *Measuring Financial Exclusion in Australia* (Centre for Social Impact [CSI], University of New South Wales, 2011).

7. Paula Gerber, "Making Indigenous Australians 'Disappear': Problems Arising from Our Birth Registration Systems," *Alternative Law Journal* 34, no. 3 (2009).

8. David Porteous, *The Enabling Environment for Mobile Banking in Africa* (2006), http://www.bankablefrontier.com/assets/ee.mobil.banking.report.v3.1.pdf.

9. Stephen Mwaura Nduati, "Challenges and Opportunities to Promote Financial Inclusion" (paper presented at the International Forum for Central Banks: Payment Systems and Financial Inclusion, Quito, Ecuador, 2012).

10. Angela Crandall et al., *Mobile Phone Usage at the Kenyan Base of the Pyramid: Final Report* (Nairobi: iHub Research and Research Solutions Africa, 2012).

11. Bill Maurer, "Mobile Money: Communication, Consumption and Change in the Payments Space." *Journal of Development Studies* 48, no. 5 (2012): 589–604.

12. Bank Negara Malaysia, "Policymakers Concur on Need to Harness Technological Advancements to Widen Access to Financial Services," http://www.bnm.gov.my/index .php?ch=8&pg=14&ac=1958 (accessed December 8, 2009).

13. Bank Negara Malaysia, "Policymakers Concur."

14. Matu Mugo, "Regulation of Banking and Payment Agents in Kenya," in *The Fletcher School: Leadership Program for Financial Inclusion—Policy Memoranda* (Fletcher School, Tufts University, 2011), 47–52.

15. Kevin Donovan, "Mobile Money for Financial Inclusion," in *Information and Communications for Development 2012: Maximizing Mobile,* ed. World Bank Group (Washington, DC: World Bank and Infodev, 2012).

16. Kevin Donovan, "What's Next for Mobile Money?," World Bank, https://blogs .worldbank.org/psd/team/kevin-donovan (accessed September 24, 2012).

17. "Is It a Phone, Is It a Bank? Mobile Banking," *Economist,* March 30, 2013.

18. Mugo, "Regulation of Banking and Payment Agents in Kenya."

19. Stephen Mwaura Nduati, "Enhancing Financial Inclusion through Technological Innovations," in *The Fletcher School: Leadership Program for Financial Inclusion—Policy Memoranda* (Fletcher School, Tufts University, 2011).

20. Nduati, "Enhancing Financial Inclusion," 39.

21. Ignacio Mas, "Don't Touch Our M-PESA!" (2012), http://www.ignaciomas.com/ announcements/donttouchourm-pesa (accessed September 24, 2012).

22. BIS Committee on Payment and Settlement Systems, *Innovations in Retail Payments* (Basle: Bank for International Settlements, 2012).

23. Siti Hidayati, "Cash-in and Cash-out Agents for Mobile Money in Indonesia," in *The Fletcher School: Leadership Program for Financial Inclusion—Policy Memoranda* (Fletcher School, Tufts University, 2011), 44.

24. David Wolman, *The End of Money: Counterfeiters, Preachers, Techies, Dreamers—and the Coming Cashless Society* (Cambridge, MA: Da Capo Press, 2012), 165.

25. CGAP, *Update on Regulation of Branchless Banking in India* (CGAP, 2010).

26. "FM Says Some New Bank Licences Expected before March 2014," *The Hindu*, June 6, 2013.

27. "Why Is India's UID Aadhar a Big Data Challenge and Opportunity?," *Information Week India*, February 7, 2013; "38 Cr Aadhaar Numbers Issued So Far; 60 Cr by 2014: Nilekani," Nextbigwhat.com, April 30, 2013.

28. Mani A. Nandhi, *Effects of Mobile Banking on the Savings Practices of Low Income Users: The Indian Experience* (Irvine, CA: Institute for Money, Technology and Financial Inclusion, 2012).

29. Chris Bold, "Does Branchless Banking Reach Poor People? The Evidence from India," November 23, 2011, http://www.cgap.org/blog/does-branchless-banking-reach-poor-people-evidence-india (accessed 2012).

30. Greg Chen, "Eko's Mobile Banking: Demonstrating the Power of a Basic Payments Product," CGAP, November 23, 2012, http://www.cgap.org/blog/eko%E2%80%99s-mobile-banking-demonstrating-power-basic-payments-product.

31. Shweta S. Banerjee, "Building India's Model of Agent Banking," http://www.cgap.org/blog/building-india%E2%80%99s-model-agent-banking (accessed September 27, 2012).

32. CGAP, "India Banking Agents Survey 2012," http://www.cgap.org/data/india-banking-agents-survey-2012.

33. International Labour Office, *Bolsa Família in Brazil: Context, Concept and Impacts* (Geneva: International Labour Office, Social Security Department, 2009).

34. Mayur Shetty, "Soon, Dial *99# to Access Your Bank Account," *Economic Times*, November 27, 2012; "PM Initiates Direct Cash Transfer Scheme," *Hindustan Times*, November 26, 2012.

35. "Aadhar-Linked Norm May Be Relaxed," *The Pioneer*, December 11, 2012; Banyan, "On the Prowl," *Economist*, December 1, 2012; Reetika Khera, "Long Road Ahead for Cash Transfers," *Financial Express*, December 4, 2012; Aditya Menon, "UPA to Milk Cash Cow for Elections: Game Changing Direct Cash Transfer Scheme for Poor to Boost Prospects in Next Elections," *Mail Online*, November 26, 2012.

36. Daryl Collins et al., *Portfolios of the Poor: How the World's Poor Live on $2 a Day* (Princeton, NJ: Princeton University Press, 2009).

37. Collins et al., *Portfolios of the Poor*, 3.

38. Collins et al., *Portfolios of the Poor*, 116.

39. Collins et al., *Portfolios of the Poor*, 3.

40. Collins et al., *Portfolios of the Poor*, 178.

41. Marianne Bertrand, Sendhil Mullainathan, and Eldar Shafir, "Behavioral Economics and Marketing in Aid of Decision Making among the Poor," *Journal of Public Policy and Marketing* 25, no. 1 (2006).

42. Sen, *Development as Freedom*, xii.

43. Nussbaum, *Creating Capabilities*.

44. Nussbaum, *Creating Capabilities*, 10.

45. Abhijit V. Banerjee and Esther Duflo, *Poor Economics: A Radical Rethinking of the Way to Fight Global Poverty* (New York: PublicAffairs, 2011).

46. "The Bank That Likes to Say Less," *Economist*, September 22, 2012.

47. Susan Johnson, "Gender Norms in Financial Markets: Evidence from Kenya," *World Development* 32, no. 8 (2004).

48. Paromita Sanyal, "From Credit to Collective Action: The Role of Microfinance in Promoting Women's Social Capital and Normative Influence," *American Sociological Review* 74 (August 2009).

49. Anuja Cabraal, "The Impact of Microfinance on the Capabilities of Participants" (PhD diss., RMIT University, 2011).

50. Abhijit Banerjee et al., "Help Microfinance, Don't Kill It," *Indian Express*, November 26, 2010.

51. "Microfinance in India: Road to Redemption," *Economist*, January 12, 2013.

52. *Islamic Microfinance: An Emerging Market Niche* (CGAP, 2008).

53. *Islamic Microfinance: An Emerging Market Niche*.

54. Mohammed Khaled, "Why Has Islamic Microfinance Not Reached Scale Yet?," last modified March 9, 2011, http://www.cgap.org/blog/why-has-islamic-microfinance -not-reached-scale-yet (accessed 2012).

55. Prahalad, *The Fortune at the Bottom of the Pyramid*.

56. Nancy E. Landrum, "Advancing the 'Base of the Pyramid' Debate," *Strategic Management Review* 1, no. 1 (2007).

57. Aneel G. Karnani, "Mirage at the Bottom of the Pyramid," in William Davidson Institute Working Paper No. 835 (University of Michigan, 2006).

CHAPTER 4

WOMEN, MONEY, AND GLOBALIZATION

Think of globalization and the images are those of the Davos Man or the Porto Allegre Man. It is men who talk big business to solve the problems of the world in Davos, and it is men who speak of inequality and justice in Porto Allegre. Where are the women? The images are of women doing piecework at home or working in a factory in a developing country, of a Third World nanny looking after children in the West, or of prostitution and sex trafficking.[1]

These images are being challenged, and there is a push for a more just globalization. International organizations have recently focused on gender and "decent work," as seen in chapter 2. For a globalization that is fair and just, women's disadvantage in the worlds of money and technology is a central concern. So why does gender vaporize in general discussions of globalization?

This is partly because we do not write of globalization as personal. Discussions of globalization most often adopt a top-down view focusing on international institutions, markets, and the nation-state rather than everyday life. Gender is missing because the grand theories of globalization tend to be male, whereas the local, ethnographic work focuses on the female. Globalization theories reiterate that the local and the global coexist, but the Russian doll version of globalization remains powerful. The local and the female are not as easily seen as the global.[2]

As noted in the first chapter, the dominant influence of economic globalization and market money pushes away gender. But when we place the social and cultural concept of global money at the center of discussions of globalization, gender issues immediately come to the fore in relation to financial inclusion, access to information and communication technologies (ICTs), migration, remittances, and diaspora philanthropy. Gender is an essential aspect of how money is managed and controlled in the family and in the household. When we see money in the family and the household, as well as the market, gender becomes crucial to the study of globalization.

Will banking and mobile money services be equally empowering for poor men and women? The question is important, for all over the world women are primarily responsible for putting food on the table. Gender is an important ingredient in effective poverty-reducing solutions such as microfinance. Women in developing countries, particularly in South Asia, the Middle East, and the Pacific, have less access to the new technologies, especially the mobile phone.

In this chapter I address the question, why do women participate unequally in the global world of money? I answer this question by discussing the gender of money. Women earn less money and financial wealth because they are often in the worst-paid and most informal occupations that have resulted from economic globalization. Men and women also approach money differently in terms of spending, expenditure, investment, and power. I then examine gender and financial exclusion and delve into the reasons behind the patterns of exclusion. Women also comprise half the migrants in the world. Women are left behind in split transnational families when their husbands migrate alone. I examine the effect of money and migration on women, both those who migrate and those who are left behind. And finally I look at women's unequal access to and use of technology, which reduces women's opportunities for connection through money and communication.

THE GENDER OF MONEY

As discussed in chapter 1, women across cultures spend more of their money than men on the household and on children. The pattern goes across generations. The reason lies partly in the personal and social pressure on mothers to put their children first. The pattern is so well recognized that Haitian authorities distributed food vouchers to the women after Haiti's devastating earthquake. Policy makers in Mexico direct conditional cash transfers to mothers to alleviate poverty and to ensure that the children go to school.[3]

Most women deal with money on an everyday basis. Why does this expertise not move to the market? Differences between men and women over money are debated in every household. Are these differences a matter of inherent discrepancies in the way men and women address investment and risk?

Some argue that there are significant differences between men's and women's attitudes toward investing money. Men talk of "freedom," "game," "risk," "speculation," "success," "prestige," "excitement," and "power." Ask women, and often one hears of "security," "old age," "the future," "a rainy day."[4] Other studies conclude that women process information differently, leading to gender differences in investment.[5] I did not find these differences in my 1997 study of marriage and banking. But I was listening to men and women speak of managing and controlling money in their married lives, rather than their investment strategies.

Women's lower tolerance of risk is connected with women having less control of money when the dominant ideology is that of male control. Women also suffer from the structural inequality of less financial wealth and lower wages. In the United States, nearly one in three single women has no wealth or has more debts than assets. Single women own 36 cents for every dollar of wealth owned by single men. This wealth gap persists across gender even for women in their twenties and thirties. The gender wealth ratio has risen since 1998. It is lower wages and less financial wealth that gives women a comparatively lower buffer for risk taking and makes them "more likely to engage in *saving* rather than *investing*."[6]

Women's work at home and in the community is seen in terms of caring. It is more in the nature of a gift than a source of profit. It is not measured or valued in the marketplace and so does not count. Women continue to get paid less for the same work as men. Occupations dominated by women often attract lower rates of pay.[7]

It is also important to note that women seldom achieve the same level of pay and conditions of work when they move into occupations previously dominated by men. Around the 1970s in the United States, there was a feminization of clerical workers, telegraph and telephone operators, waiting occupations, public school teachers, and bank tellers. This was a result of the expansion of the services sector and the resulting shortage of male workers. This greater demand was accompanied by changes in work processes and lower rewards. It meant that men migrated to more profitable work with a greater potential for mobility. At the same time there was a greater demand for women workers because they were cheaper. Women were seen to be more productive at some tasks. Antidiscrimination regulations and the growth of a female clientele also played a part. But even within these desegregated occupations, men and women were concentrated in different jobs and at different levels in the hierarchy. This meant that the wage gap did not substantially narrow for women.[8]

Women also appear to be more comfortable with money in the home, in the private sphere, than in the public sphere of the market. They often leave banking decisions to their husbands. In my marriage and banking study of 1997 among middle-income Anglo-Celtic married couples in Australia, I found that of the sixteen women studied, six deferred to their husband when it came to comparing interest rates or making major money decisions. These were women who managed the household money, paid the bills, sometimes kept the books, and balanced the checkbook.[9]

Donna, fifty-one, goes to the bank branch four times a week to conduct the family business's transactions. She also keeps the books for the family business. But when it comes to interest rates, she says, "My husband's the brains with the interest and the money. . . . He's very clever with figures."[10] Annie, now a full-time housewife, who manages the money in the household, says she leaves the interest rate decisions to her husband. "With his being out working and talking to more people, he's the one who makes more of that sort of decision. We *talk* about it but then he's more up-to-date."[11] She says she would spend time and effort on informing herself if they had $2,000 or $3,000 in the account.

Cross-cultural studies of money add to the picture of women's comfort with money in the private sphere of the home rather than the world outside. Women in many parts of Indonesia are good money managers and control finances in the home. This does not challenge the overall ideology of male superiority, because "women's control over household income does not translate into authority or power on a wider stage."[12]

This lack of comfort with market money could relate to the way women are socialized about money across cultures. A study of women university students compared thirteen middle-class women university students from the United States and thirteen women born in the Philippines but who had moved to the United States when they were around eight years old. They found that in their natural-born American sample, the daughters were taught not to ask about money. They were not encouraged to experience the earning of money at an early state. They were also not helped to manage money by setting up checking or savings accounts. "Money was made mysterious, arcane, and secret. It was represented as belonging to the world of males, and as being managed and controlled by males who do not share their knowledge."[13] Women who came from financially secure intact families desired financial independence. But their ambivalence regarding money meant that the women did not connect it with the necessity of earning their own money.

This contrasted with their Filipina sample, where money was discussed openly within the family but was seen as private outside it. Mothers taught their daughters how to manage money to gain more power in a patriarchal household. So the Filipina daughters grow up talking of money, learning from their mothers how to diminish the power of the man, but not how to equalize it.

This lack of monetary realism is an inability to think in terms of market money. In middle-income Anglo-Celtic society, women who believe in the ideology of marriage as an equal partnership do not work out the conditions and consequences of financial independence. There is little discussion of how women will achieve their desired financial independence and maintain it through childbearing and the many stages of the marital relationship.[14]

Women find it difficult to see themselves as the source of power. In her book *Fire with Fire*, Naomi Wolf discusses how difficult it was for her to deal with power and money after the publication of *The Beauty Myth*. She realized that women not only suffer from a lack of power; they also "suffer from a fear of power."[15] This connects with the two taboos around power and money that lead to women's ambivalence about claiming power. She says feminism has concentrated on pointing out economic discrimination against women and advocating equal pay. But feminism does not see "the pursuit of money as a legitimate feminine drive." It is as if enabling women to generate profits by themselves is seen as "masculine."[16]

When Wolf earned the check from her book—it was not as much as what her male peers were earning—she says, "The check was a phantom presence disrupting my sense of where I stood in the world. It felt defeminizing, like a mark of maleness stigmatizing me."[17] She had no female role models to teach her how to deal with money. It was only when she sent a large money order to a women's organization after the Anita Hill hearings in 1991[18] that she felt euphoric about her power and her money. Learning how to use her money for causes she wanted to support, mentoring younger women, and seeing how women could be supported in their microbusinesses—these were some of the steps that made money female for Wolf.

WOMEN AND FINANCIAL EXCLUSION

Gender becomes an important issue when globalization confronts financial exclusion. The greater financial exclusion of women goes beyond the insufficiency of income or lack of access to banks. The gender gap connects with women's lack of ownership of resources, primarily land. Though women are half the world, they own only 1 percent of the property. Attempts to legislate to even the gender gap, or to implement the legislation, can be blocked by male gatekeepers. Women also do not have bank accounts because money in the household is controlled by the men. It is only relatively recently that banks in high-income countries have seen women as profitable customers. In the United Kingdom and Australia until the end of the nineteenth century, legislation excluded women from having bank accounts and owning property.

The focus on credit in financial inclusion brings up the question, is being financially included good in itself? Does financial inclusion inevitably lead to greater freedom and capabilities? Financial inclusion uses the poverty line to determine who is poor and who is not poor. It is an either/or situation. You are banked or unbanked. You are financially included or excluded. But is encouraging credit at the bottom of the pyramid a good in itself? If the overall aim of financial inclusion is to encourage freedom and the development of capabilities, then debt creation has to be accompanied by sustainability. Unsustainable debt creation at the bottom of the pyramid can lead to hardship, particularly for women. Financial inclusion from a woman's perspective has to correspond with family well-being and gender equity. It has to address the structural inequalities in a society and money in the family and household.[19]

The neoliberal experiment in Chile during Pinochet's dictatorship which began on September 11, 1973, has led to the expansion of non-bank credit. In 2012, there was an average of 3.5 cards per person. Clara Han's ethnographic study of La Pincoya, a poor urban neighborhood near Santiago shows that credit has continued to be easily available. But people borrow committing themselves to fixed repayments in the context of temporary and unstable work, increased prices for services, a substantial level of addiction, and at times a history of torture. It means women and their families are living a "loaned life" and could be paying more than one-third of their household income on consumer debt. The availability of credit has offered the poor consumer goods that create a "dignified life." It has also meant increased anxiety without alleviating "pervasive economic pre-cariousness." The goods in turn have prevented households from being categorized as poor for welfare schemes. Though the credit is individual, it is the family who faces the constant danger of repossession. The need to help kin also means that cards are lent and borrowed to help tide a person over through "critical moments," further increasing the stress of credit. A failure to keep up with the fixed repayments leads to increased surveil-lance via a list of those who have not proved creditworthy.[20]

THE GLOBAL FINDEX SURVEY

The black box around the household has long ago disappeared in studies of money management and control. This black box assumed that money was equally available and distributed to everyone in the household. How-ever, the black box has until recently been a framework for data collection and the discussion of financial inclusion. Most attempts to collect data or evaluate the impact of policies have seen the household as a unit. The Global Financial Inclusion (Global Findex) database is an exception be-cause it focuses on individuals rather than households. This is why both gender and poverty become important.[21]

Women are more financially excluded than men. The gender gap is statistically significant in all regions, even when controlling for differ-ences due to education, age, income, and country-level characteristics. It persists across all income quintiles. The gender gap is seen in savings accounts held with formal financial institutions and with loans. In devel-oping economies, the gender gap averages six to nine percentage points. In high-income economies, the average difference is lower and exceeds four percentage points only for women in the poorest income quintile.

The gender gap is large in South Asia, the Middle East, and North Africa. It is relatively small in sub-Saharan Africa, where 27 percent of men and 22 percent of women report having an account.

The gender gap for the origination of new formal loans is highest in high-income countries. It is a 6 percent gap compared to the world gender gap for credit at 2 percent. This is possibly because, among the poor, both men and women are denied credit.[22]

MEN, LAND, AND CREDIT

Women seldom own land in patrilineal societies in South Asia and East Africa. When legislation attempts to even up the gender gap, the gatekeeping structures continue to be overwhelmingly male. This either stymies the legislation or prevents its implementation.

Most women in India and Pakistan do not own land. And the few women who do own land are not able to exercise full control of it. This situation has remained unchanged in the decades since the Hindu Succession Act of 1956 gave Hindu women in India considerable rights to inherit land. The passing of the West Pakistan Shariat Act of 1962, which gave Muslim women in Pakistan inheritance rights to agricultural land, also does not appear to have made a difference. Women's land ownership in South Asia has been a legal, ideological, administrative, and social struggle.[23] In India, women often cede their right to equal inheritance of inherited property to their brothers. At times women do this under pressure from the brothers and their wives, opting to preserve the valued kin relationship.[24]

The possession of arable land in rural South Asia will in the foreseeable future remain "the primary source of economic security, social status, and political power."[25] This relationship is demonstrated by a study in Kerala which shows that women who own land or a house face a significantly lower risk of marital violence.[26]

In much of East Africa as well, land is owned mainly by men. The move for financial inclusion has involved trying to get legal title for this land. Even when the legislative framework is in place, there is little evidence that this move will further the rights of women in their daily lives.

The World Bank from 2003 onward recommended that formal titles for the ownership of land would convert "dead capital" into collateral for credit and help to reduce poverty. Niall Ferguson writes that Peruvian economist Hernando de Soto says the total value of the "real estate occupied by the world's poor amounts to $9.3 trillion."[27] But without secure legal title, you cannot borrow on it.

This is a common assumption, though evidence on the ground suggests that the connection between formal titles and access to credit is not always clear. Using the example of Quilmes, a slum on the southern outskirts of Buenos Aires, Ferguson says that only 4 percent of those who had title were able to secure a mortgage.

We find the same kind of figures for Kenya. Seven years after formalization of land titles in the South Nyanza district in western Kenya, only 3 percent of the land titles had been used to access loans. In the Embu district, it was 15 percent. In the Makueini district in eastern Kenya, the formal land title was used to raise commercial loans only in two cases of the 111 interviews. This was because commercial banks showed little interest in small agricultural borrowers, with or without land title. People also knew the risks of secured commercial loans and preferred small unsecured loans through a microcredit scheme.[28]

The process of reforming land laws to incorporate gender equity can be blocked. Patrick McAuslan gives a firsthand account of this process drawing on his experience advising governments on land law reform and implementation in Tanzania, Uganda, Rwanda, Malawi, Sudan, and Somaliland over three decades. McAuslan recounts how his efforts to incorporate gender equity were blocked by male parliamentarians in Uganda.[29]

In Tanzania, McAuslan was involved in drafting legislative proposals to give procedural and substantive substance to the National Land Policy (NLP) approved in 1995. The Land Act of 1999 gave further support to land rights. One of its provisions was that a spouse's consent was required for the mortgage of a family home. The courts had the power to reopen a mortgage if the lender had imposed discriminatory terms because of the borrower's gender.

The banks in Tanzania, which were overwhelmingly South African–owned, objected to this provision, arguing that it favored the borrower. They complained to the World Bank, which directed the Tanzanian government to rewrite these provisions. The World Bank went further and made a forthcoming loan to alleviate poverty in Tanzania, conditional on redrafting.[30]

In Uganda, too, the Land (Amendment) Act of 2004 required spousal consent for land transactions to be legal. These provisions were unpopular because the lack of spousal consent voided the transaction. The commercial banks in Uganda objected to the amendment and subsequent efforts to modify the provision of spousal consent. They argued that requiring consent from spouses would make it difficult to provide loans to home owners. Tanzania's revised mortgage law and Uganda's mortgage bill now include provisions on consent. Spouses need to get independent advice on potential loans. But gender inequality with respect to land runs deep in social practice. McAuslan tells that when he visited the Ministry of Lands in Uganda to see how the provisions were working, he was told that a woman who had objected to a proposed land transaction came back the next week to withdraw her objection. It was obvious she had been the victim of domestic violence, but she was not going to make a complaint about the assault. He also learned that despite women's groups' support for joint tenancy, urban middle-class women who had acquired property for shops and investment did not want to share them with their spouses.

MALE CONTROL OF MONEY IN THE HOUSEHOLD

The gender gap in financial inclusion connects with male control of larger sources of money in the household in the global South. This is clear even from the patchy literature on household money management and control in Asia, Africa, and the Pacific.

In Kenya, among the Kikuyu, men and women control separate sources of money. Men manage and control the larger streams of income based on land whereas women have smaller sources of income. Where men and women work together on coffee and tea, the use of this money is jointly discussed. But pooling and sharing of information over money is more the exception than the rule. Married men and women, for instance, do not share details of their mobile money transfers.[31]

The segregated management of income means that men and women seek different kinds of financial instruments to manage their cash flows, gifts, transfers, borrowings, and repayments from their social network. In order to include women in formal financial processes, their lower levels of income and expenditure, and their need for privacy, will have to be taken into account. It is also uncertain whether the joint money from cash crops will go into joint accounts, because "pooling income in bank accounts requires considerable a priori agreement on use, whereas separate cash income streams does [sic] not."[32]

I found the same pattern of separate and unequal gendered finances in Morobe, a southern province in Papua New Guinea. This was accompanied by men owning the land and controlling the large incomes from mining. In Wau, a mining town that saw its heyday in the 1930s, the average income from mining is 6,000 kina a month (roughly $2,600). Of this, men may give their wives 500 kina. So, thinking in terms of household money masks the relative poverty of women. The women we interviewed in Morobe in 2011 said the men spend the rest on cards, beer, and *meri* ("women" in Tok Pisin) in Lae, the second-largest city in Papua New Guinea. Women in Wau supplement this occasional money by reselling cigarettes and betel nut bought in Lae and sold in Wau. Depending on how much they can buy, each time they sell the lot it may yield 100 kina.[33]

As in Kenya, women in Morobe manage their money by keeping savings secret from their men and from each other. When women do have bank accounts, they do not always see the bank as a safe place to store money. Linda and Jacinta, married to miners, have closed their bank accounts. Linda, over fifty years old, opened an account with a microbank in Wau five years ago with 170 kina and slowly built it up to 12,000 kina with profits from selling cigarettes and betel nut bought in Lae. Her husband found out and began asking her for money. She felt she had to give the money to him, and she has little hope of it being returned. She laughed and said more than once that if it happens, she will call me in Melbourne to tell me the good news. Jacinta, too, had an account with a bank in Bulolo, an hour's drive from Wau. She has withdrawn her money because she is worried that if she puts money in a bank account, her husband will know she has that money. Both Linda and Jacinta now keep their savings at home.[34]

In India, where only 26 percent of the women have bank accounts, money in most patrilineal families is controlled by men. I found in my research on money in middle-income urban joint families that when male dominance is linked to male management, a woman's access to money and information about money is minimal. Unlike the pattern in the West, male control is not confined to the lowest income group. The ideology of male dominance is prevalent among middle, lower-middle, and "struggling" households, particularly in nonmetropolitan Delhi.[35]

All of the sixteen men in the sample had bank accounts. Four of the twenty-four women we interviewed in twenty-seven middle-income households in 2007–8 were unbanked. Two women had no bank accounts. Another two had joint accounts only, on which they did not make transactions. They had no information about the money in the bank account or access to savings accounts or credit. For these two women, the joint account was only an inheritance device.

The stories from the field place the unbanked women in their family, social, and cultural contexts. Rina, a housewife in a peri-urban area in Delhi, does not have a bank account. She lives in a patrilineal joint family, most frequently defined as a three-generation household marked by male descent. She feels that talking with her husband about his personal bank account is like intruding into his very private domain (*dilkibaat*). She knows her father-in-law has a personal account since he is in a government job, but she does not know anything about it. She never discusses money with any member of the family.

Another housewife about forty years old says the main reason for her not having an account is that there is not enough money left over. Her husband is a tradesman, and they see themselves as struggling rather than middle income. But unlike Rina, this housewife manages the money and says that she and her husband discuss money and that major decisions are made jointly.

Another two women are in practice unbanked because they have joint accounts that they do not access. They neither manage nor control the money in the household. Amar is a widow over sixty-five, living with her son in a middle-income three-generation joint family in Dharamshala. She says that when her husband was alive, he "used to keep the money. He used to buy the rations. If I wanted to spend, I would ask for what was needed." Amar only discovered that she and her husband had a joint account after he died. Now her son looks after the money in their joint account.[36]

Her daughter-in-law Amrit, about fifty and a graduate, also does not know what is in her joint account with her husband. She says, "I don't go to the bank. He does everything. I don't have any knowledge about it." She continues, "I take from my husband what I need. . . . It is not that I get a certain amount every month. If I need to buy a shawl, I ask for money. If he says no, then there is no money."[37]

Amrit says she knows about the major investment decisions in the household, such as the purchase of land, but only after the fact. Though she helps in the family business, the information about business money is shared between the father and son. Amrit says, "He speaks with his son, not with me. I am also not interested in finding out. Even if I did take an interest, he will say, 'It is not your concern. Why do you want to know? What will you get if you know?'"[38]

WOMEN, BANKING, AND CREDIT

Stories of bankers playing golf with their clients in a small town never include women among the players. Until the last few decades, banks in the West have not seen women as suitable and profitable clients. Grameen Bank's lending to the poor attracted worldwide attention, not only because the bank's clients were poor, but because they were women.

Bank practices toward credit to women in high-income economies changed only a few decades ago. The historical male bias in laws relating to property and earnings was reflected in bank attitudes and practices. Until 1870, a married woman in the United Kingdom did not have the right to hold property in her own name or open a bank account without her husband's authority. Australia followed the UK pattern in terms of women's property and banking rights. Married women in the UK between 1780 and 1930 from wealthy families had some control of their marriage settlements through trusts. These were managed by members of the woman's natal family.[39]

Most women in the UK and Australia in the late nineteenth and early twentieth centuries had little to do with money or banks. Women in Australia in the 1960s were routinely asked to have their husband or a male guarantor sign for a loan, even when the woman was the sole earner. The assumption was that a woman did not need a loan in her own right, and she would not have the funds to service the debt.[40] Even in the early 1990s, I heard women tell how they had to get their loan application guaranteed by a husband or brother, even though they were the ones who were earning more of the money to be used as collateral. At the same time, it was usual for banks to ask women to guarantee debts by the men in their family, even when the women did not personally gain anything from the loan. This was so widespread in the 1990s that it was termed "sexually transmitted debt."[41]

In Australia, by 2005 and 2006, women in their fifties and younger were more comfortable dealing with banks. Male bankers were less comfortable. I interviewed women who reported that male bankers sometimes addressed all their remarks to their partners, even when it was the woman who was getting the loan.[42] Even now you get stories like Geraldine's which reflect bankers' dismissive attitudes toward women.

Geraldine was married and gave her age as between forty-five and fifty-four, with an annual household income of AUS$25,000 to AUS$49,999. (In Australia, age and income are seen as private, so ranges are often the preferred way of asking and responding about both.) Her husband would frequently borrow money, and she would sometimes have to pay back the debt. There was a time when he wanted a loan to buy a luxury car. He went to his bank where he and Geraldine had a joint account and a mortgage. The banker told him that Geraldine would also have to sign for it. Geraldine says,

> He [her husband] told me later that the person that was helping him get the loan was trying to give him advice how to manipulate me into signing for it. . . . He was saying, "buy her flowers and chocolates and woo her into signing the form. . . ." [My husband] didn't try . . . that with me. But after the split up, I found all the paperwork that was already filled in.[43]

WOMEN, MONEY, AND MIGRATION

Women's migration is not new, but it has only recently been recognized in official statistics and independent analyses. Women currently comprise around half of the world's migrant population. This does not include unrecorded short-term and seasonal migration. Women are the principal migrants in the Philippines, Sri Lanka, Indonesia and several countries in Latin America and the Caribbean.[44] They migrate alone to work in domestic and caregiving occupations to help improve their family's prospects. Women working as nurses are often the primary migrants, with the husband and children following the woman. Women migrate for marriage and to accompany their husbands and family.

Women migrate for varied periods, both short and long. Work is becoming one of the important reasons for migration. Single and married women migrate, including women who migrate alone, leaving their children in the care of family members in the source country. Women are also affected when men migrate on their own to work in the production and construction sectors. Families become transnational. In all these settings, women are important players in the global flow of labor and money.

I write of migrant money in greater detail in chapter 8. Migration can empower women, but it can also reaffirm gender hierarchies. This is seen in the sending and receiving of remittances. It is also evident in the negotiations around domestic work, financial management, and community participation.

Women's ability to send and manage remittances is often influenced by the kinship system and their work outside the home. Migrant women's role in the management of household money reflects the intersection of gender ideologies, class, women's and men's places in the labor market, and patterns of migration. This is particularly true when the woman is the primary earner in the household and her husband experiences downward mobility at work.

Women's migration from Sri Lanka and the Philippines for domestic and care work has in many cases been empowering. Earning money enables the woman migrant to decide how much to send and to whom. And in many cases these decisions have the desired effect of building up wealth and increasing the family's choices. But often the remitting and spending decisions lead to tension, without challenging the prevalent ideology of male control of money. Sending money to the mother, who often is the main carer for the woman's children, signals the greater importance of the mother over the husband. Sending money to the husband may have the stereotypical effect of the money being spent on drink and gambling, leaving no money for the care of the children.

The Philippines has a history of women-led migration. Women migrate to provide quality education and health care for their children. The children are more often cared for by female kin—older sisters, grandmothers, or aunts. Women earn most of the money in the household, increasing their economic power vis-à-vis men. Gender norms, however, continue to promote a view of the husband as the breadwinner. Transnational families are the norm, but the nuclear family remains the reference point. The woman is still judged in terms of her caring role. Society sees the transnational family as "broken," and the children see themselves as "abandoned."[45]

The situation in Sri Lanka, where the women migrate to work as domestic servants in the Middle East, is equally mixed. Since the early 1980s, over 40 percent of the households in a village in southern Sri Lanka had women who had migrated for two-year contracts, leaving behind husbands, children, and other family members. Most families hope women's remittances will help buy land and build a house. There are cases where this has happened. In other instances the conflict over whether the woman should send money to her husband, or to her mother who looks after the children, has led to conflict and an attempted suicide.

Kamala is a woman who migrated and sent money to her husband, though her mother looked after the two children during the day. She also secretly sent her mother Rs 1,000. When her husband came to know about this, there was a quarrel which led to the police station. When Kamala came back, she and her husband fought over controlling the money that remained. She was not allowed to give presents to her parents. These conflicts over money and control led Kamala to attempt suicide.[46]

In another case, remittances led to the dissolution of a marriage. Premasiri arranged a good marriage for his eldest daughter who had migrated to work. She had a child and after a year went back to work. She remitted money to her parents. They said they used the money for the child and to build the daughter a house. This led to problems between her parents and their son-in-law, who was working in a shop selling illicit liquor rather than as the carpenter he had been at the time of their marriage. Premasiri's status as a patron rose with his control of his daughter's wealth. His son-in-law lost standing because of his rich, employed wife. And he lost status again because his father-in-law managed the money. In the end, the husband left.[47]

Women who receive remittances are at times empowered, and at other times women feel more dependent and stressed. Despite the financial success of some migrants from Honduras, nearly every woman interviewed wished her husband or son had not migrated. Though the primary motivation for migration was to improve the family's economic situation, their men's migration had left the women with the fear that over time the family and conjugal relationship would dissolve. There was also the fear and loneliness of having to manage the additional responsibilities with the children. Most women for the first time had to manage the farm and manage the debt of roughly $5,000 that was incurred to pay the coyote (smuggler) for their men's migration. If the money did not flow adequately, there was anxiety that the land would be repossessed.[48]

Remittances had different effects on the women left behind in three poor communities in Kerala with high levels of short-term migration to the Middle East. Women in a patrilineal Muslim village were subject to the greater control of their husband's kin when the husband migrated. In a Hindu matrilineal community, the remittances revitalized female inheritance and matrilineality. In a Christian community, women were more empowered as the families became more nuclear. The interaction of religion, gender, status, and historical heritage shaped the way people from the three communities migrated and the jobs they had in the Middle East. These factors also influenced the effect of remittances on women's management and control over the money in the household. The story gains more potency as the three villages are compared.

Veni is an agrarian Muslim village. The joint family is patrilineal, patrilocal, and strongly patriarchal. The migration of men from this village is wholly organized by kin and community members who have ties of religion and a history of migration to the Middle East. The men work in the technical and unskilled areas. In Veni because of the men's migration, women no longer go to work outside the house. The wife stays with her husband's family. The husband sends his remittances to his father. He generally also addresses letters to his parents. Even when he sends gifts home, he has to make sure his gifts to his wife are not better than his gifts to his immediate natal family. The father or another male relative buys the provisions, and the wife has to ask him for money. Women have become more secluded and financially dependent. They are under the greater control of the man and his family and are watched zealously. It is only when the woman moves out of her in-laws' house that she gains some control over household decisions. Even then the husband still sends the remittances to a male relative. This relative then gives the man's wife a portion of the money for household expenses.[49]

Cherur is a matrilineal village with Ezhava Hindus. Not having the same history of migration or community ties as the Mappila Muslims, the men migrated to the Middle East via agents for skilled work. The women and children stayed with her parents, drawing on their matrilineal history. The remittances were sent to the father-in-law or the woman by postal orders. The woman continued to earn money through agricultural activities. Money was also lent out at interest rates between 36 and 60 percent. Remittances led to a greater emphasis on the education of girls and a return to the matrilineal traditions. Money was spent on gift giving within the extended family and on celebrations.[50]

Kembu is a Syrian Christian community with a history of education and contacts with overseas missions and organizations. They migrated as professionals and with their families. Women who were nurses were the primary earners, but women who accompanied their husbands were also able to be in paid work. They spent much of their money on education and on larger dowries and investments for the nuclear family. When the family did not accompany the man, the money was sent to the wife annually or semiannually through bank drafts. She made the investment decisions and also looked after the construction of the house. Ties with the extended family and community weakened. There were donations to the church, but as the churches had small congregations, the donations did not have the same community-wide effect as with the Mappila Muslims. Migration moved girls' education from nursing to a more generalized university education, which equipped them to become wives of professional men. It meant, however, that Syrian Christian women in one generation moved from being primary earners to being dependent on the man as the primary earner.[51]

Women who migrate with the husband have mixed experiences relating to remittances. In patrilineal systems of kinship, it is the men who remit. I write of this at greater length in chapter 8. A study of a Syrian Christian migrant community in the United States shows that even when the woman is the primary earner, sending remittances to the woman's family is often a source of tension for the marital couple. This is despite the fact that a woman had stated her intention to remit before the marriage was arranged.[52]

In matrilineal kinship systems, migrant women continue to have obligations to send money to their mothers and sisters in the home country. But the experience of matrilineal Akan women from Ghana who migrated to Canada shows that the need to remit has led to downward mobility at work and a comparative loss of control of money in the household. A study of fifteen Akan women interviewed in Toronto showed the pressures of remitting to their mothers, sisters, and the matrilineage led them to accept low-paid, unskilled jobs rather than hold out for the professional or management jobs they had in Ghana. Belonging to a matrilineal kinship system, they had previously managed and controlled their money independently. But the need to pool two inadequate incomes to cope with the expenses of settlement has meant that nine of the fifteen women have moved to some form of joint management and control. There is increased tension over the negotiation of money that goes to the woman's extended family and lineage—and the demands of settlement. Only one of the fifteen women owns a home in Toronto. Remittances to the matrilineage now have to be weighed for symmetry between the wife's and husband's families in Ghana. This is despite the fact that the woman's obligations to the matrilineage are traditionally greater than the man's. At the same time, conflicts have emerged in recipient households. In one instance, in a departure from traditional flows of money, the brothers objected to the money going to the sisters, saying that they would be more prudent with the money.[53]

We do not know enough about women migrants' remittances to the community because the literature has focused on men's giving. Community remittances, like family remittances, are overwhelmingly male in countries with patriarchal traditions. When men working in the Middle East send money, variable proportions of the family's remittances are used for community donations. The giving is male, though women contribute much of the on-the-ground work.[54]

Even when women are the inspiration behind the diaspora philanthropy, the project carries a male name. At times this is only a male facade for a shared family social enterprise. This is illustrated by the story of Kapoor Singh Siddhu (later spelled "Siddoo"), an Indian migrant to Canada. It was his wife Basant Kaur's dream that their two daughters train as medical doctors and go back to her village to serve. Her brother and uncle had been ayurvedic doctors in her village. To prepare for this dream while their daughters were still in school, the family bought land that could be a possible site for their hospital in Punjab. The daughters were brought up with a rich inclusive religious tradition including Sikhism and Theosophical teachings. They graduated as medical doctors from the University of Toronto. In 1952, as a graduation reward, the Siddoos took them to India for the first time. This was a difficult experience for the daughters who had grown up with an idealized notion of India. They returned to Canada to do postgraduate work. Four years later they elected to go to India to participate in the family dream of a hospital in the village. After many hiccups, the hospital opened in Aur in October 1959. The hospital is called "Kapoor Singh, Canadian, Hospital," but the continued on-site presence was that of the mother and her two daughters.[55]

Bibi Balwant Kaur's (BibiJi's) story stands out against the male landscape of giving. She migrated to Kenya from Punjab in 1925 as a young girl and then from Kenya to the UK in 1972. She engaged in charitable work when she was married with a son and when she became a widow around 1948. Over sixty years, she organized the building of a crematorium in Nairobi, went to India after the Partition to help in the refugee camps in Punjab, set up Gurdwara Bebe NanakiJi in honor of Guru Nanak's sister in India, and later established the Bebe Nanaki Charitable Trust in 1972 in the United Kingdom. The charitable work of the trust is supported by Sikhs residing overseas, but the mission is to help all communities. The trust helped with disaster relief for Ethiopia, Armenia, Bangladesh, India, and Pakistan, in addition to its focus on the welfare of women, health, and education.[56]

BibiJi perhaps drew her community spirit from "an unspoken East African Ramgarhia consciousness." Perhaps being twice a migrant was also liberating. We do not know whether the prominent role of women in the activities of the Bebe NanakiJi Gurdwaras in India and the United Kingdom will remain. BibiJi at ninety was more of a matriarchal head. As the first generation of philanthropists retired, they were replaced by men. BibiJi has died. Will women remain central to the vision, leadership, and activities of the trust and its Gurdwaras? Perhaps BibiJi's story may reinforce the male face of diaspora philanthropy.

Migrant women's experience of money management and control in the country of destination can also be more or less empowering. It is influenced by gender ideologies in the source country, the woman's position in the labor market in the destination country, and issues of class. Employed Latin American immigrant women in the United States often gain a greater role in decision making and budgeting compared with women who remain in their home countries. There is more sharing in domestic work. This is despite gender inequality in the workplace and in the labor market. Dominican women get used to this greater independence and autonomy. They spend their money on expensive durable goods and furnishings to root the family in the United States. The men prefer a more austere life to save for a possible return. A Mexican woman who had returned, said, "In California my husband was like a mariposa (meaning a sensitive, soft, responsive butterfly). Back here in Mexico, he acts like a distant macho."[57]

Syrian Christian nurses and their husbands in the United States experience changes in gendered roles with child minding, cooking, and cleaning, as well as the management and control of household finances. Typically, the women are the primary migrants. The husbands and children have followed, but the husbands have had to accept lower-status work than in India. Women's work, together with the unavailability of affordable or acceptable help and less family support, means that husbands have to have a role in child minding. Their participation in other domestic work varies. But of the twenty-one nursing households in a metropolitan area in the United States, women in eight of the households chose to plead ignorance of financial management to try and retain a sense of traditional patriarchy. Women in another eight households moved to a greater sharing of domestic work and financial management. But another five, faced with the absence of men or their financial unreliability, took control over money in the household.[58]

Women's greater earning power does not necessarily lead to a greater say in the household's finances. Women's role in financial management depends on whether the couple continues to use patriarchal norms of Kerala society as the reference point or they begin to see the greater sharing of money in the household in the United States as normal. It also shows that financial management is at times influenced by the man's attitude to his forced participation in domestic work. Women at times cede financial management as a strategy to reduce the dissonance between gender ideologies and the experience of migration.[59]

WOMEN HAVE LESS ACCESS TO NEW TECHNOLOGIES

The new information and communication technologies are potent tools in reducing financial exclusion and enabling greater social connection across distance. In low-income countries, women own, access, and use the Internet and mobile phones less than men. This is broadly linked to women not having as much education as men and less control over money and resources in the household. Men own more of the mobile phones in countries like India and Pakistan where men dominate decisions about the purchase of mobile phones and expenditure on food and electricity. The broader question is, does women's lesser access to the new ICTs mimic a society's gender inequalities?

A lack of access to technologies limits women's social and employment opportunities. Unless women have access to or own a mobile phone, they cannot be part of the mobile money transformation that is taking place in many countries in Africa and Asia. Mobile phones are so important that a recent survey showed that in Kenya, one in five of the 796 men and women interviewed were willing to forego buying food, clothes, and/or using public transport in order to pay the mobile phone expenses.[60]

Without the mobile phone and the Internet, women are also excluded from the frequent and immediate communication within transnational families. Communication now has an immediacy that was absent in letters or in the expensive three-minute telephone conversations a few decades ago. Cheaper international transportation has also made for more frequent visits to the home country and more visiting with migrant family offshoots in the country of destination.

Recently there has been a greater emphasis on measuring gendered access to technologies to provide an evidentiary base for policy. It is often difficult to compare the numbers because some studies focus on households rather than individuals, or ownership rather than use and access. As with the unbanked, a focus on the household blocks the study of gender differences within the household. It is also important to recognize that use and access can be broader than ownership. In high-income countries, ownership implies direct use. But in low-income communities with a tradition of sharing resources and expertise, intermediated access multiplies the effect of ownership and direct use. People can access a phone owned by another person as a "beneficiary-user," or have the owner use their phone to get information or connection on behalf of the "tertiary user."[61]

Gender differences in access to mobile phones in 2012 are hardly noticeable in high- and middle-income countries, especially among young people. But in low-income countries, women are less likely to own or access a mobile phone than men. Gender further exacerbates the ownership and access gap because of low income and poverty. The situation gets ambiguous as the metrics move between ownership and access.

A woman is 21 percent less likely than a man to own a mobile phone. The gender gap is highest in South Asia and the Middle East at 37 percent, followed by Africa at 23 percent. "Closing the gender gap in cell phone access would bring the benefits of mobile phones to an additional 300 million women in low- and middle-income countries."[62] The "mobile phone gender gap" is greatest at the bottom of the pyramid. GSMA's recent research in Egypt, India, Papua New Guinea, and Uganda shows that women's ownership and even the desire to own a mobile phone is influenced by social, cultural, and economic factors in each country. In Uganda and Papua New Guinea, women often acquire the second handset in the household. But in Egypt and India, the woman is third in line, after the sons, brothers, or brothers-in-law. The majority of households have a mobile phone, but women are not always able to access it. Some can borrow their neighbor's mobile, but the social costs can be restrictive. Even when women can use the household mobile, they use it mainly for voice. The most marginalized women cannot access a mobile in the household or the neighborhood.[63]

There has been a welcome push for more demand-side research on mobile and Internet use and access within households in Africa and Asia. This research provides useful evidence for the design and implementation of effective policies. Research ICT Africa (RIA) surveyed seventeen African countries—Benin, Botswana, Burkina Faso, Cameroon, Côte d'Ivoire, Ethiopia, Ghana, Kenya, Mozambique, Namibia, Nigeria, Rwanda, Senegal, South Africa, Tanzania, Uganda, and Zambia. The survey was representative at the household level and for individuals sixteen years or older.

It was conducted from late in 2007 to the beginning of 2008.[64] South African and Mozambican women are exceptional in that they own more mobile phones than men. In Cameroon, women have greater knowledge of the Internet. But in the other fourteen countries surveyed, women remain disadvantaged in terms of access to ICTs. This is because "women generally have less access to employment, education and other factors that increase the likelihood of ownership."[65] Women, particularly in rural areas, generally earn less than men and so seem to be particularly disadvantaged because of the high cost of communication.

This overall picture is changing as incomes rise and mobile handsets get cheaper. The Internet has also become more accessible on the mobile. In Kenya, the Philippines, and Thailand, women and men equally own mobiles.[66] A 2012 survey on the mobile in Kenya shows that there is no gender difference in mobile phone usage at the base of the pyramid (BOP), except for mobile Internet usage. Education was the more significant divide as most respondents without a formal education used SMS, the Internet, and M-PESA less than those with an education.[67]

The Kenyan government's removal of the value added tax (VAT) in 2009 and increased competition have reduced the cost of acquiring a mobile phone. In mid-2012, over 60 percent of people at the BOP owned a mobile phone. This is despite the fact that mobile services can cost more than a fourth (27 percent) of monthly income in Kenya.[68]

The mobile handset is a very personal device in Kenya, as a majority of the people interviewed do not share their mobile phone with anybody in the household, though they may occasionally allow others to use their phone for a call or an SMS. It raises the question, does sharing and intermediate access cease when men and women have equal ownership of the mobile phone? It would be interesting to investigate this further as this pattern of direct ownership and access is different from the community approaches to mobile phone use in Bangladesh through the Grameen Phone or those revealed in studies of intermediate access in Bangalore, India.[69]

A 2006 survey of over 8,600 persons who had made or received a call in the last three months, covering India, Pakistan, Sri Lanka, Thailand, and the Philippines at the BOP, showed that women had greater access to fixed phones than mobile phones. At the BOP in developing countries, men and women used the phone in the same way. The gender gap increases in rural areas. The study confirms that when there is one mobile phone per household, it is the male who is most likely to access it and take it with him when he leaves the house. Men used it more than women as was the case in developed countries in the early stages of adoption. Access to the Internet at the BOP in these countries was at most 10 percent.[70]

The gender divide in access to telephones was greatest in Pakistan and India. There were 2.7 men for every woman who used their own mobile as the phone they most frequently used. The gender gap was lower in Sri Lanka but was absent in the Philippines and Thailand.[71]

The main difference between South Asia and Southeast Asia relates to male decision making regarding money to be budgeted and spent on mobile phones. In South Asian countries, men dominated the decision making regarding the purchase of a mobile phone. Men made the decision for 74 percent of the women who owned their mobile phone. In Southeast Asian countries, the corresponding number was 9 percent. It was the same gendered pattern for expenditure on food and electricity.[72]

These studies in Africa and Asia show that unequal gendered access to ICTs is explained by women's lower incomes and access to education, as well as cultural patterns of male and female control over money in the household. Where women can decide on how money in the household gets spent, women own and use more mobile phones. Women's limited access to household resources, banking, and credit, particularly in South Asia, results from the same kind of male dominance that ensures women have less access to the new ICTs. This finding points to the urgency of broadening the studies of access to ICTs to include an examination of money management and control.

Policies for more gender equity in the use of technologies need to focus on broader initiatives that encourage the education and income of girls and women in areas like ICT studies.[73] Kenya has achieved gender equality in mobile phone ownership by reducing the price of a mobile handset. When the price of a handset goes down to as little as $12, women are able to afford the phones and the airtime from their own meager earnings.[74]

The push for equal mobile phone use and ownership has to be part of broader policies promoting gender equity. Women will only become equal participants in globalization once the cultural and financial inequalities between men and women are addressed. It is women's greater financial autonomy that ensures financial inclusion.

In the next chapter, from the world of the unbanked and women, we move to the center of the market. Global financial markets, banks, and electronic money are familiar settings for economic globalization. But as the next chapter will show, money in the market and money in households and families shape each other.

NOTES

1. V. M. Moghadam, "Gender and Globalization: Representations, Realities, Resistances," SHS/GED Seminar Series, http://www.unesco.org/new/fileadmin/MULTIMEDIA/HQ/SHS/pdf/Gender-Globalization.pdf (accessed November 26, 2012).

2. Carla Freeman, "Is Local: Global as Feminine: Masculine? Rethinking the Gender of Globalization," *Signs* 26, no. 4 (2001).

3. Viviana A. Zelizer, "The Gender of Money," *Wall Street Journal*, January 27, 2011.

4. P. Chesler and E. J. Goodman, *Women, Money and Power* (New York: William Morrow, 1976), 52.

5. Judy F. Graham et al., "Gender Differences in Investment Strategies: An Information Processing Perspective," *International Journal of Bank Marketing* 20, no. 1 (2002).

6. Mariko Lin Chang, *Shortchanged: Why Women Have Less Wealth and What Can Be Done about It* (Oxford: Oxford University Press, 2010), 94.

7. Barbara F. Reskin and Patricia A. Roos, *Job Queues, Gender Queues: Explaining Women's Inroads into Male Occupations* (Philadelphia: Temple University Press, 1990); M. Waring, *Counting for Nothing: What Men Value and What Women Are Worth* (Wellington, NZ: Allen & Unwin and Port Nicholson Press, 1988).

8. Reskin and Roos, *Job Queues, Gender Queues.*

9. Supriya Singh, *Marriage Money: The Social Shaping of Money in Marriage and Banking* (St. Leonards, NSW: Allen & Unwin, 1997).

10. Singh, *Marriage Money*, 159.

11. Singh, *Marriage Money*, 159.

12. H. Papanek and L. Schwede, "Women Are Good with Money: Earning and Managing in an Indonesian City," in *A Home Divided: Women and Income in the Third World*, ed. D. Dwyer and J. Bruce (Stanford, CA: Stanford University Press, 1988), 91.

13. Jerome Rabow et al., "Women and Money: Cultural Contrasts," in *Sociological Studies of Child Development*, ed. Patricia A. Adler and Peter Adler (Greenwich, CT: JAI Press, 1992), 198.

14. A. Summers, *Damned Whores and God's Police* (Ringwood, Victoria: Penguin, 1994).

15. Naomi Wolf, *Fire with Fire* (New York: Random House, 1993), 235.

16. Wolf, *Fire with Fire*, 247.

17. Wolf, *Fire with Fire*, 239.

18. Anita Hill, an attorney and academic, directed attention toward sexual harassment when she alleged that the US Supreme Court nominee Clarence Thomas had engaged in sexually harassing conduct when he was her supervisor.

19. Ambreena Manji, "Eliminating Poverty? 'Financial Inclusion,' Access to Land, and Gender Equality in International Development," *Modern Law Review* 73, no. 6 (2010).

20. Clara Han, *Life in Debt: Times of Care and Violence in Neoliberal Chile* (Berkeley: University of California Press, 2012).

21. Asli Demirguc-Kunt and Leora Klapper, *Measuring Financial Inclusion: The Global Findex Database* (Washington, DC: World Bank, 2012).

22. Demirguc-Kunt and Klapper, *Measuring Financial Inclusion*.

23. Bina Agarwal, *A Field of One's Own: Gender and Land Rights in South Asia*, 2nd ed. (Cambridge: Cambridge University Press, 1996).

24. Srimati Basu, "The Politics of Giving: Dowry and Inheritance as Feminist Issues," in *Dowry & Inheritance*, ed. Srimati Basu, Issues in Contemporary Indian Feminism (New Delhi: Women Unlimited, 2005); Madhu Kishwar, "Dowry and Inheritance Rights," in *Dowry & Inheritance*; Srimati Basu, "*Haklenewali*: Indian Women's Negotiations of Discourses of Inheritance," in *Dowry & Inheritance*; Seema Misra and Enakshi Ganguly Thukral, "A Study of Two Villages in Bihar," in *Dowry & Inheritance*.

25. Agarwal, *A Field of One's Own*, 468.

26. Pradeep Panda and Bina Agarwal, "Marital Violence, Human Development and Women's Property Status in India," *World Development* 33, no. 5 (2005).

27. Niall Ferguson, *The Ascent of Money: A Financial History of the World* (Camberwell, Victoria: Allen Lane, 2008).

28. Celestine Nyamu-Musembi, "Breathing Life into Dead Theories about Property Rights: De Soto and Land Relations in Rural Africa," in IDS Working Paper 272 (Brighton: Institute of Development Studies, 2006).

29. Patrick McAuslan, "Personal Reflections on Drafting Laws to Improve Women's Access to Land: Is There a Magic Wand?," *Journal of Eastern African Studies* 4, no. 1 (2010).

30. McAuslan, "Personal Reflections."

31. Susan Johnson, "The Search for Inclusion in Kenya's Financial Landscape: The Rift Revealed," Centre for Development Studies, http://www.fsdkenya.org/pdf_documents/12-03-29_Full_FinLandcapes_report.pdf (accessed August 19, 2012).

32. Susan Johnson, "Gender Norms in Financial Markets: Evidence from Kenya," *World Development* 32, no. 8 (2004): 1366.

33. Supriya Singh and Yaso Nadarajah, "School Fees, Beer and 'Meri': Gender, Cash and the Mobile in the Morobe Province of Papua New Guinea," Institute for Money, Technology and Financial Inclusion, http://www.imtfi.uci.edu/files/imtfi/blog_working_papers/working_paper_singh.pdf (accessed September 20, 2012).

34. Singh and Nadarajah, "School Fees."

35. Supriya Singh and Mala Bhandari, "Money Management and Control in the Indian Joint Family across Generations," *Sociological Review* 60, no. 1 (2012).

36. Singh and Bhandari, "Money Management."

37. Singh and Bhandari, "Money Management," 58.

38. Singh and Bhandari, "Money Management."

39. Sandra Stanley Holton, *Quaker Women: Personal Life, Memory and Radicalism in the Lives of Women Friends, 1780–1930* (Abingdon, UK: Routledge, 2007).

40. Summers, *Damned Whores*; Supriya Singh, "Marriage, Money and Information: Australian Consumers' Use of Banks" (PhD diss., La Trobe, 1994).

41. J. Lawton, "What Is Sexually Transmitted Debt?," in *Women and Credit: A Forum on Sexually Transmitted Debt*, ed. R. Meikle (Melbourne: Ministry of Consumer Affairs, 1991).

42. Supriya Singh and Anuja Cabraal, "Women, Money and the Bank" (paper presented at the Financial Literacy, Banking and Identity Conference, Melbourne, Australia, October 25–26, 2006).

43. Singh and Cabraal, "Women, Money and the Bank," 15–16.

44. Jayati Ghosh, "Migration and Gender Empowerment: Recent Trends and Emerging Issues," in *Human Development Research Paper* (United Nations Development Programme, 2009).

45. Rhacel Salazar Parreñas, *Children of Global Migration: Transnational Families and Gendered Woes* (Stanford, CA: Stanford University Press, 2005).

46. Michele Ruth Gamburd, "Absent Women and Their Extended Families," in *Negotiation and Social Space: A Gendered Analysis of Changing Kin and Security Networks in South Asia and Sub-Saharan Africa*, ed. Carla Risseeuw and Kamala Ganesh (Walnut Creek, CA: AltaMira Press, 1998), 282–83.

47. Gamburd, "Absent Women."

48. Sean McKenzie and Cecilia Menjívar, "The Meanings of Migration, Remittances and Gifts: Views of Honduran Women Who Stay," *Global Networks* 11, no. 1 (2010).

49. Prema A. Kurien, *Kaleidoscopic Ethnicity: International Migration and the Reconstruction of Community Identities in India* (New Delhi: Oxford University Press, 2002).

50. Kurien, *Kaleidoscopic Ethnicity.*

51. Kurien, *Kaleidoscopic Ethnicity.*

52. Sheba Mariam George, *When Women Come First: Gender and Class in Transnational Migration* (Berkeley: University of California Press, 2005).

53. Madeleine Wong, "The Gendered Politics of Remittances in Ghanaian Transnational Families," *Economic Geography* 82, no. 4 (2006).

54. Kurien, *Kaleidoscopic Ethnicity.*

55. Hugh Johnston, "The Sikhs of British Columbia and Their Philanthropy in Punjab," in *Sikh Diaspora Philanthropy in Punjab: Global Giving for Local Good*, ed. Verne A. Dusenbery and Darshan S. Tatla (New Delhi: Oxford University Press, 2009).

56. Navtej K. Purewal, "Gender, Seva, and Social Institutions: A Case Study of the Bebe Nanaki Gurdwara and Charitable Trust, Birmingham, UK," in *Sikh Diaspora Philanthropy in Punjab: Global Giving for Local Good*, ed. Verne A. Dusenbery and Darshan S. Tatla (New Delhi: Oxford University Press, 2009).

57. Patricia R. Pessar, "Engendering Migration Studies," *American Behavioral Scientist* 42, no. 4 (1999): 585.

58. George, *When Women Come First.*

59. George, *When Women Come First.*

60. Angela Crandall et al., *Mobile Phone Usage at the Kenyan Base of the Pyramid: Final Report* (Nairobi: iHub Research and Research Solutions Africa, 2012).

61. Nithya Sambasivan et al., "Intermediated Technology Use in Developing Communities" (paper presented at CHI 2010: HCI and the Developing World, Atlanta, Georgia, April 10–15, 2010).

62. World Bank, *World Development Report 2012* (Washington, DC: World Bank, 2012), 262.

63. GSMA, *Striving and Surviving: Exploring the Lives of Women at the Base of the Pyramid* (2012).

64. Alison Gillwald, Anne Milek, and Christoph Stork, *Gender Assessment of ICT Access and Usage in Africa* (Research ICTafrica.net, 2010).

65. Gilwald, Milek, and Stork, *Gender Assessment of ICT Access*, executive summary.

66. Gilwald, Milek, and Stork, *Gender Assessment of ICT Access*, executive summary; Ayesha Zainudeen and Dimuthu Ratnadiwakara, "Are the Poor Stuck in Voice? Conditions for Adoption of More-Than-Voice Mobile Services," special issue, *Mobile Telephony* 7, no. 3 (2011); Rohan Samarajiva, "Mobile at the Bottom of the Pyramid: Informing Policy from the Demand Side," special issue, *Mobile Telephony* 7, no. 3 (2011).

67. Crandall et al., *Mobile Phone Usage.*

68. Crandall et al., *Mobile Phone Usage.*

69. Sambasivan et al., "Intermediated Technology Use."

70. Ayesha Zainudeen, Tahani Iqbal, and Rohan Samarajiva, "Who's Got the Phone? Gender and the Use of the Telephone at the Bottom of the Pyramid," *New Media & Society* 12, no. 4 (2010).

71. Zainudeen, Iqbal, and Samarajiva, "Who's Got the Phone?"

72. Zainudeen, Iqbal, and Samarajiva, "Who's Got the Phone?"

73. Gillwald, Milek, and Stork, *Gender Assessment of ICT Access.*

74. Personal communication, Angela Crandall, January 12, 2013.

CHAPTER 5

BANKING

CONNECTING MARKETS
AND INTIMATE LIVES

In this chapter I focus on banks and bankers. They occupy a special place at the intersections of globalization, money, and information and communication technologies (ICTs). Banks are national, and banks are global, illustrating that globalization can be local and global at the same time. Banking is where personal lives and markets connect. This multisided aspect of banks reflects some of the main themes of this book. ICTs have changed banking and payments. Traditionally banking and payments have been part of a single package. But with the unbanked on the one hand and the digital generation on the other, payments often stand alone. Banks move into a supportive though necessary role as they are the ones that are regulated to take deposits. But the role of banks in money management, payments, and lending is in flux. This story of change begins in this chapter and continues in chapters 6 and 7.

In this chapter, I first position banks in the global financial markets. I argue that the financial markets are social institutions. I then focus on how banks are national, reflecting their social history, and subject to national regulations and goals regarding economic policy and financial inclusion. Drawing on my research on marriage, family, and banking in Australia and India, I illustrate how personal money and market money are intertwined, each shaping the other. I do this by detailing how the values of *marriage money* in Australia and *family money* in India structure the characteristics of bank accounts in the two countries. I then focus on how the new ICTs are changing the role of banks in money management, payments, and lending across the world. Most often the pathways to change are digital, though at times the interface is physical but backed by complex technology platforms.

BANKS IN GLOBAL FINANCIAL MARKETS

Banks are important market institutions, but in terms of scale they rank behind derivatives and bond markets. The total assets of banks in June 2012 were $33.4 trillion.[1] The over-the-counter derivatives market was nineteen times larger at $639 trillion.[2] Bond markets, counting international and domestic debt securities (March 2012), were nearly three times larger than banks at $99.9 trillion.[3] Yet the evolution of banking was "the essential first step in the ascent of money."[4]

Banks take in deposits which they lend to other households, corporations, and governments. For most of us in households, it is the deposits and loans that are the most visible aspects of banking. But as told in the derivatives story in chapter 2, banks are part of the global derivatives market. Banks on-sell loans through securitization and use their capital to lend some more.

In contrast to the familiar picture of banks, there is a virtuality about the other players in the global financial markets, with a lack of connection to economic activity on the ground. Financial markets do not produce or distribute goods. They trade financial instruments that circulate rather than being consumed by end consumers. This "shift from concrete funds to abstract entities epitomizes the decoupling of financial markets from the ordinary economy of production, consumption, and exchange."[5] Deregulated markets around the world are not subject to national regulations, policies, currencies, taxes, and welfare systems. Some financial markets like currency markets are inherently transnational. Bond and equity markets are becoming more global.

Financial markets are social institutions. Money is traded in specific social and cultural contexts. The social aspects of money in the market are well illustrated in the open-outcry pit futures trading room in the Chicago Board of Trade (CBOT) and a London futures (LDF) trading room with numbers on a screen. These are quintessential global market sites. We again meet up with the gender dimensions of markets and globalization, for it is a male world. Of the six hundred traders in CBOT, two were women. At LDF, there was one woman and sixty men.[6]

In both environments traders attempt to interpret fast-moving bids and offers within a social and narrative context. They need to get a "feeling" of the market. "The first thing traders learn is that *numbers tell very little*."[7] "Flexible interpretation rather than formal calculation characterizes the styles of reasoning common in financial futures markets, both in the pits and on the screen."[8]

In Chicago, the social context comes from the physicality of the open-outcry system, the sheer noise, and the color, with each cry wanting to be heard and seen. It is the controlled loud voice that is needed, with routinized hand gestures giving the numerical signals. Where bulk and stature is against the crier, he jumps high in the air to catch a trader's attention. Traders are recognized on the street not only because of their colorful jackets but their raised shoes.[9]

The traders in the digital futures trading room in London also try to get a sense of the market by placing the numbers in a social context and working out which characters are operating that day. They do this by listening to the market chatter of other traders and injecting a narrative around the patterns of numbers. With the help of coworkers, traders assign personalities and motivations to the persons behind the numbers. There is great symbolic capital attached to a trader who can "take out" the Spoofer, a recurring character who uses a large number of bids to try and make the market go in his favor.[10]

Financial markets only work because there is trust and a sense of social responsibility. Markets, financial institutions, investors, borrowers, and savers are "part of wider social arrangements, rather than operating in an entirely separate economic domain."[11] These social arrangements include the regulation of markets, property rights, and norms and conventions about proper ways of conducting economic activity. The simplistic notion that markets work only through a rational pursuit of self-interest has to be replaced by the two-way influences between the economy on the one hand and political, legal, and cultural processes on the other.[12]

People expected that if banks lent to them, they were creditworthy. This was the way banks used to work. Corporations assumed that banks would not trade against their clients or knowingly sell them toxic securities. Investors depended on ratings agencies to verify the quality of the complex securities sold. Governments and societies expected that banking regulators would have adequate oversight of the banks and their trading activities. The global financial crisis resulted in a deep gash of disbelief because these social expectations were not fulfilled.

BANKS ARE NATIONAL AND GLOBAL

It is a fascinating journey to study the history of a society through a history of its banks and bankers. Having written of central bankers in Malaysia, I studied Australian bankers when I moved from Malaysia to Australia in 1986.[13] The location and number of banks, their place in society, the maleness of banks, their relationship with the government—these characteristics have been shaped by social history.

Australian banking is dominated by four large banks with a large national branch network. Australian banks expanded with the gold boom of the 1850s and the opening of the wheatlands in the 1860s. Hence Australian banks were found across the rural hinterland. The story was often told that a bank together with a church and a school were the first buildings to come up when new land was opened.

Banking history in Australia is also a story of bankers making do in tents in the goldfields and riding for days to get to the nearest branch. Banking history is a good way to learn local history—what the small town of Eden in Victoria was like in the gold rush, how a banker after eleven months in Advale, Western Australia, spent a Saturday afternoon, half nude and drunk, running in the streets.[14]

I noted this large rural banking network in Australia because in Malaysia the colonial banks with a branch network were concentrated in cities. The small Chinese banks were also in cities but without a national branch network. In Malaysia the central bank had to "strongly encourage" banks to open branches in rural areas. When that happened, it was an event to be celebrated, as it made banking more accessible.[15]

In Australia, the chief executives of the four major banks in 1989 had joined the banks at fifteen or sixteen as juniors. Most successful banking stories at that time were of how the sons of teachers, farmers, clergymen, and traders started as juniors and rose to head the banks. Bob White, who retired as managing director of Westpac Banking Corporation in 1987, came from a farm of dry mallee land in New South Wales. He had a scholarship to go to the University of Sydney, but his father decided Bob should go to the bank, for it represented a secure opportunity. When Bob reported for duty at Echuca in Victoria, the manager had just taken delivery of a navy-blue Chevrolet sedan. Bob's voice goes silky talking of it forty-seven years later. The manager also lived at the top of the bank, a building with a big stone facade and large, high-ceilinged bedrooms.[16]

There are no family-owned banks in Australia as in the United Kingdom, Singapore, Malaysia, Hong Kong, and Thailand. This explains the lack of a banking dynasty. The boards, however, prized family connections and social status. In 1989 Westpac had six knights among its fifteen directors. There was also a religious divide. Private Australian banks drew their recruits mainly from the Anglo-Saxon Protestant majority. This was such an accepted part of the private banking tradition that Bill Gurry, chief executive of the National Mutual Royal Bank established in 1986, was deeply conscious that he had made it in banking as a Catholic boy.[17]

In Malaysia in 1984, banking was an elite profession. Many bank chief executives came to banks after a foreign education, often in Australia. There was a "Melbourne Mafia" in banking in Malaysia, for many chief executives had graduated from universities in Melbourne, developing relationships over Sunday curry lunches. This included the then governor of Bank Negara Malaysia.

Some aspects of banking were the same in Malaysia and Australia. Banking in both countries was male. In Malaysia in 1983, if I met a woman at a central bank dinner, I assumed she was the wife of a banker. However, in September 1998, Tan Sri Dato' Sri Dr. Zeti Akhtar Aziz, was appointed acting governor of Bank Negara Malaysia, becoming governor in May 2000. She has been judged one the world's top central bankers each year since 2010. In Australia, Miss Tennyson Beatrice Miller was the first woman hired in the Bank of New South Wales (now Westpac) in 1886 and was called "Lady Typewriter." A woman had to be unmarried and without children to make it even to the middle tiers of banking. And as we saw in chapter 4, women were not seen as desirable bank customers.

In 1989, the appointment of a woman general manager was so unusual that Westpac issued a press release. Now Westpac is led by Gail Kelly, a South African–born Australian businesswoman.

In Australia and Malaysia, central bankers saw banks as social institutions with a social and national responsibility. Nugget Coombs, the first governor of the Reserve Bank of Australia, told me in 1998, "I saw being a banker as the use of intellectual understanding for social purposes."[18] He held to an "old-fashioned view that, whether you are in a public or private institution, you have a social responsibility."[19] Tun Ismail Ali, the first Malaysian governor of Bank Negara Malaysia, was a nationalist. He was an austere disciplinarian and strove to build the bank to become a premier financial institution. But above all, he wanted the bank to serve the national interest. When Tun Ismail became governor in July 1962, a senior Western central banker told him, "You must be independent like us." Tun Ismail Ali said, "I don't remember what I told him. But I had no doubts at all . . . that Bank Negara must be involved with the development of the country."[20] He saw the bank as "being independent within government but not of government. After all . . . the objectives of government must prevail."[21]

Many central bankers in developing countries would agree with Tun Ismail. They see themselves as following a social agenda set by the government. Kenya's and India's central banks have financial inclusion as one of the main objectives of banking. It is one of the ways of achieving a more equitable and economically developed society.

Banks' deep roots in social history do not conflict with the global nature of their operations. In today's world, banks have to operate in a global context of money as they lend and borrow from each other, as well as lend domestically and internationally. In the past, Australian and Malaysian banks have survived global linkages that threatened to destroy their banking systems and economies.

Australian banks began lending for land directly or indirectly in the 1870s. Competition in the late 1880s became frenzied. More than a quarter of banks' deposits came from London. They had borrowed short and were lending long. At the same time the general depression of the late 1880s saw wool prices fall by a third between 1884 and 1891. Melbourne land prices collapsed. In 1893, fifty-four of the sixty-four deposit-taking institutions closed. A whole generation had their savings frozen for long periods. The image of the big bad banks became firmly entrenched. It led to the establishment of the publicly owned Commonwealth Bank of

Australia in 1912 and an attempt to nationalize banks in 1947. Bankers and the Catholic Church campaigned against this proposal. It contributed to the end of the Chifley government in 1949. As described in chapter 2, Malaysia, too, was singed by its open economy and lack of capital controls during the East Asian Financial Crisis of 1997–98.

BANKS CONNECT MARKET AND PERSONAL MONEY

Banks are national institutions central to the market in a global network of money flows. Banks deal with market money when they lend to each other or buy and sell derivatives. Banks also bring personal money from the household to the market. Banks deal with multiple monies when they mediate households and engage with the market. First there are the multiple monies in intimate relationships. The characteristics of these monies change across cultures according to marriage ideology, forms of family and household, and patterns of money management and control. Second, there are multiple monies in the bank, because banks move between the banking money applicable to households and market money for transactions between market institutions. These different kinds of money in the bank are reflected in the structure of their accounts.

I draw on my research in Australia and India to show how values around money in intimate relationships are reflected in the way people bank. In both countries, multiple bank accounts are the banking version of money in jars on the mantelpiece. People need to separate money from business and money from other sources. Money from consultancies, tax refunds, bonuses, or occasional activities like umpiring is kept apart from wages. Money from inheritance is put in a different account so that it does not get spent on groceries. Money for personal spending is separate from joint expenses. Money to be remitted to parents overseas does not mix with family expenses. Money from an investment property or a retirement package is parked in a separate account for taxation purposes. Loan accounts are separated from savings accounts. Money is separated according to the ways it is paid, withdrawn, or transferred—via the passbook in the old days, the checking account, or the Internet.

The differences are seen best in the representation, structure, and use of joint accounts. In Australia it is the married or de facto couple who shares the joint account, whereas in India joint accounts are also routinely held between adult children and parents. This pattern of joint accounts reflects the different boundaries and values around domestic money. As noted in chapter 1, in Australia, money is private to the marital or de facto couple. Information about money is seldom shared with adult children.[22] In India, money is also private, but the boundaries of domestic money extend to the joint family and other kin. Information about money is at times shared more easily between the father and son or between brothers than between husband and wife.[23] The characteristics of *marriage money* in Australia and *family money* in India shape the structure and use of joint bank accounts.

MARKING TOGETHERNESS AND DEFLECTING POWER IN MARRIAGE IN AUSTRALIA

In my study of banking and marriage in Australia in the early 1990s,[24] I heard couples tell how after their wedding they went to the bank to open a joint account. They took their marriage certificate—sometimes still with a ribbon tied to it—and rolled their individual accounts into the joint account, now in the husband's name and the wife's changed name after marriage. Oprah, forty-five, in part-time paid work, said the jointness of accounts was part of the mechanics of getting married. "It was just a matter of course. It was one of the things we did when we were married," she said.[25]

The personal joint account made the married couple visible to themselves. It symbolized commitment, jointness, and the togetherness of marriage to those under sixty-five years of age. This was despite the fact that most of their parents were in long, committed marriages without having joint accounts. The generational change in the way couples did their banking was accompanied by a greater proportion of married women being in paid work. There was also more joint home ownership. The Privacy Act of 1988 led banks to encourage these joint accounts. Banks could no longer look up the wife's credit record through the husband's account. Separate files for husbands and wives led bankers to prefer joint accounts and joint loans.

The joint account represented jointness rather than necessarily indicating joint management and control. The joint account also deflected questions about the quanta of financial contributions to the marriage. It masked tensions between the ideology of marriage as a partnership and the reality of women's lower earnings. The joint account helped focus on the togetherness of marriage by theoretically converting separate and individual earnings to joint ownership of money. It avoided discussion of issues of power and financial inequality in an ongoing marriage.

The generational change became clear when I interviewed Betsy, eighty-one, her son Barry, forty-four, and Barry's wife Beth, forty-one. Betsy lived in a Housing Commission house in an older Melbourne suburb, less than half an hour's drive from her son's house. Her house was simply furnished with a TV, white arum lilies in a vase, a green lounge set, and photographs of the grandchildren when they were young. Her husband—she called him Dad—was sitting in his chair. They had been married for fifty-six years. He had been suffering from Alzheimer's for the past three years and had a stroke twenty years before. Each of them was on the old-age pension of some AUS$250 a fortnight. Every now and again in telling her story, Betsy said she had had a fortunate life.[26]

Betsy did not have a bank account until she was fifty-seven when she went into paid work. She did some tailoring after leaving school at age thirteen. She was paid in cash and gave all her wages to her mother. Her mother would then give her some money if she wanted to go for a dance. When she got married fifty-six years ago, her husband worked as a mechanic fixing equipment in farms. Talking of forty years ago, she said, he earned £5 a week. He used to give Betsy the "envelope," with his wages in cash, in the classic whole-wage system of money management and control. Then Betsy had to work out how to pay the bills and stretch out the money. She would give her husband the fare to work, which she remembered may have been 10 shillings, and something in his pocket.

She stressed, "I never owed a penny." Often she would be left only with a "shilling in me pocket" until the next payday.[27] So there was never any money left over to save in a bank account. However, the prospect of life on an old-age pension and paying rent was daunting enough for Betsy at fifty-seven to go back to paid work at the cafeteria of a large department store. She no longer had to look after her diabetic mother, as she had died after living with them for twelve years. Betsy opened a passbook account with the State Bank of Victoria near her workplace. She was paid in cash and would put some in the account first and use the rest. She paid off the house, and with their combined savings they treated themselves to three holidays in Tasmania, Perth, and Darwin with the Elderly Citizens' Club. Betsy continued to ensure that her husband had something in his pocket when he went for a walk.

Barry and Beth, Betsy's son and daughter-in-law, lived in more affluent surroundings. But like Betsy, Beth and Barry did not spend on personal wants. Barry said he sometimes bought two pairs of shoes when he needed one or donated when they were short. But they paid off their house in eight years. Barry managed a small private company and earned AUS$40,000 to AUS$45,000 a year. Beth worked part time at a kindergarten and earned less than AUS$5,000 a year.

Barry's money was paid by check—we are talking early 1990s—and went into their joint bank account. Beth's salary went into her separate housekeeping account. "So everything starts off in the bank," Barry said, comparing it with his parents' time. "In their day only the leftover got into the bank." Joint accounts were also important for the way they saw themselves as a married couple. It also meant that the whole-wage system or the housekeeping-allowance systems of money management no longer applied.

For Beth and Barry, the joint account reflected their joint management of money and their togetherness as a married couple. Beth said they managed their money "together . . . together!" The money was "pooled together" when they got married and both were earning. It remained pooled after the children came and she went into part-time paid work.[28]

Beth saw the joint account as symbolic of her trust in Barry and as fundamental to their relationship. Beth, forty-one, talking of her marriage and banking, said, "We are pretty joint. . . . I totally trust Barry with every cent we have."[29] The idiom of jointness was so central to the way they dealt with money that Beth's separate accounts hardly rated a mention. She explained her separate housekeeping account as one where they just have not gotten around to registering Barry on it. There was also her passbook account at the State Bank of Victoria that was still separate. She used the savings in it to buy the garage. "I think there's [AUS]$2 there still. . . . When things are bad, I go and get my [AUS]$2 out."[30]

Women's consciousness of financial dependence did seep through in other ways. In my first interview for the marriage and banking study which began in 1990, I interviewed a couple together. We sat in the living room, and the wife began to tell how she felt constrained using the joint account for personal expenditure. The husband was cut to the quick. He remonstrated that he had never objected to her spending money as and when she wanted. The wife demurred that it was not him, but it was something she felt. It went from bad to worse, signaling to me that open talk about money between married couples could be awkward. So I changed the research strategy and from then on interviewed the husband and wife separately, coming together afterward for coffee.

There is an uneasy tension between money that is earned and spent and money that is spent without being earned. Nellie, forty-four, in full-time work, said she could spend what she wanted. But since she had been earning, she said, "I've been having my nails manicured, which is something I've never ever done."[31]

Joint accounts have remained important for married couples since the 1960s. The 2006–7 longitudinal and random Household, Income and Labour Dynamics in Australia (HILDA) Survey, with an overall sample size of 12,905 persons, revealed that 83 percent of married persons had joint accounts, either only joint or combined with separate accounts. De facto relationships presented a mirror image, as 85 percent of persons in de facto relationships had separate accounts, with or without joint accounts.[32]

I studied banking and information in Australia again between April 2005 and July 2006, covering 108 people in Australia. My research showed that marriage often meant a move from separate to joint accounts. As de facto relationships before marriage became more popular, couples started off with separate accounts. Having a joint account for some became part of the transition from the de facto relationship to marriage.[33]

Shane, twenty-five to thirty-four years old, had only separate accounts when he and his partner were in a de facto relationship. When they got married, Shane pushed for having only joint accounts, mainly because his parents had joint accounts. He said, "I wanted to have joint accounts because I saw that as being . . . almost a symbol or a practical application of our functioning as a team."[34] Shane's wife at the time earned more than he did. He said his wife was wary about moving from separate accounts to joint accounts because she was afraid of losing her independence with handling money. Moreover, her parents had a mix of joint and separate accounts. Shane and his wife compromised by trying out joint accounts for a year. As the joint accounts worked out, they kept with the arrangement.

Further research combining the previous two qualitative studies and the HILDA database showed that more married women in Australia had a mix of separate and joint accounts compared with married men, who were more likely to have only joint accounts.[35] This was not an example of a growing individualism and a lack of continued commitment, where relationships are becoming "more porous, and of course more fragile."[36] It also was not a move toward what Giddens calls a "pure relationship," which promised more equality and was more democratic.[37] Women's greater use of separate accounts also did not suggest that bonds "need to be only loosely tied, so that they can be untied again, with little delay, when the settings change— as in liquid modernity they surely will, over and over again."[38]

Separate accounts allowed women the freedom of personal spending. Women particularly value this because they seldom feel free to use joint accounts for personal expenditure. Separate accounts also give married couples the flexibility to deal with split and multiple responsibilities in step, blended, and migrant families. But having this separateness does not necessarily translate to separate management and control of money in marriage.

So money in marriage, that is, *marriage money*, in Australia is a "special money." It is domestic, private, personal, joint, and cooperative. It is nebulous because in an ongoing marriage, it is seldom quantified as to who put in how much. It differs from the ideal type of market money described in economic and classical sociological theory. Market money is impersonal, individual, contractual, and calculable. The nature of marriage money also shapes banking money in Australia, which is also a "special money." When banks deal with married couples, they present ways of banking that are joint, personal, and cooperative. It is only when the banking relationship or marriage dissolves that banking money reverts to market money.

PROTECTING FAMILY AND INTIMATE RELATIONSHIPS IN INDIA

In India in middle-income urban families, the joint bank account does not have the same connotations of jointness for the married couple as in Australia. The joint account in India is predominantly a way of ensuring that money in the account goes to the surviving account holder, who may be a spouse, a child, or a sibling. It is primarily an inheritance device to protect members of the family. The Indian joint account may only nominally be a joint account for the sake of protection rather than transaction. Often it is used as a separate account. In some cases, as we saw in chapter 4, it means that women who are the second-named account holders will be unbanked in practice.

It has been difficult to find nationally representative data about the relative incidence of separate and joint accounts in India. I conducted a qualitative study between November 2007 and January 2008 about money, information, and privacy in metropolitan and peri-urban areas of Delhi and the small town of Dharamshala. I studied forty predominantly middle-income and upper-middle-income persons from twenty-seven households. In the study, twenty-four of the thirty-nine married persons in the sample had joint accounts, with or without separate accounts. Less than half (eleven of the twenty-four married persons with joint accounts) could transact on these accounts.[39]

The joint account often substitutes for the separate account because it offers superior legal protection to the survivor and the convenience of emergency access. Balu, in his fifties, said he had a joint account for the sake of convenience. Since he traveled a lot, he wanted his wife, Beatrice, to conveniently withdraw money as and when required. Beatrice, too, had her own joint account for her professional fees and inheritance. She said, "It is totally my account. I withdraw. I deposit."[40]

Mahesh, a retired professional, said all their accounts are joint in name but managed separately. He said,

> In India the salaries go into separate salary accounts for . . . the income tax lawyer wants separate streams of money coming in and going out. . . . The joint account is a matter of contingency, either or survivor. But the income tax rules are that the owner of the account is the first name on the account.[41]

In the two cases above, the married couple had information about each other's joint accounts. The money was meant for common use. But there were also three cases in the study where there was no information or transactional access to the joint account. Neera, an upper-middle-class businesswoman in Delhi had a joint account with her husband and a separate business account. She did not access the joint account even when her husband was away. She also had no information about money in the account. She said,

> He has never said, "I don't want to tell you." . . . I myself have not taken the initiative. Many times he tells me, "You should know. You should take more interest." I feel he is better at it than I would be. He knows better what to do.[42]

The other two women we met in chapter 4 were unbanked in practice because they only had this one joint bank account. In addition, Santokh, over sixty-five, in Dharamshala says his wife, who lives in another city, has never withdrawn money from the joint account.

Though joint accounts between spouses were most common, parents and adult children also had joint accounts. So did siblings. This is because in India it is the family in its different forms, rather than the couple, which is the boundary of domestic money, as noted in chapter 1. A two-way flow of money between parents and children is central to *family money*. Parents acknowledge an obligation to help their adult children. Adult working children, particularly sons, including those not living at home, recognize an obligation to help their parents. This is true even when their parents can survive without the additional money.

This obligation is couched in terms of "duty" (*dharma*) on the children's part and a "right" (*haq*) on the parents' part. In the study, there were five instances where a parent had a joint account with his or her adult children, making it easier for money to flow between parents and children. The two-way flow was accepted by parents and children. There were two cases of upper-middle-income parents who had the ability and the wish to be financially independent but said their adult children kept offering them money.[43]

Accounts with the children are for protection and convenience. Gauri, a housewife about fifty years old, with an annual household income of INR 5 to 10 lakhs ($10,000 to $20,000), had joint accounts with her two working sons so that she could deposit and withdraw money for them. Tara in Dharamshala, also about fifty, with an annual household income of under INR 90,000 ($1,800), had one joint account with her husband and a child and another joint account with a second child. These joint accounts enable the children who are studying away from home to withdraw money from an ATM. Urmilla, about sixty years old, in a Dharamshala middle-income nuclear family household, did not have a joint account with her working son. But he gave her an ATM card so that she could withdraw money from his account. These accounts are all with unmarried adult children. Avinash, sixty-two, and his wife Asha, sixty, used to have joint accounts with their unmarried daughters. These accounts have ceased now that the daughters are married.[44]

Some of the stories I heard in India suggested there has also been a generational change toward joint accounts, joint money control, and female money management among urban middle-income couples. Preeta's story showed how differently she and her mother-in-law managed and controlled money in the joint family.[45]

Preeta, a housewife, was in her late forties or early fifties and was part of an upper-middle-income three-generation joint family with an annual household income of over INR 30 lakhs ($60,000). She was married to the only son of the family. Preeta, her husband, and their two boys lived on the ground floor, and her mother-in-law lived on the first floor. They had their meals together on the first floor. Preeta and her husband had a joint account. Preeta accessed and transacted via the joint account. She said she knew "absolutely what my husband has."[46] She ensured she was well informed so that she could be part of the decision making about money. Preeta's husband gave Preeta money to give to his mother. Preeta's mother-in-law controlled and managed her own money.

This is a different situation compared to Preeta's mother-in-law's experience as a married woman. When Preeta's mother-in-law (a graduate) got married and lived in a joint family, she had little access to money. If she wanted more, she had to ask her mother-in-law. Her husband, that is, Preeta's father-in-law, was a professional. He would give most of his money to his mother. He gave his wife a small amount when he wanted to. He only began giving his wife the money he earned after his mother died. But even then, he discussed his investments with his son, but not with his wife. It turned out he had a joint account with his wife. The family only discovered it after the father-in-law's death.

Both Preeta and her mother-in-law have a BA degree and are part of high-income households. So the key to this generational change is neither income nor education. Preeta said her father-in-law felt "it was very important to be a good son. He forgot it was important to be a good husband as well."[47] Preeta said the shift happened because her husband thinks it is equally important to be a good son and a good husband.

This emphasis on family relationships rather than the primacy of the conjugal relationship shapes the pattern and use of joint accounts. *Family money* in India is private and protective. It can be private while being joint with the spouse, child, parent, or sibling. It is protective, anticipating dissolution at death. These characteristics shape the structure of the joint account in India. The joint account makes clear how the money will be transferred when one of the joint bank owners dies. The account may be either or survivor, former or survivor, or latter or survivor. The Reserve Bank of India has also asked banks to prompt account holders to nominate who would inherit the money in different bank accounts.[48]

NEW WAYS OF BANKING

New ways of banking are sparked by the recognition that banks don't understand customers' experience of banking. This includes the unbanked, the underbanked, and the banked. The question before bankers is, will banks get relegated to the back room? Banks will be needed because they are the regulated deposit-taking institutions. But different aspects of

banking are being offered by alternative services. Aggregators already offer money management. Other organizations facilitate online lending and
borrowing. Mobile network operators enable payments.

New ways of banking most often will be digital. This will be true for
the young professionals in the US who have grown up with electronic
money and electronic banking. The digital will also be part of extend-
ing the reach of banking and payments to serve half the world that is
unbanked and underbanked. The mobile phone, the Internet, physical
branches, prepaid cards, and cash are coming together in new combina-
tions. The challenge is to offer the poor ways of saving small amounts of
money frequently, flexible credit and insurance, and a choice of payment
options. At the same time the business model should ensure that the bank,
the banking agent, and the telecommunications provider can make a sustainable profit. I addressed these challenges in chapter 3. In chapter 7, we
will see how the mobile phone has revolutionized the transfer of money
in sub-Saharan Africa.

While celebrating innovation in banking services, it must be noted
that new ways of banking seldom address the needs of the underbanked
in high-income countries. Guarantees for credit to the poor increasingly
have to be based on confidence in a person's moral ability to repay rather
than on economic and legal guarantees. The use of moral capital as a
guarantee for credit will in time move from the poor to ways of serving
the underbanked.[49] In the next chapter, I write of Green Dot, a company
that offers prepaid cards at an affordable fee to this group in the United
States and is making a profit. But payday lenders who charge exorbitant
rates of interest continue because there are no alternative sources of small
amounts of immediate credit at an affordable rate.

THE MOVE TO DIGITAL MONEY MANAGEMENT

Banks are in danger of losing their central role in helping people manage
their money. They continue to organize themselves around the branch
as the primary channel and the checking account as the basic product.
Banks see the electronic channels as alternatives, and yet 90 percent of
daily transactions in the United States are done electronically. Banks have
not responded to the fact that most young people in the West have never
written a check in their lives and seldom go to a branch. Young people use
the Internet and the mobile phone for their banking transactions. Banks
continue to treat the different channels and product divisions as silos and

treat each as an independent profit center. So banks are ill equipped to cater to the use of a changing mix of payment instruments and channels. As a result, the person dealing with the customer seldom has a picture of his or her relationship with the bank.[50]

In the United States there is a move away from banks because of their high fees and their failure to satisfy customers' need for money management. Aggregators dealing with banks will increasingly offer services that have the customers' aims of money management at the center. An aggregator layer is emerging as with SmartyPig, Goalmine, Mint, and Simple in the United States. It brings banks, payment methods, and other financial service providers together to offer the customer a satisfying financial experience.[51] But these new means of online money management have not gone global. At present they are confined to the United States because they only partner with US banks. These new forms of quasi-banking services are addressed to young people who "have digital in their DNA" as Paul Braund, cofounder of RIOS Institute (Research and Innovation for Organizations and Societies Institute) in Berkeley and Silicon Valley, told a seminar in Melbourne on March 21, 2012.

In one way, these new services go back to an incompletely remembered past. The simple and sure statement of money saved for different goals is a much-missed feature of multiple passbooks. Reading about the design of aggregator services for money management, where progress toward savings goals is clear, reminds me of a woman who told me she had six passbooks, each relating to a separate savings objective. Aggregator services are also trying to deliver the personal attention we thought we got in the past at a branch.

Some of the greatest enthusiasm on the Internet is for Simple, cofounded by Joshua Reich, thirty-three, an Australian who moved to the United States. Simple has been three years in the making. It opened to its first invited customers in November 2011. It has more than one hundred thousand people who have asked to be invited. Receiving the white Simple Visa debit card is celebrated in blogs.

Simple is a technology company that partners with the Bankcorp Bank, an FDIC-insured bank in the United States. It is a front-end alternative to a bank. The money sits in the bank. Simple looks after the user's experience through its Web and mobile interface. It is geared toward simplifying banking services and giving relevant information. There are no hidden fees. Simple's revenue will come from sharing the interest rate margin with the bank and the interchange fees with the card issuer. For international funds transfers, it will charge the customer what it costs. A real person will answer the phone. It is hoped that it will be the same person every time if possible. This has led to doubts about its sustainability over time, but it has already attracted $13.1 million in funding.[52]

Simple is still a work in progress and expects to be continually changing as it responds to customer feedback. In December 2012 it did not offer small business accounts or joint accounts, though they are being considered. It offers a checking account for US residents. Its customer base so far is drawn from "college-educated adults earning between $40,000 and $100,000 a year who don't demand complex financial transactions and who get mad at checking-account fees."[53]

Simple does nothing new, but does it better. It tags and can map where you have spent your money like Mint and Quickbooks. It makes it possible for you to send a picture of your check, like Chase, USAA, and Citi. It uses a debit card. It offers free ATM withdrawals at the forty-three thousand ATMs on the Allpoint network. It offers savings goals and strategies like other banks.[54] The key is that Simple has made it an enjoyable experience.

New ways of banking appear attractive, for they promise a more individualized and personal online experience. Even if these start-ups don't challenge traditional financial institutions in terms of market strength and global reach in the short term, they act as catalysts in showing that a different way of banking and paying is possible. Cutting down banking and payment fees and having money management at the center can only mean that traditional banking will be pulled in more desirable directions.

New Ways of Borrowing, Lending, and Managing Money Online

People have begun in small ways to borrow and lend online, bypassing banks. Peer-to-peer (P2P) lending in the United States, United Kingdom, and Australia has parallels with previous movements that led to the formation of credit unions and building societies as more humane, personal, and community-centered financial institutions. The strong feeling against banks, particularly in the United States, is behind some of these new developments.

These peer-to-peer transactions are in some ways similar to the borrowing and lending relationships of the poor. The decision to lend is based on the P2P lenders' credit scoring and assessment of risk. The lender gets more than he or she would, compared to fixed deposit rates. The borrower pays less than he or she would pay with credit cards. The risk is often spread through a portfolio of borrowers, but it is unsecured risk. It is an unsecured loan. The difference is that among the poor, the borrowing and lending is embedded in established social networks with a physical base and history, whereas online there is a fleeting virtual connection with the borrower assessed by the assigned credit score. Alternative forms of borrowing and lending bypass banks, whereas one of the main aspects of financial inclusion is to include people in formal financial channels, possibly banks, in a culturally appropriate way.

The main players in this field are Zopa, set up in 2005 in the United Kingdom, and Prosper (2006) followed by Lending Club in the United States. This sector is being seen as a credible alternative to banks, given the lack of confidence in the banking sector. Zopa has arranged more than £200 million in loans over the last eight years. This includes a monthly record of 1,621 loans totaling £8m in July 2012 alone. This is up by 72 percent on the same period the previous year.[55] This sector has been given a boost with the British government announcing that it would channel £100 million in loans to small business through P2P lenders. Bank of England executive director Andy Haldane has said that P2P lending through online sites could eventually replace old-fashioned banking.[56]

Prosper and Lending Club in the last year have been attracting institutional investors who want a higher yield than they can get with junk corporate bonds. Questions being asked in the media revolve around the higher risks of P2P lending to people who may not have the best credit histories. But the returns are greater than from most government or corporate bonds.[57]

Kiva is the not-for-profit sector's poster child, where loans blur into donations. I tried kiva.org. It felt good lending—that is, donating $25 to a nineteen-year-old single woman from Guatemala who applied for a loan to purchase threads for her weaving. I chose my borrower for her story. I received an e-mail thanking me for making my first Kiva loan. After that, there was nothing for a while. I did not hear from kiva.org whether the woman attained her target amount or how she was doing. When I went back to the site after nearly a month, I found that her loan of $925 was fully funded. Jonathan O'Donnell, one of my colleagues in Melbourne, was surprised because he gets updates on his borrowers.

Paul Braund of RIOS told us in Melbourne that my borrower most likely had already received a loan through the local microfinance institution

(MFI) network that is aligned with kiva.org. My loan through kiva.org was backfilling loans already made to partners in the field. My borrower most likely does not know that this MFI network receives its money through kiva.org donors. The money is free to the MFIs, who then charge interest rates—sometimes high—on their loans. So this direct "feel good" image is based on incomplete information and one-way communication between the lender and kiva.org. I did not feel a sense of connection after that first bit of a glow. My borrower has repaid the $25, and it is sitting there in my Kiva account for me to donate or relend as e-mails keep reminding me.

Jonathan, unlike me, is enthusiastic about kiva.org. He made his first Kiva loan on July 1, 2008, after he had heard of it in a discussion group. He has made seven loans since then. It is not so much a loan as a "renewable donation." The most recent is to a woman in Bolivia. He will get his money back by March 2013, and he will most likely give another loan. Jonathan is so happy with Kiva that he has given thirty-eight gift certificates to friends and family, of which twenty-seven were redeemed and turned into Kiva loans. The other eleven were not redeemed after a year and were turned into donations for Kiva's operating costs.

Jonathan has also lent to Kickstarter, which helps support artistic, creative, and design projects. He has supported game designers, jewelry designers, comic book authors, and a couple of singers. Kickstarter raised more money in 2011 than the annual budget of America's National Endowment for the Arts.[58]

He says he has also been satisfied with his experiment with crowd funding where money is solicited for arts projects or social enterprise. With social enterprise, they have a donor who will put up an equal or multiple amounts of the money raised through crowd funding. It is a more targeted way of donating money because the money goes toward a specified project with an organization you want to help.

A MORE SATISFYING BRANCH EXPERIENCE

A face-to-face initiative also geared toward a satisfying customer experience is progressing in India with the Kshetriya Gramin Financial Services (KGFS) in a totally different market. KGFS focuses on the poor who have no or few formal financial services. As with the US developments, the aggregator model with money management and wealth creation is at the center of the customer experience. Banks and other formal financial institutions remain part of the picture, for their mediation of deposits into credit is something they alone are regulated to do.

KGFS began operations in June 2008 in three different rural areas in India. Its emphasis is on providing local, immediately accessible branches in rural areas that are not served by private banks. The branches are painted green and orange with an open front. There are rows of wooden benches and a teller window. Two online computers and three uniformed staff complete the picture. The branch staff seek to enroll all households within a five-kilometer radius.

The focus is on wealth management and helping a household achieve its financial goals. Information about the household's financial situation and its aspirations are the starting point for advice about products, services, and strategies. Staff members visit village households when they establish the branch and then every six months to update their reports and financial advice. The wealth managers at the local level are evaluated according to how well they have helped households achieve their goals.

This approach has had noticeable success. Branches have expanded to five areas serving two hundred thousand customers. The earliest KGFS has enrolled 76 percent of all households in its geographic area. Of these, 89 percent use some of the fifteen financial products available at the branch. Insurance and pension services are the most widely used.[59] There is euphoria around the model that is customer centered and that appears to be succeeding. The first KGFS expects to be profitable in 2012. However, we await the greater scrutiny that an independent evaluation will offer sometime in 2014.

In the next chapter I analyze the rapid adoption of the new information and communication technologies that have led customers to use a different mix of channels and payment instruments for a variety of activities. ICTs have changed the way customers pay and transfer money, though old forms and channels of money continue to remain important. These changes make us rethink the characteristics and constancies of money.

NOTES

1. Bank for International Settlements, *Detailed Tables on Preliminary Locational and Consolidated Banking Statistics at End-June 2012* (Basel: Monetary and Economic Department, Bank for International Settlements, 2012).

2. Bank for International Settlements, *Semiannual OTC Derivatives Statistics at End-June 2012* (2012).

3. Bank for International Settlements, *Securities Statistics and Syndicated Loans* (Basel: Bank for International Settlements, 2012).

4. Niall Ferguson, *The Ascent of Money: A Financial History of the World* (Camberwell, Victoria: Allen Lane, 2008), 65.

5. Karin Knorr Cetina and Alex Preda, Introduction to *The Sociology of Financial Markets*, ed. Karin Knorr Cetina and Alex Preda (Oxford: Oxford University Press, 2005), 4.

6. Caitlin Zaloom, "Ambiguous Numbers: Trading Technologies and Interpretation in Financial Markets," *American Ethnologist* 30 (2003).

7. Zaloom, "Ambiguous Numbers," 261.

8. Zaloom, "Ambiguous Numbers," 269.

9. Zaloom, "Ambiguous Numbers," 263.

10. Zaloom, "Ambiguous Numbers," 267.

11. Robert J. Holton, *Global Finance* (New York: Routledge, 2012), 2.

12. Holton, *Global Finance*, 2–3.

13. Supriya Singh, *Bank Negara Malaysia: The First 25 Years, 1959–1984* (Kuala Lumpur: Bank Negara Malaysia, 1984); *The Bankers: Australia's Leading Bankers Talk about Banking Today* (North Sydney: Allen & Unwin Australia, 1991).

14. Singh, *The Bankers*.

15. Singh, *The Bankers*.

16. Singh, *Bank Negara Malaysia*.

17. Singh, *Bank Negara Malaysia*.

18. Singh, *The Bankers*, 49.

19. Singh, *The Bankers*, 51.

20. Singh, *Bank Negara Malaysia*, 335.

21. Singh, *Bank Negara Malaysia*, 335.

22. Supriya Singh, *Marriage Money: The Social Shaping of Money in Marriage and Banking* (St. Leonards, NSW: Allen & Unwin, 1997).

23. Supriya Singh and Mala Bhandari, "Money Management and Control in the Indian Joint Family across Generations," *Sociological Review* 60, no. 1 (2012).

24. Singh, *Marriage Money*.

25. Singh, *Marriage Money*, 43.

26. Singh, *Marriage Money*, 87.

27. Singh, *Marriage Money*, 88.

28. Singh, *Marriage Money*, 91.

29. Singh, *Marriage Money*, 2.

30. Singh, *Marriage Money*, 91.

31. Singh, *Marriage Money*, 106.

32. Supriya Singh and Clive Morley, "Gender and Financial Accounts in Marriage," *Journal of Sociology* 47, no. 1 (2011).

33. Supriya Singh, "Balancing Separateness and Jointness of Money in Relationships: The Design of Bank Accounts in Australia and India," in *Human Computer Interaction International* (San Diego, CA, 2009).

34. Singh, "Balancing Separateness," 508.

35. Singh and Morley, "Gender and Financial Accounts in Marriage."

36. Elisabeth Beck-Gernsheim, *Reinventing the Family: In Search of New Lifestyles* (Cambridge, UK: Polity Press, 2002), 41.

37. Anthony Giddens, *The Transformation of Intimacy: Sexuality, Love and Eroticism in Modern Societies* (Stanford, CA: Stanford University Press, 1992), 58.

38. Z. Bauman, *Liquid Love: On the Frailty of Human Bonds* (Cambridge, UK: Polity Press, 2003), vii.

39. Singh, "Balancing Separateness and Jointness."

40. Singh, "Balancing Separateness and Jointness," 510.

41. Singh, "Balancing Separateness and Jointness," 510.

42. Singh, "Balancing Separateness and Jointness," 510.

43. Singh and Bhandari, "Money Management and Control."

44. Singh, "Balancing Separateness and Jointness."

45. Singh and Bhandari, "Money Management and Control."

46. Singh and Bhandari, "Money Management and Control," 63.

47. Singh and Bhandari, "Money Management and Control," 63.

48. Banking Codes and Standards Board of India, "Code of Bank's Commitments to Customers," http://www.bcsbi.org.in/Code_of_Banks.html (accessed May 7, 2008).

49. Ariel Wilkis, "Morality and Popular Finance: Moral Capital as a Kind of Guarantee," *Estudios de la Economía*, http://estudiosdelaeconomia.wordpress.com/2012/10/23/morality -and-popular-finance-moral-capital-as-a-kind-of-guarantee (accessed April 1, 2013).

50. Brett King, *Bank 2.0: How Customer Behavior and Technology Will Change the Future of Financial Services* (Singapore: Marshall Cavendish Business, 2010); "Bye-bye Checking and Current Account," last modified May 29, 2012, http://www.finextra.com/community/fullblog.aspx?blogid=6586.

51. Ignacio Mas, "Making Mobile Money Daily Relevant," http://papers.ssrn.com/sol3/papers.cfm?abstract_id=2018807 (accessed September 13, 2012).

52. Eric Chaves, "Simple's Pitch: A No-Fee, No Hassle Bank Account," CNN Money, http://money.cnn.com/2011/12/20/technology/simple_bank/index.htm (accessed November 26, 2012).

53. Nancy Cook, "Deploying Electrons to Battle . . . the Biggest and Baddest Banks," *National Journal*, June 7, 2012.

54. Benjamin Jackson, "First Look: Simple Reimagines Banking," http://thenextweb .com/insider/2012/08/01/first-look-simple-reimagines-banking (accessed November 26, 2012); Owen Thomas, "Simple Is Ramping up Its Revolution in Banking—Square's Cofounder Just Got His Card," *Business Insider*, June 16, 2012.

55. Andrew Hagger, "Money Insider: Peer-to-Peer Lending Gathers Pace as Faith in Banks Falters," *The Independent*, September 22, 2012.

56. Milind Sathye, "Could Peer-to-Peer Lending Challenge Our Banks?," *The Conversation*, June 28, 2012.

57. Joe Light, "Would You Lend Money to These People?," *Wall Street Journal*, April 13, 2012.

58. "The Digital Age: Reaching Out," *Economist*, January 12–18, 2013.

59. Bindu Ananth, Greg Chen, and Stephen Rasmussen, *The Pursuit of Complete Financial Inclusion: The KGFS Model in India* (Washington, DC: CGAP and IFMR Trust, 2012).

CHAPTER 6

ELECTRONIC MONEY

INFORMATION AND TIMELINESS

There has been a great change in the nature of money and banking and it is taken for granted in middle- and high-income countries. We have to go back many years or to older generations to remember the world of savings passbooks, checks, and branches. Reading of Betsy opening a passbook account or her son Barry receiving his wage by check takes us back to what seems to be a long-gone era of banking and payments. Today Betsy and her husband would be receiving their pensions by direct credit in their bank accounts. Her son Barry would also be receiving his wage by direct credit.

Just as financial markets have changed because of information and communication technologies (ICTs), money has become electronic information for households in the West. Money has been information for banks ever since they exchanged money through IOUs and bills of payment. In 1977, money became electronic information with SWIFT

(Society for Worldwide Interbank Financial Telecommunication). SWIFT provided a secure standardized network for financial institutions to send messages to each other about financial transactions. For retail customers, money became information around the same time with credit cards in the 1970s and then with ATMs and direct credit in the 1980s. Internet and mobile banking and online payments furthered this transformation.

In this chapter I describe how electronic money and the new forms and channels of money that have resulted prompt us to think of the "reality" and nature of money. Electronic money changes the way we pay and get paid for goods and services. It changes the way we manage money. Yet multiple forms and channels of money remain part of a changing mix. I use the available quantitative data on payments in different countries, focusing on consumers. I supplement this with my qualitative research on the use of electronic money in Australia to show how timeliness and cultural values around activities influence which form and channel we use for money in different contexts. I illustrate how electronic money has changed the way we manage money within marriage. At the same time, customers' values of sharing in marriage and family, together with issues of access and accessibility, have influenced the use of banks' privacy and security settings for electronic money.

Innovations in electronic money have led to novel currencies and ways of payment. Through it all runs a constant theme that we are moving toward the end of cash or at least a displacement of cash by electronic money. Part of it seems to be a wish to fit the payments world to that of young professionals who grew up with electronic money. Once we get rid of cash and/or the older people who use it, we can move to a more efficient payment system. As I write this, I remind myself that cash and face-to-face transactions are at the center of the financial lives of half the world that is unbanked. Poor men have little access to the new technologies, and poor women have even less. This is a useful corrective for those of us who live in a digital world.

IS ELECTRONIC MONEY "REAL"?

Two decades ago, it was common to worry about the "reality" of electronic money. In my marriage and banking study in the early 1990s, Heath, a forty-four-year-old teacher, spoke of his preference for cash as "real money." He liked to "keep tabs" on his money. So he preferred to go to the bank branch to withdraw AUS$600 in cash on payday. He then divided it up for the different expenses. He took out AUS\$30 in AUS\$2 coins to pay for his son's basketball game and tae kwon do in exact change. His wife Hilary, forty-five, was comfortable with this approach. She, too, had compartments in her purse to separate housekeeping money; money for *Quest*, a children's science magazine; basketball money; and petrol money. "You know it is dwindling," she said. "You've actually got physical tabs."[1]

Though Heath used four credit cards and the ATM, he talked of plastic money as "pretend money." He said that when he used a credit card,

> no money has passed through my hands. There is just this thing that con-
> tinually goes around. Whereas if you open up your wallet and you've got
> \$5 left, it is a lot harder to take that \$5 out and spend it. . . . This is why
> I am certain that young people have so much trouble overspending—be-
> cause it's almost not real.[2]

I spoke of this with Robert M. Janowiak, executive director of the International Engineering Consortium in the United States over dinner in Melbourne. He asked whether I had read *The Velveteen Rabbit*. Having grown up in India on the British fare of Enid Blyton, I had not. He sent me a handsomely illustrated version. It is a much-loved story of a velveteen rabbit, a boy who used to love him, and an old skin horse who also lived in the same toy cupboard as the velveteen rabbit. One day the rabbit asked the skin horse, "What is real?" The skin horse replied, "Real isn't how you are made. . . . It's a thing that happens to you. . . . You become. It takes a long time."[3]

Money is real because you think it is real. Trusted networks are the defining characteristic of money.[4] Money is abstract, impersonal, and symbolic.[5] But electronic money is "virtual," in that, compared with cash, checks, and the branch, the payment instrument and/or channel is no longer physical. We still speak of "handling" money when we are really managing money as information.

People used to talk of electronic money as impersonal, for it replaced face-to-face transactions. Often the choice to transact across the counter—despite unsatisfactory service—was an attempt to retain a valued personal sense of money. But banking itself has become impersonal, so electronic money may offer a greater measure of personal control. The new forms of money management that are emerging in the United States and India, as we saw in chapter 5, are built around individual goals for money and a person's life. These new forms of money management, even when they are digital, could feel more personal than waiting in line at a bank branch.

USE OF ELECTRONIC MONEY FOR PAYMENTS

Money became global for me in 2008 when I could go to an ATM in Dharamshala, a small town in the foothills of the Himalayas, and withdraw money from my banks in New Delhi and Melbourne. The ATM works most of the time. The electricity is on and the ATM functions. Before 2008, when I went to my Himalayan home, I had to bring cash from New Delhi while traveling in an overnight bus or give a check to the temple priest. He would lend me the money for the three weeks it took the bank to clear a New Delhi check.

My use of payment instruments in Dharamshala is a timely reminder that electronic money does not rule in all parts of the world. I pay my rent by check, but for everything else in Dharamshala, I still need cash. I cannot use my credit card in Kotwali Bazar, the main market in Dharamshala, though I can use it in some of the Tibetan shops in the more tourist McLeod Ganj where the Dalai Lama lives. I need cash to pay the vegetable seller who calls out his vegetables below my unit and to pay the maid who comes to help. I need cash for the daily offering at the Sikh temple. I particularly need cash for the ritual gift of *shagun* to bless a new bride or baby.

Money is becoming increasingly electronic in form and channel in much of the Western world. The Bank for International Settlements' data on twenty-three countries shows that people pay more often by card, followed by direct debits. The traditional electronic payment instruments, such as direct transfers and credit and debit cards, are growing in the number and value of transactions. Overall, checks remain most important in terms of value, followed by direct debits.

The use of the check is declining in number and value, though there is great variation among the twenty-three countries in the use of checks. In 2011 in Singapore, checks accounted for 67.1 percent of the value of noncash payment transactions. People in the United States continued to issue 68.3 checks a year—these accounted for more than half their transactions—and were worth 39.2 percent of the value of transactions. In the Netherlands, Switzerland, Sweden, Germany, Belgium, the United Kingdom, Mexico, and Russia, checks accounted for less than 5 percent of the value of transactions.[6] The use of checks has also declined in the United Kingdom and Australia, but attempts to phase out the check have been abortive. There was vocal opposition from older citizens and the nonprofit groups that benefit from charity checks.[7]

Cash still remains the most popular way to hand over person-to-person payments. Its use is declining, but it is not fading as fast as predicted by many futurists of money. In Australia people use cash for payments under AUS$40. Cash accounts for 64 percent of a person's total number of consumer payments, but just 34 percent of their value. Compared to 2007, the use of cash has declined about 5 percent in value and number.[8]

Cash is used differently across countries. In Germany cash is used for around 87 percent of all payments, whereas in Norway the use of cash declined from 84 percent to 24 percent between 1993 and 2007. Face-to-face transactions remain the most important, though some cash payments have been replaced by debit cards and online transfers.

People use a mix of forms and channels of money for different kinds of payments. The size of the transaction and its timeliness influence their choice. In Australia, less than 40 percent of customers still use checks. Older people use checks more than younger people do. Check use is declining, but for some payments, we do not have electronic alternatives. Cards are used for midsized transactions, while BPAY, Internet/telephone banking, and checks are used for transactions above AUS$500. Internet and phone payments account for one-tenth the number and one-third the value of transactions. About 40 percent of bills are now paid online.[9]

Australians have started using electronic money for a wider range of activities than before. I interviewed women in 1996 for a study about money online who were horrified by the idea of using a credit card for groceries. There has traditionally been a strong Anglo-Celtic cultural norm against buying food on credit. One woman professional said that using cash for grocery shopping was a habit from the early years of her marriage when money was tight. With cash, she knew how much she had spent and how much was left. Only two women from two of the twenty-three households bought groceries on credit to accumulate loyalty points. The feeling against buying food on credit was so strong that one of them stopped and went on to EFTPOS (electronic funds transfer at point of sale), withdrawing money from her bank account.[10] This situation has changed. In 2010 only 54 percent of payments in supermarkets were in cash, the closest merchant category to grocery shopping.[11] This may mean consumers feel a greater sense of control over electronic money transactions. It may also mean that domestic transactions such as grocery shopping are no longer invested with the same cultural meanings.

Electronic channels and forms of money have also changed how we manage money in intimate relationships. The social nature of use remains the same. The use of information and communication technologies, as in ATMs, EFTPOS, direct transfers, phone banking, and Internet banking, gives greater access and information about earnings, expenditure, and money in a joint account. When direct crediting of wages was introduced in Australia in the 1980s, some workers and their unions strongly resisted the move. These workers used to receive their money in envelopes with the total amount written in pencil. The envelope was resealable. This made it possible for the man to remove some of his wages, particularly his overtime, before handing the rest to his wife. So it was only with direct crediting—to a joint account—that women came to know how much the man was earning. In Australia, the direct crediting of wages also means that earnings are no longer cash in hand. Savings become the money that is left over after expenditure.

The use of electronic channels also increased the available information for joint accounts. ATMs give up-to-date figures of money still left in the account. Credit cards and EFTPOS give an itemized account that can be monitored by either partner in a joint account. These statements have the added advantage of supplying the answers without the spouse asking the questions. I have heard women say that if they think they are buying something extravagant, they "split the plastic" so that the transaction gets divided into two statements. This increased information that comes with the use of electronic money means that the housekeeping-allowance and whole-wage systems of money management are no longer important in Australia. Controlling physical access to money is no longer the key to controlling money in a marriage. A person with a joint account can access cash through ATMs and EFTPOS and spend on the credit card without prior division of the household money.[12]

In Chile, it is customary for people to lend store credit cards to their family and trusted network of friends. Clara Han describes how people lend each other cards to enable them to deal with "critical moments" when the need for credit is immediate.[13] In Santiago, it is not unusual for a housewife who has no access to bank accounts to lend her card to her son and daughter-in-law. "People do not lend money, but the capacity to borrow and go into debt."[14]

SHARING PASSWORDS IN INTERNET BANKING

There is a greater comfort now with Internet banking. About 90 percent of Australians have Internet access at home or work. Some 80 percent have purchased online. Just over 60 percent of those with Internet access pay most of their bills online. Almost 60 percent have transferred money online to a family member or friend.[15]

Consumers remain concerned about fraud, security, and privacy. Some use Internet banking despite these concerns because they trust the consumer protection measures that have been in place for credit cards. In Australia, the Electronic Funds Transfer Code of Conduct, first issued in 2001, capped consumers' liability for unauthorized transactions to AUS$50 on their credit card. In 2012 the code was amended so that the consumer has no liability unless it can be proven that he or she contributed to the loss. These protections have been extended to electronic funds transfers (EFTs) via any authorized access method.[16]

Banks' attempts to shore up security minimize the banks' liability. Current systems for banking authentication require that customers not reveal their access codes, even to members of the family. This does not connect with the way customers use Internet banking. I found that more than two-fifths (43 percent) of Australians with bank accounts share their banking passwords and personal identification numbers (PINs). These conclusions are drawn from a 2007 study based on a random representative sample of 669 Australians over eighteen and with a bank account. One-third (33 percent) had shared their banking passwords or PINs with their partners. Seven percent had shared them with their children, 6 percent with other family members, and 5 percent with their parents.[17]

These findings confirmed my qualitative research, which shows that it is routine for people to share passwords in some contexts. This is based on a study of banking, security, and information among 108 people in Australia (Melbourne, rural Victoria, and Brisbane) between April 2005 and July 2006. Some married and de facto couples see password sharing as a practical way of managing money and demonstrating trust in each other. When one person in a couple relationship manages the money, it is not unusual for that person to manage the joint accounts as well as all the individual accounts, including the accounts of the partner. The Internet in that sense is breaking down the traditional boundaries limiting access to money or information about money in the individual account.

Erin, an administration assistant, twenty-five to thirty-four years old, with an annual household income between AUS$75,000 and AUS$100,000, queried the banks' instructions on passwords. She said,

> As far as the bank is concerned, they say that no one else should have your password and that sort of thing but (my husband) trusts me as his wife to have that information and do the transactions that need to be done. We

could be breaching security as far (as) the banks are concerned but as a married couple it's a trust thing. But I wouldn't go giving it to anyone else.[18]

Benjamin, a farmer aged thirty-four, and his wife have a joint account. Each of them also has an individual account. All bills associated with their house are paid by Benjamin from his account, and his wife usually pays for things for their baby. The joint account has their savings. Each of them knows the other's log-ins. Sometimes his wife logs in as him to pay the bills. "Now that she is at home (on maternity leave) it is easier for her to do this," Benjamin said. He had also logged in as her a few times to conduct some transactions.[19]

Sharing PINs is a common practice among remote indigenous communities in Australia. In areas with poor banking access, this is the only way to access cash. Sanna, a Torres Strait Islander, is between forty-five and fifty-four years old, has a BA, and earns more than AUS$50,000 a year. She is now working in Brisbane. Speaking of banking on her island, she says there is only one bank on one of the islands, Thursday Island, where you can go to replace a passbook or get a keycard. There are no mobile bankers. Giving a sense of the remoteness of the islands and the poor access to banking, she says,

> There are seventeen inhabited Islands apart from Thursday Island. We're spread out over 180,000 square kilometers of ocean. . . . Usually you get on a plane and you've got to do the milk run. It goes to every other Island before it gets to Thursday Island. So you can start at 10 o'clock in the morning and arrive there at 3. . . . That will cost you $250–$300, depending on what season you're traveling. And then you've got to stay overnight, because you can't fly back the same day.[20]

You also have to book weeks in advance. There are four hundred people on Sanna's island, and the plane seats eight to twelve persons. She says, "When one person goes into Thursday Island they [do] everybody's business and shopping." This means they take others' keycards with the PINs. "You have to," says Sanna. "It's a matter of survival."[21]

People with certain disabilities have to share passwords with carers and PINs with retail clerks. Inaccessible banking services leave little choice. Fiona, who has a physical disability, is thirty-five to forty-four years of age, with a master's degree and a household income of AUS$50,000 to AUS$74,000. She says she withdraws money via EFTPOS so that the cashier can help with swiping the card. She says,

When I go to do EFTPOS I tell the shop assistant my PIN. . . . I do that on a random basis. Not at the same time every week. Some shop assistants say they can't do that and I say they have to because I can't do it.[22]

Grant, seventy-five, is deaf. He depends on tellers to help him. He says,

Before I go to a bank I write a list explaining I am deaf and what I want. The woman then reads it, looks at me and reads it again and gives me the thumbs up. And she does not shout. I say, "don't shout, I'm deaf." And when I go to the bank another day, I try to go to the same teller who knows me.[23]

Placing people at the center, we find that in varied social contexts, security practices diverge dramatically from what bankers and regulators see as best practice. The situation at present remains opaque. Banks are not designing for user-centered security, but they are also ensuring that no cases come to court where trust in the Internet can be questioned. This is important, for the Internet still remains the online channel of choice in the West.

NOVEL CURRENCIES AND PAYMENTS

Over a few decades, there have been many new currencies and many new methods of payment. Some hark back to a nostalgic sense of community. Others aspire to money that is not controlled by the government. What brings them together is that they remain bound to a community defined by location or a worldview. Some electronic payments that were seen as new in the 1990s are now traditional ways of paying in the second decade of the twenty-first century.

For the most part, central banks are sanguine about these new currencies, as they have not seriously challenged national currencies. Only the central bank of China has issued a warning about the QQ coin that is used for digital purchases on China's most popular instant messaging site, Tencent QQ. Other currencies, like the peer-to-peer (P2P) digital currency bitcoin, have attracted attention from law enforcement authorities because they have been used to buy drugs. But for the most part alternative currencies have tried to recreate or sustain a sense of local community or are part of game worlds that can appear real to the players.

The new methods of electronic payment that I write about in this section have not replaced traditional card payments and direct transfers over the Internet. There is a constant refrain that we are moving toward the end of cash. This is partly a statement of fact in that we use less cash than before. But it is also part of discussions of the future of money. I keep in mind Kahneman's wisdom that people fail to predict the long-term future or know the past.[24] But the anthropological impulse is to interpret "the way we and others picture the future."[25] This is important because the pictures of the future often influence the present.

NOVEL CURRENCIES

Most novel currencies have the national currency as a reference point. China's QQ coin is worth one renminbi, though it can be exchanged for more or less depending on the context. An Ithaca HOUR, which circulates in the Ithaca community of New York State, is worth $10. Game money like Linden dollars used in Second Life has to be bought in real cash. Bitcoin, a P2P digital currency, differs in that its reference point is digital even though it can be exchanged for legal tender.

Currencies like Ithaca HOURS are "local," "complementary" in relation to the national currency, and a "community" currency. They hark back to a nostalgic past when the economy was connected with community, locality, and beliefs.[26] Ithaca HOURS have been circulating in Ithaca since 1991. Ithaca is a community of thirty thousand people. There were over eleven thousand HOURS worth $110,000 issued between 1991 and March 2011.[27] Experimenting with novel currency forms is "trying to reweave the social organization of money, but not necessarily according to the same old patterns of national capitalism."[28]

There is tension around alternative currencies when they become competing rather than complementary currencies. The new currency is suspect if it is shrouded in privacy and/or is suspected of being used for money laundering and illegal activities across national borders, as has happened with bitcoin. An alternative currency can also become a threat when it is as widely used as China's QQ coin.

Other currencies like Disney Dollars, which began in 1987, are more like tokens that can only be used at Disney resorts. Private virtual currencies used in games are also like tokens in that they are specific to particular games, as with the QQ coins issued in 2002 by Tencent Holdings Inc. The company, founded in November 1998, is best known for its instant messaging program, QQ. In the first quarter of 2012, about 750 million people used its service at least once a month. It has used this strength to drive traffic to its social media and video gaming sites.[29]

QQ coins are a virtual currency pegged to one QQ coin equaling one RMB. Coins can be transferred to others. About 45 percent of the $900 million worth of trading in virtual items in China is now for items on Tencent QQ. The coins are also said to be used by other online sites because credit cards are not yet common in China. There is no information on the volume and value of QQ coins in circulation.

Virtual currencies used for games also raise the question of whether they are real and trustworthy. Virtual currencies may seem like make-believe money. But when they are translated to legal tender, there is little doubt they are real. The exchange of large amounts of virtual currencies like QQ coins, in the absence of proof of transfer, can involve face-to-face cash transactions. This also brings the virtual players into face-to-face contact, adding a physical dimension to the game and the money.[30]

Some users have also started using QQ coins to buy real-world goods such as CDs and cosmetics. Exchanges have come up to buy QQ coins at a slight discount. QQ coins are now reportedly being used outside the QQ program to be traded on the black market for use in online gambling and telephone chats with "QQ" girls. In June 2009, the Ministry of Commerce banned the use of virtual currencies to purchase "real goods and services." Tencent supported the new order.[31]

Bitcoin is a digital P2P currency. On November 1, 2008, a man who called himself Satoshi Nakamoto described his design for a new digital currency, bitcoin, in a research paper submitted to an obscure cryptography listserv. Bitcoin makes possible instant payments to anyone anywhere in the world.[32] The only information available on Nakamoto is that he (or she) lived in Japan, but even that information is doubted. Could he be British? Was he a person or a collective? But Nakamoto had succeeded in creating digital money when trust in banks, the central bank, and the government was at its lowest in the United States. Digital money that was untraceable by governments and banks fed into the 1990s cypherpunks movement of libertarian cryptographers.[33]

Previous efforts to create digital money had failed. This included David Chaum's ecash. Bitcoin was generated digitally and is based on solving difficult mathematical problems. The first miner who solved complex cryptographic puzzles containing data from irreversible transactions would be awarded 50 bitcoins. Nakamoto was the first miner of 50 bitcoins. After warning against Wikileaks accepting donations in bitcoins, little else was heard from him.[34]

Behind bitcoin is the desire for privacy, moving away from government control of currency, and from banks and fees for payment transactions. Unlike national currencies, there is a cap of twenty-one million bitcoins that can be mined, harkening back to the language of gold. The difficulty of the puzzles would increase with time while the award would decrease. It was expected that the twenty-one-million cap would be reached around 2140. The transactions are open and transparent, but the identities of the transactors are private.[35]

Bitcoin was lauded by cryptographers. The Electronic Frontier Foundation, which advocates digital privacy, began accepting donations in bitcoins. Bitcoins began trading in April 2010. The value of one bitcoin was below 14 cents. Rising enthusiasm and media coverage led to bitcoins soaring to $29.57 on June 9, 2011. On the market site Silk Road on the so-called secret Internet, people could buy anything from drugs to kits for machine guns with bitcoins. In the United States and Australia, the digital currency has attracted the attention of the government, especially money-laundering and anticrime authorities.[36]

Bitcoins went on a downward slide because of theft and hacking and a lack of trust. In mid-June 2012, someone calling himself Allinvane reported that twenty-five thousand bitcoins had been stolen. About a week later, a hacker withdrew tens of thousands of other people's bitcoins from Mt. Gox, which handled 90 percent of bitcoin exchanges. The price plummeted and trust was shaken. The Electronic Frontier Foundation stopped accepting bitcoin donations. Moreover, some bitcoin donors to Wikileaks could be identified. Other disasters followed with the Polish exchange. The oldest wallet service was suspected to have defrauded those who had deposited with it.[37] There remained clusters of bitcoin enthusiasts in Berlin, New Hampshire, San Francisco, and Helsinki.[38] Coinbase, a company that wants to make a digital wallet for bitcoins, has raised over $600,000 through crowd funding.[39] As Benjamin Wallace said in *Wired* magazine, "while people have stolen and cheated and abandoned the bitcoiners, the code has remained true."[40]

Then came the Cyprus proposal on March 16, 2013, that money be confiscated from every bank deposit. Two days later, Bitcoins rose from $45 to $55 to rise to $103 in early April. There is circumstantial evidence that the demand is coming from Spain. It illustrates a collapse of trust in the euro and central banks, at least among some of the European countries. The US Financial Crimes Enforcement Network (FinCEN) also came out with its guidelines as to how it will or will not regulate virtual currencies. Moreover bitcoins are being accepted by a growing number of online businesses. But as Gavin Andersen, Bitcoin Foundation's chief scientist, says, bitcoin still remains an experiment.[41]

NEW WAYS OF PAYING

A 2010 survey of 101 central banks revealed that there were 173 innovative retail payment instruments and methods. Innovations in retail payments revolve around speedier processing times. Electronic money wallets are used in many countries, particularly for transport, but they have failed to become multifunctional. Few of the recent innovations have had a significant impact on the market. One-fifth of the number of reported innovations are driven by the need for financial inclusion in unbanked markets,[42] as we will see in greater detail in the next chapter.

New ways of paying direct attention to new players like PayPal, Square, and Dwolla. PayPal has the greatest market and global reach of new ways of payment. Founded in 1998 as a way for people to switch between global currencies, it has become an online payment mechanism particularly for auctions.[43] It can bypass credit cards as well as use them as a source of funds, while undercutting their fees. PayPal said it had 117 million active users in 2012. It is "the leading global online payment company," operating in 190 markets and twenty-five currencies around the world. PayPal's 2011 value of total transactions was $118.7 billion.[44]

Square and Dwolla are not global at this stage. Square moved from the United States to Canada in 2012. In the meantime, PayPal's version of Square, PayPal Here, is in Australia, and mPowa and iZettle are in the United Kingdom. Dwolla is only available in the United States. Square was cofounded in 2010 by Jack Dorsey, thirty-five, who created Twitter. It has simplified the way businesses pay and receive money. Square enables small businesses to accept credit cards via a small, free, white credit card reader that plugs into the headphone jack of a smart phone. The sign-up process takes a few minutes. There are no other permissions needed to process credit card payments. There are no equipment fees and no monthly fees. At least 60 percent of the Girl Scouts, artists, farmers, taco-truck vendors, and babysitters who use Square had never accepted credit cards before. Larger businesses are also finding it attractive because Square charges the business a fee of 2.75 percent on the transaction value instead of the more usual 4.8 percent.[45]

The customer swipes his or her credit card on the reader. The money is deposited into the business's account the next day. As Square owns all the data on the transaction, it also analyzes customer and payment data for the business as an add-on. By November 2012, Square was processing $10 billion worth of transactions a year and was used by two million Americans.[46] In its most recent iteration in June 2012, Pay with Square, the customer does not have to swipe his or her card. The customer's phone app with a photo linked to a credit card allows the customer to be recognized by the business. The payment is completed with a tap.

Simplifying business payments meant building software that would talk to the Automated Clearing House (ACH) system designed in the 1950s. This system moves electronic money between banking and customer accounts. Matthew O'Connor, director of engineering at Square, says "his young 21st-century programmers—used to building cool stuff on top of open, modern platforms—were initially stymied. 'It's older than their parents.'"[47]

Being able to pay for coffee at Starbucks from late 2012 is a big step for Square and for mobile money. Starbucks has invested $25 million in Square, and its chief executive sits on Starbucks' board. This partnership brings Square to the retail shop front in Starbucks' seven thousand shops and takes it one step closer to becoming an everyday, routine way of paying.[48] Though this rollout has not been seamless, as Bill Maurer said at an RMIT seminar on March 19, 2013, the advantage for Starbucks is that having the wallet in the mobile phone will help "enclose" the customer, assuring Starbucks of a loyal customer base.

Dwolla is also getting enthusiastic reviews for peer-to-peer payments in the United States. Ben Milne, twenty-nine, who started Dwolla (a combination of "dollar" and "web") in 2008, also had to connect with the ACH. People can send a payment from their checking account or through e-mail, Facebook, Twitter, or LinkedIn. By the beginning of 2012, the company had signed up more than 100,000 users and was processing $30 to $50 million a month in transactions.[49]

Ben Lyon of Kopo Kopo in Nairobi uses Dwolla to send money to his friends in the United States, "immediately with no hassle." He says,

> Dwolla is linked to my social account. . . . You say, "Add my Facebook account. Add my Twitter handle." When I send money to my friends in the US, I start typing their names, and I see their names and their pictures, for Dwolla is pulling this information from my Facebook and Twitter ac-

counts. Like, "Are you trying to send money to . . . ?" I say, "Yes." All his
details are there. I say, "Send $25." Then it asks, "Would you like to pay
the transaction fee on his behalf?" Which is 25 cents. A transaction under
$10 is free; over $10 is 25 cents. No frills, no additional fee.

These different ways of paying are aimed at young, banked persons who
see the digital as traditional. Even the founders and cofounders of Square
and Dwolla are under thirty-five. However, a different kind of innovation
in the United States is directed to the 20 percent of the population that is
underbanked. Green Dot, a US company that began operating eleven years
ago, distributes prepaid debit cards with an average fee of $7 a month.
It had $16 billion in transactions in 2011. The cards are old technology,
physical, most often used in face-to-face transactions. But behind these
cards is a sophisticated technology platform allowing for secure and relatively inexpensive loading of the card. It also integrates with the Visa and
Mastercard payment networks.[50]

New ways of paying are not only about new players and different ways
of organizing transactions. Bill Maurer, an anthropologist of money and
banking, is one of the few people who have done fieldwork on emerging
payment systems. He focuses on the social nature of payments and directs
our attention to the infrastructure issues that distinguish payments using
the Automated Clearing House (ACH) and new networks. When new
players deride the ACH, Bill Maurer admits he is "actually a fan of the
ACH. It is a public-private hybrid, federally mandated, and operating for
the public good. It may be old, but it's reliable and trusty. And it settles
transactions at par. There is no interchange fee."[51]

The metaphors of payment move from those of exchange and transfer of value to those of transit engineering when thinking of payment
networks. The talk is of "interchange," new mobile "rails," "ramps,"
"plumbing," and "scaffolding." The difference between the old and new
infrastructures is like going on a free public highway as against paying
"tolls" for every transaction on privately owned roads that connect in a
user-friendly way with the highway.[52] The move is from networks designed for the public good to privately owned networks. The new owners
also ride the free rails of the ACH when they connect with banks and then
make money on their new payment network.

The infrastructure aspects of payments are obscure. But there is a lot of
money in payments. Some estimate that the size of the payments industry
is greater than biotech, Hollywood, global venture capital investment,

or the airline and lodging industries. All of us contribute to the revenue whenever we use a credit or debit card, prepaid card, or gift token. When you and I pay $100 in cash or checks, the merchant receives $100. The transaction is settled at par. But when cash or money in the bank gets converted into electronic money, the merchants, and indirectly the consumers, bear the cost of the transaction. A merchant in the United States would receive $97 of the $100 the customer has paid. And if you and I had paid by Facebook credits—they were discontinued in the third quarter of 2012—then the merchant only receives 70 cents on the dollar. This toll on the means of payment leads to a nonpar transaction and generates a large revenue stream.[53]

A large part of the revenue comes from the interchange fee charged by the credit card companies for moving money from a customer's bank to the merchant's bank and then to the merchant. The average cost of credit card transactions for American merchants is "six times as much as cash transactions and twice as much as checks or PIN-based debit cards."[54] Corporate cards and reward cards can cost the merchant twice as much.

These costs have been hidden from customers because there were no transparent price signals reflecting the cost of different means of payments. Credit card rules incorporated in merchants' contracts prevented them from adding surcharges on credit card payments. There was also the "honor all cards" rule, which meant that merchants had to accept all cards of a brand at the same fee, even though they came with different costs. These "merchant restraints"[55] have been regulated away in Australia and in some European countries, bringing down the price of transactions.[56] An antitrust suit in the United States settled by the credit card companies on July 13, 2012, for $7.25 billion means that merchants can now impose a capped surcharge on credit card transactions. It is not clear whether this will actually lead to merchants surcharging customers or whether this would lead to a lowering of prices.[57]

"The payments industry is fracturing"[58] as players ranging from mobile telecommunications network operators to social networking devices issue different kinds of prepaid products. The revenue, then, is increasingly likely to come from mining the data rather than tolls on transactions.

New ways of paying are at best a signpost to a possible future in payments and electronic money in the West. The present is far more prosaic. Mobile banking and mobile payments still remain limited in number and function in the United States and Australia. Nonbanks such as mobile telecommunication providers are becoming more important, but banks remain the most significant payment service providers.[59]

It is in the low-income countries that the mobile phone has become the channel of choice for the transfer of money. Paying via mobile is widely advertised in Australia. So I tried to send money to my son via mobile phone in Melbourne in August 2012. It was easy from my side, but my son received a message to put in his account details, my mobile phone number, and the code for the payment. He assumed it was a scam. When he did try, there were repeated error messages. He gave up. The bank kept my money for a fortnight before depositing it back into my account. Mobile Internet payments worked fine. No wonder a Kenyan taxi driver in Melbourne hearing us talking of M-PESA broke in excitedly to ask, "Are we going to get M-PESA here?" When I went to Kenya, I understood his enthusiasm.

THE END OF CASH?

The future of money in one way or another involves the end or a reduction in the use of cash. This is despite the fact that using cash for small transactions costs less than any other means of payment.[60] One banker in Melbourne who is involved in mobile banking talked of the "displacement of cash." Listen to technologists, and the message is that cash is not cool. Most people who participate in such discussions are young male professionals in the West living in a world of digital money.

David Wolman, a contributing editor with *Wired*, spent a year living without cash. He says cash is expensive to produce, distribute, and protect. Cash is dirty in that it is handled by several people in a variety of situations. Cash lubricates the black market, graft, and crime. Cash can be counterfeited.

Wolman describes how he was tripped up only a few times in the year without cash. The first was when he had to buy a train ticket on the train in the United States. The ticket collector would only accept cash. He also had to overlook lemonade stands. He had to look the other way when the collection plate was passed around in places of worship. But Delhi defeated him. He had to give up his ambition to go cashless in the week he spent there. That was where the cash was the dirtiest. But he says it would have been more difficult if he had decided he would only pay in cash.

Wolman meets people who devise alternative currencies, those who design legal tender, those who counterfeit currencies, and those who are implementing mobile money. He talks to Ignacio Mas, formerly from the Bill and Melinda Gates Foundation, who tells him it is cash that entraps the poor. They have no option but to earn and pay and save in cash. That is where mobile money has been so liberating. People have the option to pay and save in e-money, even if they choose for the moment to go with cash. But at the end of their lunch at a café near the Gates Foundation offices, Mas paid with a $20 bill. Seeing the surprised look on David Wolman's face, Mas says, laughing, "'I don't actually have a problem with cash.' . . . Advantages such as universal acceptability, anonymity, and simplicity, he says, are tough to beat. And he, like me, has the luxury of choice."[61]

David Wolman ends his year even more phobic about the germs on cash. He is convinced that cash is on its way out, though nobody quite knows when. He bets on mobile money of some sort. It has the best characteristics of cash in that it is easy to use, universally acceptable, and fungible, but it also does not come with the disadvantages of cash.

The majority of the experts and Internet stakeholders surveyed by the Pew Research Center agree that by 2020 the need for cash or credit cards will nearly be eliminated. It must be noted that most of these experts are from the West and work in digital worlds. They say that most people will have "fully adopted the use of smart-device swiping for purchases they make."[62] A third of the experts felt that people will not trust the security, privacy, and anonymity of the new devices. This means that cash and credit cards will remain important in the advanced countries. This division in opinion was stark because respondents were asked to select the positive or negative side. However, a number of respondents thought the true outcome will be a mix of both scenarios. The process will develop generationally. Younger users will stop using cash and credit cards. Their parents and grandparents may slowly move to mobile payments, if at all. There is the unspoken message that when this older generation dies, cashless payments will be the norm.

David Wolman's experiences with cash may have been different if he was traveling the villages and small towns of Asia and Africa. If Delhi was difficult for him, he should have gone to Dharamshala. Even in Kenya, where two-thirds of the households use M-PESA—that is, money transferred over the mobile phone—the initial result has been the better distribution and availability of cash. Some cash has been replaced by digital money, but most of it goes in as cash with the cash-in agent and comes out as cash with the cash-out agent. Digital technologies have made for the better distribution of cash. In one sense it is a repeat of what ATMs and EFTPOS did to make it more convenient to get cash at any time and at many more places than just the bank branch.

In the next chapter we meet the world of M-PESA in Kenya. Money is transferred via a mobile phone through cash-in and cash-out agents. Senders and receivers do not need bank accounts. It is one of the most successful stories of technology and regulation leading to an innovation that serves the needs of the banked and the unbanked. It is global in that different countries are trying to replicate versions of M-PESA to address issues of financial exclusion and gender.

NOTES

1. Supriya Singh, *Marriage Money: The Social Shaping of Money in Marriage and Banking* (St. Leonards, NSW: Allen & Unwin, 1997), 28.

2. Singh, *Marriage Money*, 128.

3. Margery Williams, *The Velveteen Rabbit or How Toys Become Real* (New York: Fremont & Green, 1995), n.p.

4. Nigel Dodd, *The Sociology of Money: Economics, Reason and Contemporary Society* (Cambridge, UK: Polity Press, 1994).

5. Georg Simmel, *The Philosophy of Money* (London: Routledge & Kegan Paul, 1990).

6. BIS Committee on Payment and Settlement Systems, *Statistics on Payment, Clearing and Settlement Systems in the CPSS Countries—Figures for 2011—Preliminary Release* (Basle: Bank for International Settlements [BIS], 2012).

7. BIS Committee on Payment and Settlement Systems, *Innovations in Retail Payments* (Basle: Bank for International Settlements, 2012).

8. John Bagnall and Darren Flood, "Cash Use in Australia: New Survey Evidence," *Reserve Bank of Australia Bulletin*, September 2011; John Bagnall, Sophia Chong, and Kylie Smith, *Strategic Review of Innovation in the Payments System: Results of the Reserve Bank of Australia's 2010 Consumer Payments Use Study* (Reserve Bank of Australia, 2011).

9. Bagnall, Chong, and Smith, *Strategic Review of Innovation*; Bagnall and Flood, "Cash Use in Australia."

10. Supriya Singh, *The Use of Electronic Money in the Home* (Melbourne: Centre for International Research on Communication and Information Technologies, 1996).

11. Bagnall and Flood, "Cash Use in Australia."

12. Singh, *Marriage Money*.

13. Clara Han, *Life in Debt: Times of Care and Violence in Neoliberal Chile* (Berkeley: University of California Press, 2012), http://RMIT.eblib.com.au/patron/FullRecord.aspx?p=896312.

14. José Ossandón, "The Economy of the Quota: The Financial Ecologies and Commercial Circuits of Retail Credit Cards in Santiago, Chile," Institute for Money, Technology and Financial Inclusion, http://blog.imtfi.uci.edu/2012/11/the-economy-of-quota-financial.html (accessed April 1, 2013).

15. Bagnall, Chong, and Smith, *Strategic Review of Innovation*.

16. Australian Securities and Investments Commission (ASIC), "Electronic Funds Transfer Code of Conduct: As Revised by the Australian Securities and Investments Commission's EFT Working Group," http://www.asic.gov.au/asic/pdflib.nsf/Lookup-ByFileName/EFT-Code-as-amended-from-1-July-2012.pdf/$file/EFT-Code-as-amended-from-1-July-2012.pdf (accessed October 27, 2012).

17. Supriya Singh, "Secure Shared Passwords: The Social and Cultural Centered Design of Banking," *Journal of Financial Transformation* 23(2008).

18. Supriya Singh et al., "Password Sharing: Implications for Security Design Based on Social Practice" (paper presented at the SIGCHI Conference on Human Factors in Computing Systems CHI '07, San Jose, California, 2007), 898.

19. Supriya Singh et al., "Password Sharing," 899.

20. Supriya Singh et al., "Password Sharing," 900.

21. Supriya Singh et al., "Password Sharing."

22. Supriya Singh et al., "Password Sharing," 901.

23. Supriya Singh et al., "Password Sharing."

24. Daniel Kahneman, *Thinking, Fast and Slow* (New York: Farrar, Straus & Giroux, 2011).

25. Sandra Wallman, "Introduction: Contemporary Futures," in *Contemporary Futures: Perspectives from Social Anthropology*, ed. Sandra Wallman (London: Routledge, 1992), 2.

26. Bill Maurer, *Mutual Life, Limited: Islamic Banking, Alternative Currencies, Lateral Reason* (Princeton, NJ: Princeton University Press, 2005).

27. Nilsa Garcia-Rey, "Ithaca Hours: An Interview with Paul Glover," *Reality Sandwich*, March 22, 2011.

28. Bill Maurer, "Money Nutters," *Economic Sociology: The European Electronic Newsletter* 12, no. 3 (2011): 6.

29. Paul Mozur and Juro Osawa, "Internet Breadth Helps Buoy Tencent," *Wall Street Journal*, August 14, 2012.

30. Yang Wang and Scott D. Mainwaring, "'Human-Currency Interaction': Learning from Virtual Currency Use in China" (paper presented at the in CHI 2008, Florence, Italy, April 5–8, 2008).

31. Ministry of Commerce, People's Republic of China, "China Bars Use of Virtual Money for Trading in Real Goods," http://english.mofcom.gov.cn/aarticle/newsrelease/commonnews/200906/20090606364208.html (accessed November 26, 2012).

32. Benjamin Wallace, "The Rise and Fall of Bitcoin," *Wired*, November 23, 2011.

33. Wallace, "The Rise and Fall of Bitcoin."

34. Wallace, "The Rise and Fall of Bitcoin."

35. Wallace, "The Rise and Fall of Bitcoin."

36. Adrian Chen, "The Underground Website Where You Can Buy Any Drug Imaginable," http://gawker.com/5805928/the-underground-website-where-you-can-buy-any-drug-imaginable (accessed January 16, 2013); Rohan Pearce, "Money Laundering Using Virtual Worlds, Bitcoin on Watchdog's Radar," *Computerworld*, August 15, 2012.

37. Wallace, "The Rise and Fall of Bitcoin."

38. "Berlin Becomes Latest 'Bitcoin Hotspot,'" http://www.bitcoinmoney.com/post/35733263353/bitcoin-clusters (accessed November 25, 2012).

39. "Coinbase, First Crowd Funded Bitcoin Company, Raises over $600k," https://www.privateinternetaccess.com/blog/tag/crowd-funding (accessed November 25, 2012).

40. Wallace, "The Rise and Fall of Bitcoin."

41. Maria Bustillos, "The Bitcoin Boom," *New Yorker*, April 2, 2013.

42. BIS Committee on Payment and Settlement Systems, *Innovations in Retail Payments.*

43. Daniel Roth, "The Future of Money: It's Flexible, Frictionless and (Almost) Free," *Wired*, February 22, 2010.

44. PayPal, "Get the Latest on Paypal," https://www.paypal-media.com/about (accessed November 26, 2012).

45. Ellen McGirt, "For Making Magic out of the Mercantile," FastCompany, http://www.fastcompany.com/most-innovative-companies/2012/square (accessed November 27, 2012).

46. Sean Ludw, "Bank of America Who? Square Now Processing $10b in Payments Annually," *Venture Beat*, http://venturebeat.com/company/square (accessed November 27, 2012).

47. McGirt, "For Making Magic out of the Mercantile."

48. Claire Cain Miller, "Starbucks and Square to Team Up," *New York Times*, August 8, 2012.

49. Eric Markowitz, "30 under 30: America's Coolest Young Entrepreneurs 2012," *Inc.*, 2012.

50. Lee Gomes, "Money for the Masses," in *The Future of Money* (MIT Technology Review, 2012), http://www.technologyreview.com/news/427333/money-for-the-masses/.

51. Personal communication, January 4, 2013.

52. Bill Maurer, "Payment: Forms and Functions of Value Transfer in Contemporary Society," *Cambridge Anthropology* 30, no. 2 (2012).

53. Maurer, "Payment: Forms and Functions."

54. A. Levitin, "Priceless? The Economic Costs of Credit Card Merchant Restraints," *UCLA Law Review* 55 (2008): 1323.

55. Levitin, "Priceless?," 1321.

56. Michele Bullock, "A Guide to the Card Payments System Reforms," *Reserve Bank of Australia Bulletin*, September 2010.

57. Douglas A. King, "The Debate on Credit Card Surcharges," Retail Payments Risk Forum, http://portalsandrails.frbatlanta.org/2012/07/debate-on-credit-card-surcharges.html (accessed January 13, 2013).

58. Maurer, "Payment: Forms and Functions," 17.

59. BIS Committee on Payment and Settlement Systems, *Innovations in Retail Payments*; Aaron Smith, Janna Anderson, and Lee Rainie, "The Future of Money in a Mobile Age," in *Imagining the Internet* (Pew Research Center, 2012); Bagnall, Chong, and Smith, *Strategic Review of Innovation.*

60. Carl Schwartz et al., "Payment Costs in Australia" (paper presented at the Payments System Review Conference, Sydney, Australia, November 29, 2007).

61. David Wolman, *The End of Money: Counterfeiters, Preachers, Techies, Dreamers—and the Coming Cashless Society* (Cambridge, MA: Da Capo Press, 2012), 159.

62. Smith, Anderson, and Rainie, "The Future of Money in a Mobile Age," 3.

CHAPTER 7

MOBILE MONEY

THE POWER OF IMMEDIACY

"Do you use M-PESA?" I ask people I meet in Kenya. Personal conversations begin. Margaret, a senior personal assistant in a government office in Nairobi, clicks on to the M-PESA menu on her mobile phone with a special password and shows me how the M-PESA messages document her transactions over the last two days.

- On August 27, 2012, at 4:19 p.m., she loaded KSh 2,000 on her phone, giving her a balance of KSh 2,045.
- At 4:21 she bought KSh 500 of airtime.
- At 5:03 she sent her aunt KSh 1,030, leaving her with KSh 485.

Margaret explains that this aunt, though not closely related, "was supportive when my mother died. She came in person and gave me money. Now I am sending her money because she is bereaved. Her friend's husband has died."

- Back comes her aunt's message: "Thank you very much, Margaret. God bless you."

I am in Kenya mainly to get a feel of M-PESA and find out what has made for its astounding success in moving nearly twenty million people to formal payment systems. M-PESA is the world's most successful mobile money, that is, money deposited, transferred, and paid via mobile phone. It is an example of the way innovation, technology, and enabling regulation have come together to produce a global success story empowering unbanked women and men.

Margaret has only praise for M-PESA. "Without M-PESA," she says, "I would have to go across town to give her the money. That would have been two days later over the weekend. But now with M-PESA it means the money reaches my aunt when it is most important, not two days later, when she would just put it in her savings account."

Margaret has not connected either of her two bank accounts to M-PESA. She wants the discipline of having to decide to go to the ATM to withdraw money. She wants to make it difficult for herself to withdraw her savings. Knowing she needs to prepay her electricity, she goes one floor up to the canteen with me to the M-PESA agent. The agent, however, has exhausted his KSh 800,000 float by 12:30 p.m. It will be another ten minutes before he gets more float. But he has closed the M-PESA business to serve the canteen customers between 12:30 and 1:45 p.m.

At first, Margaret says she uses M-PESA only for airtime, sending money, and to prepay her electricity. Then she says that when she is traveling she takes perhaps KSh 10,000 in cash and KSh 10,000 in M-PESA. She can pay a reservation fee for a room in Mombasa and the reservation is recorded. She also calls her watermelon and fish sellers to deliver the goods to her at the car park at 5 p.m. "That way they are fresh," she says. She pays the shop by M-PESA, but the tip is in cash.

M-PESA enables people to save, send, and receive money via their mobile phone. This is possible even without a bank account. M-PESA is intimately grounded in people's everyday lives and relationships. It is now used by two-thirds of the households in Kenya.[1]

"Do you use M-PESA?" I asked the senior government official as we both sat in the waiting room of the governor of the Bank of Kenya, with framed currency notes to our right and the *Economist*, *Newsweek*, and *African Review* in front of us. He said, "I can't imagine life without it." He comes from Garissa, 380 kilometers from Nairobi. "It has made my life easy," he said. "I can immediately respond to a problem of money." The governor's secretary called him in. "Wait," he said, continuing the story. He sends money to his mother, money for school fees directly to the school. Before M-PESA—and that is something many people say, using 2007 as a reference point—he used the *mutatus*, the passenger buses, or sent it with people he knew. He said that if anyone tried to do anything with M-PESA, there would be protests in the street. "We can do without banks, but not without M-PESA."

My guide at Maasai Mara could not do without M-PESA, and neither could the others, from the assistant manager of my lodge to the omelet maker. I go with my guide to a Safaricom agent in the market town of Talek, an hour away from the lodge. It is an unappetizing-looking square, nearly empty as it is not market day. There is a barbershop, computer services, a hairdresser for women, and a community clinic. We stop at a dark provision store stocked with sacks of sugar, bread, Coke, and glass for windows. M-PESA is advertised on signs outside. It also advertises "BamlaHapa," that is, M-PESA credit for airtime.

There were two people I met in Kenya in the nine days I was there who did not use M-PESA. The first was my host who has a family business. He pays and is paid through the bank rather than M-PESA, as his clients include large businesses and the government. The second was the driver who took me to the airport. He used to send money to his mother via M-PESA, but now he sends it to her with anybody who is going to his village. He said, "She keeps losing her phone. This is the third phone she has lost. She forgets it when she is milking the cows." In time, he will buy her a new phone, he said.

My experience with getting M-PESA started off inauspiciously. The network was down until 5:30 p.m. that day. So I experienced for myself how M-PESA's network is not always able to cope. The next day I found I could only load M-PESA on a Safaricom phone. It is, I learned, a product of Safaricom, Kenya's near-monopolistic telecommunications provider. Senders and recipients of funds via M-PESA must be Safaricom customers. So I had to get a Safaricom subscriber identity module (SIM) for KSh 100. After asking for an identification document, the agent at a mobile phone shop in the local shopping center filled in all the details on her mobile phone to register me. My Australian driver's license was sufficient. Nothing happened. She called Safaricom and tried again. This time a message came back instantly. I was asked to activate M-PESA, choose a password, and enter my birth date. I could now save and send money, though I would earn no interest on the money saved in the phone. I handed her KSh 5,000 to deposit in my account. She gave me a receipt, and back came a message confirming the amount.

Having heard stories from my host about money going astray to wrong mobile numbers, I followed Margaret's practice of writing the number down on a piece of paper. As it was a new number, I tried to confirm it with a telephone call. I was sending money to my host's retired maid in her village. I called, but there was no answer. Later I learned she lives in a village with no electricity and so only charges her phone infrequently. I sent KSh 1,000 together with the withdrawal fee of KSh 25 with some trepidation. Back came a message that Lucy A. had received the money. The agent said that Lucy must be registered with M-PESA, and hence her name came up. I was comforted by this confirmation, but later I learned at a conference in Mauritius that this was also one of the disturbing issues around privacy and M-PESA.

I sent her the remaining KSh 3,000 with the 40 bob as the withdrawal fee. That transaction was also confirmed. There was also a message in Swahili reminding me to keep my PIN private. The sending fee of KSh 30 for each transaction was deducted from my M-PESA balance.

The participant observation became a bit too real when I misplaced my SIM within a week. After a phone call to Safaricom, I went back to the original agent—I could have gone to any agent—for a replacement SIM for KSh 50. She filled in all the details on her mobile phone, and after a fair wait my replacement SIM was activated. I hung around for an hour or so, watching a woman buy a mobile phone and seeing people stream in to send and withdraw money. Unlike the canteen agent at the government office who had gone through his e-float of KSh 800,000 during the morning, the agent at the shopping center only had a KSh 100,000 float. Every time somebody deposits money, the float contracts as e-money is exchanged for cash. When a person withdraws, the e-money goes up. So the agent at the shopping center—I saw at least one other Safaricom agent and an Airtel Money shop on the same floor—was able to manage with a much lesser float as the deposits and withdrawals were more balanced.

She showed me the ledger for the morning—perhaps because I had come with an introduction to the Indian owner. There were six sending transactions and seven withdrawals in the hour and a bit that I was there. The withdrawals ranged from KSh 1,000 to KSh 70,000, whereas the money sent varied from KSh 1,000 to KSh 50,000.

I then withdrew the money left in my M-PESA account. This ability to get your money back even if you lose your SIM or your phone contributes to the trust in M-PESA. As David in the iHub building on Ngong Road said, "M-PESA money is good money." He tells the story of how they were caught in a remote part of the country and their helicopter was grounded. The commercial flight was leaving in an hour. They were able to buy a ticket with M-PESA. He was also saved by M-PESA when he was fined because his car insurance was out by a day. He was able to instantly pay the fine.

The enthusiasm around M-PESA was so great that I found myself taking a step backward to realize that this was basically a payment service. If I was living in Kenya I would connect it to my bank account(s). But for credit and for the storage of larger sums of money than the KSh 800 I had in my M-PESA account for four days, I would need a bank. In the end, it is not a case of M-PESA or banking. It is M-PESA *and* banking. And perhaps for money management I would go even further to an organization that would help me manage my money rather than just offer me deposits and credit. As Ignacio Mas argues, it is the ability to manage money, to save for a goal, and to get credit and insurance if need be to achieve that goal that is at the center of financial services.[2]

THE STORY OF M-PESA

Kenya, a low-income East African country with a population of 41.6 million (2011), has become the capital of mobile money. With mobile money, the center of financial and technological innovation has moved to Africa. Though mobile money transfer projects first started in 2001 in the Philippines, it was the astounding success of M-PESA in Kenya in 2007 that changed the payments landscape. It is one of the most successful stories of poor unbanked men and women using flexible, convenient, and cheaper financial services to become part of a connected interpersonal web of money transactions. M-PESA differs from most mobile money systems in that it is a payments-led model. However, the difference between the payments- and bank-led models will become outdated as third parties emerge to offer a money management experience connecting the two. M-PESA has already become a channel to open a bank account with the Commercial Bank of Africa and offer microloans through its M-Shwari service. In its first four months of service to the end of March 2013, it has already attracted deposits of $47 million. The average loan is $12.[3]

In Kenya there remain long-term issues of consumer protection, deposit security, and the power of monopolies in the finance space. Dependence on private exchange networks would need to be supplemented by an exchange system that serves the public good and does not depend on tolls for every transaction.

M-PESA is the dominant mobile money service in Kenya, with Safaricom having 80 percent of registered mobile money users and 60 percent of the registered agents in 2012. It overshadows competing mobile money services in Kenya such as Airtel Money, Orange Money, and YuCash. Others are operated by banks (such as Equity Bank's Eazzy 247 service and KCB Mobile Banking), and still others are operated by independent players (such as Mobicash).[4]

Daily M-PESA transactions in Kenya outnumber the global transactions of Western Union. "One out of every two people in the world who sends money over a mobile phone is a Kenyan."[5] Though the number of smart phones is increasing in Africa, most versions of mobile money work on a basic handset. Mobile money is built on earlier practices of prepaid airtime. "Once you have minutes (airtime) in your phone, you are storing value, which you can use or send to others."[6] Mobile money differs from mobile banking in that money can be transferred without having a bank account. The more it is used, the more profitable it is for the provider. The bank model differs, as it is based on float, that is, accepting deposits and lending them.

M-PESA has been a win for financial inclusion. In the early years, M-PESA was used by those who were well off. In 2012 more than four-fifths (84.4 percent) of the Kenyans at the bottom of the pyramid used M-PESA (or any other money transfer service). This is despite the fact that sending money via M-PESA at KSh 42 is the single most expensive item in the weekly expenditure on the mobile phone. It is, however, cheaper and faster than the informal methods used before or the formal banking system.[7]

M-PESA was launched in December 2007 by Safaricom, the dominant mobile network operator (MNO) in Kenya. But the story began with Nick Hughes at Vodafone in London in 2003. Nick Hughes at the time was head of social enterprises at Vodafone, which owned 40 percent of Safaricom. He thought of the mobile phone initially as a way the unbanked could repay microfinance loans. He was granted one million pounds by the British development agency Department for International Development (DFID). Vodafone contributed a matching amount in cash and staff time.[8]

The pilot in 2005 was conceived as a partnership between the Commercial Bank of Africa, Faulu Kenya (a microfinance institution), and Safaricom/Vodafone. Susie Lonie, with a background in mobile commerce in Europe with Vodafone, joined the team for three months to manage the project in Kenya. Some of the features of M-PESA were established during the pilot phase. Targeted at the unbanked, the product had to work without a bank. So the money in the system was deposited with the Commercial Bank of Africa on behalf of the customers. The product was based on the SIM toolkit that was present in all the basic phones. SMS (text messaging) was a familiar use of the phone. As most of the expected customers would have little education, both Swahili and English were used. The team recognized the essential role of the agents who would take the cash to be sent and give out the cash withdrawals. This cash would be converted to e-money as it transmitted through the phone and would come out as cash at the other end.

Safaricom's network of roughly one hundred thousand airtime dealers was an initial recruiting ground for M-PESA agents. Like most mobile phone services around the world, a Safaricom customer purchases credits or "airtime" on a pay-as-you-go basis rather than paying a monthly subscription fee. A local ad agency suggested the name M-PESA. "Pesa" is the Swahili word for money. It is based on the paisa of the Indian currency that was introduced in Kenya in 1896 to pay Indian workers on the Kenya-Uganda railway.

Hughes and Lonie observed that people were repaying other people's loans in return for services and that businesses were using this mode of payment between themselves. People were also using M-PESA as a way of keeping money safe overnight if they had not been able to get to a bank or if they were traveling. People also sent airtime purchased through M-PESA to their relatives in villages.[9]

Though the pilot was conceived as a way of making it easier to repay microfinance loans, sending money to relatives emerged as the most important application. The campaign honed in on the central aspect of M-PESA. "Send Money by Phone" later became "Send Money Home." This slogan spoke to Kenyans sharing money in the family and tapped into the large flows of money resulting from rural-urban migration.

The Commercial Bank of Africa fell away early in the pilot as it became clear it introduced greater levels of complexity to the technology needed. It became the repository for M-PESA's trust fund and has since become an active partner for deposits and loans. Since Safaricom was not licensed as a bank, the funds in the system were put in a trust account rather than being leveraged to make more money for the company or being fed back to cover operating expenses. Faulu Kenya's manual back office system could not handle the record keeping. So Safaricom remained the only provider of M-PESA.[10]

The service needed to be significantly redesigned for a full national launch. The consumer proposition "Send Money by Phone" had been tested. There was a cultural fit with domestic remittance patterns and familiarity with sending airtime. But in order to go ahead, the Central Bank of Kenya had to be convinced that M-PESA was not a deposit-taking institution and did not intend to give loans. The Central Bank also had to be confident the money sent by phone would not be used for money laundering.

Responding to these concerns, the funds in the M-PESA system were held in a trust account through the M-PESA Holding Company in the Commercial Bank of Africa. Interest that accumulated had to be given to a foundation to be used for all Kenyans. The M-PESA team also put in place a customer registration process with national identity cards. To help implement anti–money laundering policies, there was a transaction limit of KSh 50,000 (about $625). This has since risen to KSh 70,000 (about $843). An IT consultancy firm, Consult Hyperion, conducted an audit of operational risk and security. There was a long legal review and many conversations with the Central Bank.

Safaricom's CEO Michael Joseph said, "We talked a lot with Jecinta Mwatela, who was acting Governor of the Bank, and got lots of encouragement, but we got the blessing when Njuguna Ndung'u became Governor." He says this happened "because he came from academia and could think outside of the box! He knew that most of Kenya's economy is in the informal sector. The Bank has . . . no records for 70 percent of the economy."[11]

After ensuring that consumers would not lose their money and that M-PESA would not become a means for money laundering, the Central Bank issued a letter of no objection. Joseph set out to quickly build an exclusive agent network. Each agent was required to set up in three places. Agreements were reached with Housing Finance (a mortgage financier), Caltex Fuel Stations, and Post Bank. Reflecting on those early days, Michael Joseph said in 2011, after he had stepped down as CEO, "When we launched in March 2007, I decided that this is going to be big." But nobody had anticipated it would become as big as it did.[12]

Part of Safaricom's success was due to its dominance. Until 2011, it was the largest company in East Africa. One-third of Safaricom is owned by the government of Kenya. It is said that Michael Joseph was able to access government officials with ease. As one observer says, "It was a mix of power and influence. The government had a stake in it." It is also said that some of the top people in government have an individual share in the company.

Safaricom was able to put in place an extensive network of agents. The transactions are numerous enough so that being a Safaricom agent means good business and profitability. The typical M-PESA agent in urban slums and rural areas earns 4.3 times greater profit from being an agent (US$5.01 per day) than selling airtime (US$1.55 per day).[13]

The challenge for Safaricom was to educate customers not to share their PINs. More functionality was added to M-PESA. People could re-pay microfinance loans, pay for utilities and other bills, and buy airline tickets. The bulk payment function allowed employers and others to pay e-money to large groups.

Though the banks initially had little interest in the 70 percent of the unbanked, by 2008 M-PESA had more customers than all the banks combined. Money was flowing from the cities to villages. Banks cried foul, querying the Central Bank of Kenya's decision in 2007 that M-PESA was not a bank. They asked why Safaricom could employ agents when banks could not, and why Safaricom had looser identity require-ments. They argued that M-PESA was unsafe and dangerous. With 80 percent of the mobile market and 60 percent of the agents, Safaricom could charge banks for using the mobile channel. Competing mobile network operators Zain (now Bharti Airtel) also complained that Safari-com had an unfair advantage.

Kenya's acting finance minister, John Michuki, asked the Central Bank to audit M-PESA so that consumers would remain protected. The Central Bank showed that M-PESA was moving less than half the money in ATMs as its average transaction was $25. Typical e-money balances in M-PESA accounts were less than $2. M-PESA was still operating at the margins.

The Central Bank had also commissioned another survey in 2008, which showed that most people were satisfied with M-PESA's service. This reaffirmed the initial audit of security and operational risk. Less than a month after the request for an audit, M-PESA was declared safe and could continue to operate legally in Kenya. At the same time, a bill that allowed banks to create a nonexclusive agent network would be fast-tracked. The rush began for banks to engage with M-PESA, leading to customers being able to get cash from ATMs with the code in their mobile phones. Banks also set up their own agent networks to offer mobile money and banking products.

THE CENTRAL BANK OF KENYA AND M-PESA

In 2006 when the Central Bank of Kenya received the proposal for M-PESA, three-fourths of Kenya's adult population were financially excluded from formal banking and payment services. Banks were not part of most people's lives, as they served only 14.2 percent of the adult population.[14]

Banks did not see the poor as a viable market. In order to open a savings account, commercial banks asked for two letters of introduction from customers of the bank. The minimum deposit was KSh 500 to KSh 1,000. If a person had deposits of less than KSh 6,500, a fee of KSh 75 would be levied. As a result, the savings of most of the households in Kenya remained outside the formal financial system. Micro and small enterprises were excluded from credit from the formal banking sector. Hence in 2006 the Central Bank of Kenya had no oversight over money for nearly three-fourths of the population. But the Central Bank had a mandate to oversee the payments system as well as banking. M-PESA offered a way to bring payments into the formal sphere, perhaps as a first step to broadening access to banking.

M-PESA was proposed at a time when Kenya Vision 2030 sought to make Kenya a middle-income country by 2030, giving specific attention to the development of the financial services sector. Announced in 2006, one of its aims was to expand banking services to people who did not have bank accounts, especially in rural areas. The governor of the Central Bank of Kenya, Prof. Njuguna Ndung'u, says (interviewed August 29, 2012), "I came into the Central Bank with an idea that what we need in the country was financial inclusion." Appointed to the position in March 2007, he saw two barriers to entry. The first

> can be related to the cost of opening and maintaining your bank account. The other barrier is that of physical distance to the bank. You can spend 20 percent of your time that day just [to get to a bank]. . . . All of a sudden an opportunity came [with] M-PESA. . . . You solved the physical distance cost effectively, and . . . you don't have to have a bank account.

... Other countries ... said they want a bank-led model. I said, "No, we want a payments-led model." Once you get a platform, it is much easier to open a bank account.

The governor says that when Safaricom started the project, they advertised for banks to show interest. "Only one bank and one microfinance showed interest. Essentially they have no business talking against this because they did not show interest. Now they think they are being left behind." He said many banks, including international banks, told the Central Bank that it was going to get into a banking crisis.

> They believed there will be an exodus of deposits from banks. I said, "No, this is a payments platform." And I advised some of them [the banks], saying, "What you need to do is to integrate with the mobile phone platform. If you integrate with the mobile phone platform it means your customers can operate their account through the mobile phone." Five years down the line, most of the banks have integrated.

With M-PESA, cash is converted into electronic units of money. The governor says, "You are moving electronic units of money, not money, which can be changed anywhere in any location, into money." He says that some maintain there are two institutions issuing money—the Central Bank and the mobile phone. "No, this is not correct. When you go to a point of sale or an agent, you give cash, and he gives you an electronic unit of money."

The governor sees this movement of electronic units of money as moving Kenya toward a "cash-lite" society. "Before, you needed cash because most of your transactions were in cash. But now you can use your mobile phone. . . . The financial sector has deepened, and that is very good."

In the beginning, M-PESA was seen as a way of helping the poor and of contributing toward financial inclusion. The governor says, "Now it is for everyone. Even the government . . . is using M-PESA to deliver benefits." He notes that M-PESA has become a platform, and people are using it to pay in the supermarket, for their electricity, and even for their satellite TV, DSTV. The governor says, "It is interesting. We wanted M-PESA for the poor. But DSTV is for the elite. It is a tool that can be useful for everyone." He himself uses it to send money to his farmworkers. He says,

> I come from a rural area. I have tea, I have coffee. . . . Every Friday morning—somebody would come from my home—it is about eighty kilometers

away—to say this is the amount of wages we need for Saturday afternoon or for cattle feed. Today, they send an SMS saying there are five workers picking tea, there are five workers blah blah blah. So you save the transport. You save one day's work. You sit in the comfort of your home and you have the float from your bank account to your mobile phone and send it to whomever you want. Now with some mobile phone operators you don't even need the two-stage process from your bank account to the mobile phone account and then send. Now you go to your bank account on your phone and you can send from there to whomever. . . . You can even get microinsurance.

He says now the wages go directly to the mobile phones of his permanent workers. A worker then goes to the shopkeeper where he has credit for the week. He just transfers the money from his phone to the shopkeeper.

The governor says that mobile money has brought down banks' cost of doing business with the poor. In 2007, there were 2.5 million microaccounts under KSh 100,000—that is, about US$1,200—that were insured by Deposit Protection Insurance. Now, in August 2012, there are over 15 million deposit accounts.

Keeping limits on the amount of money that can be transferred via mobile money in any one day caters to anti–money laundering concerns. The daily limit has been raised from KSh 50,000 to KSh 70,000 per customer. At the same time the Central Bank also required mobile money operators to offer the ability to transfer less than KSh 100 at a time, for even transferring KSh 10 was important for the poor. The total amount transferred is about US$1 billion a month. The median is about KSh 2,500. The governor says "the fraud that you see is people trying to defraud each other. But it is not the system. The system is so good."

Having to attend the funeral of the wife of the ex-minister of finance, Prof. Njuguna Ndung'u handed me over to Stephen Mwaura Nduati, head of the National Payment System of the Central Bank of Kenya. An engineer with an MBA and a law degree, he came to the Central Bank in 2004 via a policy research center, KIPPRA. He has been involved with M-PESA from the beginning. Stephen showed me a copy of the letter sent to M-PESA in 2006, which said that the Central Bank had no objection to them starting the service, provided they kept to "Know Your Customer" (KYC) and anti–money laundering guidelines.

Spending much of the day with Stephen, I began to understand why bloggers of mobile money have been rapt by his enthusiasm. He is passionate about payments, seeing their regulation as connected but different from banking. Over a late lunch in the garden at Fairview, he asked about the consumer protection of electronic funds transfers in Australia and savings in Malaysia. He is excited to hear of the account nominee system in India, for he thinks that is the answer to unclaimed mobile money accounts after a person's death.

The Central Bank's involvement in M-PESA was through its mandate to oversee the payments system. Nduati (interviewed on August 29, 2012) said it is important to remember that the regulation of banking and the regulation of payments have to focus on different things. When you regulate banking, you need to remember that in banking "the mischief" is around the safety of deposits, and hence ensuring their safety is paramount. In payments it is the efficiency, effectiveness, and safety of the payments system that is most important.

This separation of banking and payments also flows down to the Central Bank's approach to financial inclusion. He said the Central Bank believed that financial inclusion in the narrow sense means being banked, being a customer of a bank. But in the broader sense, financial inclusion means using financial products. Hence, being part of a formal payments system is a broader indicator of financial inclusion. The sequence is that being part of formal payments may lead to the use of cost-effective banking services.

The problem for the Central Bank of Kenya is that unlike 2008 when the banks protested, mobile money payments in May 2012 were greater in value than either the ATMs or electronic funds transfers (EFTs). The value of M-PESA at a daily average of KSh 4,140 million transactions is only marginally lower than the combined value of ATMs and EFTs at KSh 4,292 million.[15] Savings without interest on M-PESA have also risen, though we don't have the figures for the total value saved. M-PESA wants to distance itself from the accusation that it is a deposit-taking institution. However, the difference between interest and noninterest deposits at the lower end is miniscule at 0.5 percent. Jack and Suri's report says that 81 percent of people in 2009 kept savings with M-PESA.[16]

The "mischief" of banking and payments may be coming together with regard to keeping money safe. At present the value of the e-money circulating in M-PESA is held in trust with a number of commercial banks in Kenya. Questions are being asked about the safety of these funds. How are these increasingly large funds insured against bank failure? Are individual deposits of 70 percent of adult Kenyans protected in case of bank collapse? Are these funds protected by deposit insurance?

Can consumer protections be enforced? Is there an appropriate risk-based regulatory framework that guides the MNO financial payment transaction process? How do the authorities prevent one actor in the mobile money transfer ecosystem from becoming too big to fail? These questions are important in light of the subprime mortgage and derivatives issues that led to the GFC. They also become important if one recognizes that payments are a public good and the infrastructure being created is one that has to be open to all.[17]

SEND MONEY HOME AND SAVE A BIT

People use M-PESA to send money to family and friends to respond to need and to express care and relationship. The use of M-PESA has grown because it offers a more convenient, cheaper, faster, and trusted channel compared to previous options. People have been saving money in M-PESA from the pilot stage. This is in addition to traditional methods of saving, such as keeping money under the mattress. The sums accumulated vary according to different studies.

Sending money home still rings the loudest bell when we look at the way people use M-PESA. Money is sent to the nuclear family and a wide network of family and friends to express relationship. In rural areas, money sent to and received from other family members and friends represented half the transactions, compared with one-third sent to or received from immediate family and household members. This money was sent for a variety of purposes by different people. Husbands and children working away from home sent money back. There were money transfers and gifts for weddings, the birth of a child, Christmas, or a funeral. M-PESA is frequently used to pay for school fees and as payments for work done on the tea and coffee farms. In the three small towns where Susan Johnson studied the use of M-PESA, it was still mainly used for interpersonal money transfers rather than for business and other payments. The median amounts sent and received were KSh 1,500 and KSh 1,100, lower than the national figure in 2012, which was KSh 2,500.[18]

Tonny Omwansa, in his home in Nairobi (interviewed August 27, 2012), reflects that he more often sends money to his mother than to his father. The neighborhood children are on a loquat tree outside the gate. While I eat loquats, he says his father controls the large chunks of money for investments like land. His mother has smaller amounts of money that come in with a higher frequency from her cow, vegetables, and shop. So she easily gets out of money. Her problems are smaller and can be solved immediately, whereas addressing his father's problems could require six months of planning.

I ask, "Does it also change your mother's negotiation with your father for money?" He says it makes her more powerful with an ability to execute things. There is also the comfort that she needed money and her son sent it to her. Jack and Suri note that M-PESA, being less visible than other money transfers, could have the effect of empowering household members like women who have traditionally had less bargaining power.[19] M-PESA's impact on money management and control remains a matter for future research.

M-PESA increased the frequency of remittances, enabling people to send it "in bits." This allowed remitters to better control their money while getting it to the family when the money was most needed. At one level, this frequent sending of money enhanced the continuing relationship between the urban migrant and the rural family. But at another level, it also decreased the need to visit to deliver cash personally.[20]

M-PESA was not conceived as a savings medium—and Safaricom does not promote it as such because of regulatory concerns. People began to use it for small, instant savings right from the pilot stage. Women especially use it to save small amounts of money on their phone. It is more convenient than going to the bank. The money is accessible and at the same time hidden from their husbands.[21]

A random, representative study of 2016 households in 2009 showed that 81 percent of households saved on M-PESA.[22] Another study of three small towns showed that the median amount was KSh 300. These amounts of money are stored for future expenditure and emergencies, rather than the banks' view of savings as residual after expenditure.[23]

By 2009, 70 percent of Kenya's households were using M-PESA, including an increasing number of the unbanked.[24] Usage grew because M-PESA was cheaper, faster, and more reliable than sending money via previous options such as buses, taxis, friends and relatives, or going yourself to hand over the cash. It was the preferred channel even though agents sometimes did not have the float. It was the senders in urban areas who pushed forward the use of M-PESA, persuading their families to register to reduce the expense of sending money. During the violence following the elections in December 2007, M-PESA stepped into the breach because other ways of sending money home were no longer safe. People trusted the service because they trusted Safaricom.[25]

People also send money via different channels. A survey of eight thousand persons in eight African countries found that a quarter (26.9 percent) of the 124 million persons who had sent or received money in the previous thirty days had sent or received cash delivered in person. This translates to 62 million persons in these eight countries. In Kenya, the figure was 21 percent, or 5 million persons. For the eight countries, mobile money transfer accounted for 44.4 percent, and the rest were transfers from financial institutions and money transfer services like Western Union.[26]

M-PESA Money Is Instantaneous and Interpersonal

Hearing people speak of M-PESA makes me ask, is M-PESA money a new kind of money? Has the mobile phone changed the nature and meaning of money? The meaning of money changes by its instantaneous transmission via the mobile phone. M-PESA money is interpersonal money embedded in a wide range of family and nonfamily relationships. It is a kind of money that makes fuzzy the distinction between the medium of communication and the communication itself. It is a verb, that is, "to M-PESA" money. The activity of sending and receiving money, the meanings of that communication, and the channel of money is M-PESA money. "Mobile money complicates consumption research because the commodity consumed slips between being a service and becoming money."[27] Maurer adds, "With mobile money, people are potentially setting in motion new media of exchange, methods of payment and stores of wealth and possibly measures of value."[28]

M-PESA's instantaneous transmission is made possible by the conversion of cash into e-units of money which can be converted to cash or be transferred again as electronic units of money. The immediate sending and receipt of money is caught in the title of Omwansa and Sullivan's book on M-PESA, *Money, Real Quick*. The immediacy of the money transaction gives M-PESA money its special potency in affirming a wide range of relationships.

Timeliness changes the value and empowerment of money for the sender and the receiver. As Margaret, the senior personal assistant in Nairobi, said, money sent to help for a funeral is more valuable if it arrives on the same day rather than two days later. For both my Maasai guide in Maasai Mara and his daughter, the gift became more meaningful as it was sent and received on the same day he heard of her success in the

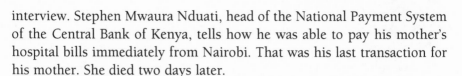

interview. Stephen Mwaura Nduati, head of the National Payment System of the Central Bank of Kenya, tells how he was able to pay his mother's hospital bills immediately from Nairobi. That was his last transaction for his mother. She died two days later.

Tonny Omwansa speaks of how M-PESA has changed the use and meaning of money for him (interviewed August 27, 2012). Tonny says that because of M-PESA, money for him has become "more powerful." He can do many things at the same time by pressing a few buttons. There is time saved. He gets instant feedback and confirmation that the money has been received. It has "greater impact," he says. "It empowers me. Before, I used to be afraid of receiving a call asking me to send cash to any of the properties I own, located in remote places. It would take painfully long to get funds over there. Now it's absolutely easy. It is instant!"

The emotional content of the instantaneous nature of M-PESA money is that it allows immediate response and gratification in terms of relationship. Tonny says it makes him feel good being able to send money by M-PESA to his mother as soon as she asks.

This instantaneous nature of M-PESA money also makes for a more insistent asking for money. Tonny says that now on invitation cards for functions, there is an M-PESA number. Even if you cannot attend, you are expected to contribute. The governor of the Central Bank, Prof. Njuguna Ndung'u, says, "It can also be exploitative. Before, they only come to you when you get home. Now with fundraising, they say, this is the M-PESA account."

The success of M-PESA lies in the interpersonal nature of M-PESA money as opposed to banking money. M-PESA is able to capture the vast array of flexible and interpersonal financial transactions that operate in the give-and-take of everyday life. Help is received and given in many ways, including cash. These transactions are embedded in traditional relationships of kin and lineage. They also extend to networks of friends and peers across varied social contexts of home and work life. Susan Johnson says there is a kikuyu saying, "*kuheananikũiga*," which means "giving is keeping."[29] By giving, you save with others. When you are in need, you can ask for help and borrow resources or receive them as a gift.

M-PESA money differs from cash and other electronic money. Tonny Omwansa says he treats M-PESA money less seriously than cash. "It is a number on a device where he has serious or informal conversations with kin and friends." This is one reason why people like Margaret erect barriers so that money does not flow easily from their bank accounts to M-PESA.

M-PESA by itself is not bringing the governor's cash-lite society closer. M-PESA facilitates the storage and movement of cash. The large majority of M-PESA transfers are in cash. A recent study shows that small businesses like restaurants, pharmacies, and groceries continue to pay for 90.4 percent of goods and services in cash. Mobile money and cards make up the rest.[30]

Another study focused on a rural site in eastern Kenya with eight thousand people and an economy dominated by cereal production and cattle rearing. It also concluded that M-PESA was not ushering in a cash-lite society. Each of the thirteen M-PESA agents bring in KSh 440,000 a week to accommodate withdrawals. This means that KSh 23 million flow into the rural site, the country hub, and a nearby village. M-PESA agents are the largest suppliers of cash to the local community. The agents, however, are not big enough to deal with the cash needs of the grain and mango traders. These traders bring cash in person to pay each farming household KSh 20,000 to KSh 100,000 per season in one payment. Noncash payments to nonlocal traders are done by check. Household payments for agriculture, informal work, plowing, *bodaboda* (bicycle taxis), and water sale are also wholly in cash. Business payments are 92 percent in cash, with 8 percent by M-PESA. Teaching and dividends are paid via the bank. Remittances are the only sphere where M-PESA dominates—79 percent by M-PESA compared with 16 percent by cash and 5 percent by the bank.[31]

BUILDING ON THE M-PESA PLATFORM

At the Central Bank of Kenya, the governor and the head of national payments speak of the M-PESA platform on which other services can be built. Others speak of M-PESA being part of an ecosystem including other financial players, the regulator, and customers. Yet others liken M-PESA to a network, the rails that make other developments possible. Philip G. Machoka, lecturer of information systems and technology at the US International University in Nairobi (interviewed August 29, 2012), says, "M-PESA is like a road. Once it exists, then other things come up on the side. It also enables other kinds of activities." The main point being made is that M-PESA is not just a discrete service but has become an enabling mechanism for other services and activities.

Banks have now partnered with M-PESA. People fall into two groups about their enthusiasm of the bank–M-PESA connection. The first group includes people like Margaret, Philip Machoka, and my Maasai Mara guide. They put up a wall between their bank account(s) and M-PESA for discipline purposes or find that the transfer fees are higher than going to an ATM to withdraw. The second group includes many professionals such as Stephen Nduati and Ben Lyon of Kopo Kopo who see this bank–M-PESA connection as one of the most valuable aspects of M-PESA. Lillian Nduati of iHub says she wanted to open an account with a bank in her building. But she only opened the account when the bank said it would partner with M-PESA in three months. Though she does not send money home, she pays by M-PESA in restaurants and cabs.

A recent study of savings for the poor in Kenya estimates that at the beginning of 2011, more than seventy-five financial institutions—commercial banks, microfinance institutions (MFIs), and savings and credit cooperatives (SACCOs)—were linked to M-PESA "with different degrees of integration."[32] M-PESA's November 2012 offering of M-Shwari, a paperless, virtual banking platform through a partnership with the Commercial Bank of Africa (CBA), integrates mobile money in a seamless fashion with flexible banking deposits and microloans. Unlike M-KESHO, the much publicized partnership between Equity Bank and M-PESA that began in March 2010, moving money between M-PESA and CBA is free. M-Shwari, however, offers a limited deposit and loan experience. Unlike Equity, which has the largest number of banking customers in Kenya, with a stated focus on low-income customers, CBA has a limited retail presence. M-Shwari does not offer withdrawal of deposits at CBA branches. Individual loans are more like payday loans for a month and range between KSh 100 and KSh 20,000. Interest in December 2012 was 7.5 percent per month. If the loans are not repaid within a month, they are rolled over, and M-Shwari deposits up to the amount owed are frozen. After sixty days of nonpayment, the customer's account is closed, and a report is sent to the credit bureau.[33] This integration of one bank with M-PESA for a limited banking experience is not perhaps the integration that the Central Bank of Kenya had in mind.

There is passion and enthusiasm about other developments of the M-PESA platform like business payments aggregation for small and medium-sized businesses. These services are hidden behind the business payments and customer interactions. Ben Lyon, director of Kopo Kopo (interviewed August 27, 2012), came to Nairobi two years ago. We sat outside in the winter sun on a balcony of a new building on Nairobi's Ngong Road, which hosts a number of information businesses. There was a buzz about the place. It was swarming with young African and Western graduates having a cappuccino from the café on the fourth floor.

Kopo Kopo is the middle person between individual M-PESA transactions with a business and putting the money into the business's bank account of choice. Each business gets a unique M-PESA account that Kopo Kopo manages and for which it provides customer support. The money comes into a parent account managed by Kopo Kopo, and then their software directs it to the particular business account.

Currently they serve the higher-end businesses in all the malls, large restaurants, and large franchise operations. Ben says, "Almost all of our merchants do have a point of sale machine. . . . That means they are reporting value added tax (VAT) to the revenue authorities. . . . There is a secure record of all the business transactions, accessible any time from a computer."

The customer value proposition is that the payment cannot be reversed. Businesses do not need to search for agents with enough liquidity and pay the withdrawal fees. Often a business has to go to three agents and pay three withdrawal rates. They don't have to queue to deposit the cash in the bank. With the aggregator model, there is a flat rate of 1.5 percent compared with up to 5 percent for cards. "Intelligent payment reports" are generated for the business. For Ben, this is the exciting part of the business. He says,

> We are a payments company. We do transactions. But what is interesting to me is what it means. When you see transactions at the end of the month and people run out of cash, what businesses are they shopping in? What is the effect of the exchange rate on purchasing behavior? I am much more interested in feeling the pulse of society.

With the intelligent customer reports, the merchant can better know its customers and drive loyalty revenue. Kopo Kopo has ten fields of information for every transaction. Ben says, "We are thinking big on the long term. This is much, much more interesting than getting 1.5 percent on the transaction." He talks of creating a "platform." He says,

> We don't see ourselves as a product. . . . We are a platform in that the service we provide is generic and is the same for every merchant. . . . But we also own the merchant relationship . . . and we can continue developing and adding new services on top of it. We are the super highway in the financial system that can potentially shed some light on the data.

Privacy concerns emerge with the linking up of business M-PESA accounts and bank accounts. Ben says the danger is that the Kenya Revenue

Authority will receive permission to get inside M-PESA's account not only to see the aggregate numbers but also to see who paid what to whom and for what. They could examine whether the value added tax of 16 percent has been paid. As most small businesses work with a 3 percent margin and do not pay the tax, this may reduce the push to move from the informal to the formal economy.

MOBILE MONEY IN THE PHILIPPINES

M-PESA is the most successful mobile money service, but it was not the first. Smart Communication's Smart Money started in the Philippines in 2001. It was provided by a mobile network operator (MNO) Smart Communications partnering with Banco de Oro (BDO), plus a number of retail merchants who acted as their agents overseas. Globe's GCash launched in November 2004. Unlike Smart Money, GCash was run wholly by a subsidiary of an MNO, Globe Telecom. In 2009 Globe Telecom also became part of a new mobile savings bank called BPI Globe BanKO.

I am tempted to tell the story of mobile money in the Philippines, highlighting its strengths with M-PESA as the reference point. The Philippine model has some advantages. There has been competition in the market of mobile money services since the early days. Mobile money started with international remittances and now covers customers in the cities in the Philippines and in remote rural areas. There isn't the same kind of tension between MNOs and banks in the mobile money space in the Philippines, because the MNOs and the banks have become increasingly "integrated." Mobile money meshes with mobile banking more easily in the Philippines. Financial inclusion in the Philippines involves the coming together of mobile payments and mobile banking. The mobile phone is increasingly a way for banks to increase their reach to the remote, rural, and unbanked in the country. Mobile money has become a channel for the distribution of cash transfers in the government's welfare program. Mobile money is linked with rural banks and microfinance in the partnership between the MNOs, rural banks, and the USAID-supported program Microenterprise Access to Banking Services (MABS).

Mobile money in the Philippines is similar to M-PESA in many ways. Both have central banks working cooperatively with MNOs and allow nonbank agents as a way of increasing financial inclusion. In the Philippines in 2012, only 27 percent of adults in the Philippines had an account with a formal financial institution. This included 4 percent of the poor.

Women were more banked than men at 34 percent.[34] In Kenya and the Philippines, consumer protection was enabled by limiting the amount of money that could be transmitted. Mobile money was supported by equivalent amounts in trust accounts in regulated banks.

Yet mobile money in the Philippines does not have the same international buzz around it that M-PESA does. Have Smart Money and GCash "transformed" the way money is managed and controlled? Has mobile money changed the intensity of connection between families working at a distance? Have the money relationships between married women and men changed? Some of these questions cannot be answered even with M-PESA. At present mobile money in the Philippines is being studied in terms of "success stories" and performance indicators, and the evaluation needs of corporations and international organizations. This prevents mobile money from becoming part of the muddles and complexities of everyday life. The story of mobile money as part of the everyday life of money and relationships in different parts of the country still has to be written.

FROM INTERNATIONAL REMITTANCES TO RURAL MICROFINANCE

Smart Money and GCash started with international remittances that were cheaper than the available alternatives. They serviced the needs of persons from the Philippines working overseas to provide better opportunities for their children. Pawnshops had traditionally acted as an informal money transfer service. Many customers selling goods to pawnshops needed to send money to help a friend or family member. Pawnshop owners realized that their businesses could improve if they helped people send money and if they could help their clients get their money back to reclaim their pawned assets.[35]

The Philippines provided a favorable environment. Mobile phones were common in the Philippines, and its people had taken avidly to texting. Cards were widely accepted. The two MNOs were well established. The mobile money transfer was similar to M-PESA in that it used SMS and cash-in and cash-out agents. Smart Money could also be withdrawn from a bank branch or an ATM and came with a more formal registration process.

Mobile international remittances changed the frequency of remittances and the number of recipients. The lower costs of remitting meant that migrants were able to better control their remittances by sending smaller amounts to more people. It became possible for a Filipino maid in Hong Kong to send some money to her mother who looked after the children, some money to the husband, and some money straight to the school for the fees. This separation and earmarking of money helped a woman manage the gender tensions that arise from working overseas, as detailed in chapter 4.

This early push into international remittances by Smart Money and GCash contributed to the hope that mobile international remittances would make remittances more transparent and yield large profits for the industry. International remittances are still an important part of mobile money in the Philippines. A person can send GCash to the Philippines from thirty-five countries via more than one hundred partner money transfer organizations. But as of February 2012, only three hundred thousand of the twenty-nine million Globe Telecom subscribers have used GCash wallets for international remittances.[36]

As most of the mobile money projects around the world have discovered, the domestic payments market is larger than that of international remittances and involves a greater percentage of the population.

Early indications are that mobile money in the Philippines has helped bring formal payments to the unbanked. In 2009, half the mobile money users in the Philippines were the unbanked, with a quarter (26 percent) being below the US$5-a-day poverty line in the country. There is an impressive level of awareness of mobile money. More than two-thirds of consumers (68 percent) with multiple SIM cards use their mobile money SIM as the primary one for texting and calling. One in ten unbanked already save $31 on their mobile wallet. Low-income consumers use mobile money to send and receive domestic remittances. The average amount sent is $57 and received is $48. Twelve percent of low-income unbanked users of mobile money do not have a mobile phone. The use of mobile money extends beyond remittances, for one-third of mobile money users do not send or receive money. They purchase airtime and make remote purchases.[37]

The reach of mobile money has increased with the partnership between rural banks, MABS, and mobile money providers. This added another 1,100 rural agent outlets, 390,000 new clients, and over $400 million in mobile money–enabled transactions. Globe also participated in a pilot transmission of World Food Program's Cash for Work Program in 2010 and the Conditional Cash Transfer (CCT) Program administered by the Department of Social Welfare and Development (DSWD) and LandBank. In 2011, Globe serviced three hundred thousand CCT grant beneficiaries to distribute an estimated $23 million in grants to almost seventy areas in sixteen of the most remote districts. It meant a savings for the government for it no longer had to take the cash in helicopters to remote areas. It also helped the grant beneficiaries who sometimes used to spend 30 percent of their benefits to travel to collect their money.[38]

The stories most often told about GCash today are about rural school-teachers and workers receiving their salaries in their mobile banking account. This can often save a day of onerous travel to the bank branch and also some $17 in transport expenses.[39] Other stories are of poor households receiving their cash transfers from the government in the country's large social welfare program. Like Bolsa Familia in Brazil, these cash transfers are conditional on the children remaining in school. These transfers also have health-related conditions attached to them like having the children vaccinated.

Despite these positive moves, mobile money in the Philippines has not seeped through the lives of most of the people in the country. In the Philippines, 15 percent of adults have used mobile money in the last twelve months. This is a creditable achievement when compared with the rest of the world, but it falls behind the 70 percent in Kenya. Countries in Africa report higher figures, but the Philippines is the highest in Asia. Only 4 percent in India said they used mobile money in the past twelve months. China was even lower at 2 percent. The only countries outside of Africa that rate equal to or higher than the Philippines in terms of mobile usage are Haiti, Tajikistan, Kosovo, Macedonia, and Albania.[40]

Comparisons with M-PESA are hard to ignore. In the Philippines, Bangko Sentral ng Pilipinas (BSP) imposed stricter conditions on its mobile money providers. Mobile money senders as well as the recipients had to be registered. The regulator also required that any cash receiving or transmitting agent be registered and undergo a day's training in "Know Your Customer" and anti–money laundering (AML) guidelines. It took a strict view of these guidelines as the Philippines had been blacklisted by the US Financial Action Task Force for not being compliant with anti–money laundering procedures. The Philippines came off the blacklist in 2005.[41]

These strict guidelines meant that the agent network in the country was sparse, particularly in rural areas. Even urban mobile money users in 2009 reported that there were four times as many ATMs and bank branches as mobile money agents within fifteen minutes of their house. The agent network was limited because the MNOs' airtime resellers were not willing to forgo a day's income to go away for training. Moreover, the percentage of fees from airtime reselling was up to four times that from cash transfers. Unless the MNOs could get the marketing and the agent network right, mobile money could not tap into the estimated $450 million held by low-income Filipinos in informal savings.[42]

In 2010, Bangko Sentral ng Pilipinas allowed Globe to go to the resellers' locations to administer KYC/AML guidelines and commercial training. This increased Globe's agent network to eighteen thousand, making it the widest remittance network in the country. They were able to add the resellers and cellular phone shops to their network of pawnshops, rural banks, financial institutions, and mini-grocery stores.[43]

GLOBAL DEVELOPMENTS IN MOBILE MONEY

Mobile money projects and pilots now dot the developing world. The GSM Association has counted 130 live mobile money deployments across ninety-three countries. It has been difficult to replicate M-PESA's success. Vodacom in Tanzania claims nine million registered users for its M-PESA rollout and more than fifteen thousand cash in/out agent locations. The active customer base is likely to be nearer two million. The competing services, Tigo Pesa, Airtel Money, and Easy Pesa, are also likely to grow given the more fragmented mobile telephony and widespread use of multiple SIMs.

In Uganda, MTN's MobileMoney service may have more than one million active users, with competition from Airtel Money, UTL's M-Sente, and the recently launched Warid Pesa. Mobile money has had some success in Pakistan and Afghanistan. Pakistan's Easypaisa by TameerTelenor is probably used by more than a million customers for paying bills or sending money over the counter rather than through registered services.[44]

On the other side of the world in Haiti, mobile money began in November 2010. Mobile money was introduced with the financial help of the Bill and Melinda Gates Foundation and the USAID-funded Haiti Integrated Finance for Value Chains and Enterprises (HIFIVE) after the catastrophic earthquake in January 2010. It was hoped that mobile money would not only allow money to move more freely but in the long term would also introduce more effective ways of paying for goods and services, facilitate trade, and increase the banked population. Research shows that it is still a work in progress. Mobile money is adopted most easily for Me2Me transfers, that is, for sending money to oneself, for the storage and safe keeping of cash.[45]

Mobile money thus enables a person to store money in his or her own mobile money account. Sending money home is not a prominent part of mobile money in Haiti, as most of the country is urban. International remittances as yet cannot be transferred by mobile. Using mobile money for trade would require the ability to transfer larger sums than currently possible. The agent network also needs more training and reliability. But the potential for setting up a new infrastructure for payments remains strong.

Despite Smart Money and GCash, mobile international remittances is a market in its early stages. Of the seventeen possible mobile international remittance ventures in 2010, only six were launched in 2012.[46] M-PESA teamed up with Western Union in March 2011 to send money from forty-five countries to Kenya. Theoretically this should combine the strengths of M-PESA's agent networks in Kenya and Western Union's sending networks across the world. Barclays is currently testing Pingit, developed in the United Kingdom. It is said to allow people to send and receive money instantly on the mobile.[47] Vodafone announced in October 2012 that it had joined up with HomeSend, an international remittance hub, to enable international remittances via M-PESA. Nation Media Group, the biggest media group in Kenya, connected with the diaspora through news coverage, launched NationHela (wealth) in 2012.

Mobile international remittances have also been long awaited in the Pacific. Sending $200 from Australia to Tonga, Fiji, or Samoa in the third quarter of 2011 used to cost $23.21, $29.94, or $25.30, respectively. Sending money to these countries from New Zealand was not vastly different. This corridor was one of the most expensive in the world.[48] The banks have some of the highest costs of remittances. Costs have fallen with the recent partnership of Digicel, the dominant MNO in the Pacific, with KlickEx, a peer-to-peer (P2P) currency exchange provider that matches individuals and companies who want to change currencies. Digicel Mobile Money was launched in October 2011, catering for remittances from Australia and New Zealand to Fiji, Samoa, and Tonga. It is an mWallet service. Funds are transferred instantly in less than an hour and can be used to pay bills, top up, or make purchases in stores.

To send $200 from Australia to Fiji in February 2012, Digicel Mobile Money was the third-cheapest, costing 6.48 percent. It was less than the money transfer organization (MTO) average of 8.12 and the bank average of 17.54 percent. Western Union charged 10.67.[49] As a result of the competition, the ANZ Bank transfer price has dropped to $8. Western Union has also offered discounts on transaction fees. Early reaction is said to be good, with repeat use and referrals. Digicel also claims to have more agents than any other money transfer service in the Pacific. In February 2012, there were 35 agents in Samoa, 50 in Tonga, and 150 in Fiji to offer help, service, and cash-out facilities.[50]

The introduction of mobile money in Africa has transformed the lives of people, particularly those who are poor and who previously had little access to formal payment channels. M-PESA has been the stellar success story, and attempts are being made to replicate its success around the world. However, mobile money, for all its promise, has yet to move into international remittances—what the *Economist* has dubbed "the rivers of gold."[51]

NOTES

1. Bill Maurer, "Mobile Money: Communication, Consumption and Change in the Payments Space," *Journal of Development Studies* 48, no. 5 (2012).

2. Ignacio Mas, "Making Mobile Money Daily Relevant," http://papers.ssrn.com/sol3/papers.cfm?abstract_id=2018807 (accessed September 13, 2012).

3. "Is it a Phone, Is It a Bank? Mobile Banking," *Economist*, March 30, 2013.

4. Anjana Ravi and Eric Tyler, *Savings for the Poor in Kenya* (New America Foundation, 2012).

5. Tonny K. Omwansa and Nicholas P. Sullivan, *Money, Real Quick: The Story of M-PESA*, Kindle ed. (London: Guardian Books, 2012), Kindle location 38.

6. Omwansa and Sullivan, *Money, Real Quick*, Kindle locations 59–62.

7. Angela Crandall et al., *Mobile Phone Usage at the Kenyan Base of the Pyramid: Final Report* (Nairobi: iHub Research and Research Solutions Africa, 2012).

8. Omwansa and Sullivan, *Money, Real Quick*.

9. Omwansa and Sullivan, *Money, Real Quick*.

10. Omwansa and Sullivan, *Money, Real Quick*.

11. Omwansa and Sullivan, *Money, Real Quick*, Kindle Locations 343–56.

12. Omwansa and Sullivan, *Money, Real Quick*, Kindle Locations 363–66.

13. CGAP and DFID, "Scenarios for Branchless Banking in 2020," CGAP and DFID, www.cgap.org/gm/document-1.9.40599/FN57.pdf (accessed December 6, 2009).

14. Financial Sector Deepening (FSD) Kenya, *Financial Access in Kenya: Results of the 2005 National Survey* (2007).

15. Stephen Mwaura Nduati, "Challenges and Opportunities to Promote Financial Inclusion" (paper presented at the International Forum for Central Banks: Payment Systems and Financial Inclusion, Quito, Ecuador, August 2, 2012).

16. William Jack and Tavneet Suri, "Mobile Money: The Economics of M-PESA," (NBER Working Paper No. 16721, 2011).

17. Bill Maurer, "Note from IMTFI: Mobile Money Regulation—A Story Arc of Best Practices and Emerging Realizations," Microlinks, last modified December 6, 2011, http://microlinks.kdid.org/learning-marketplace/notes/note-imtfi-mobile-money-regulation-story-arc-best-practices-and-emerging; Maria C. Stephens, "Promoting Responsible Financial

Inclusion: A Risk-Based Approach to Supporting Mobile Financial Services Expansion," *Banking and Finance Law Review* 27, no. 2 (2012).

18. Susan Johnson, "The Search for Inclusion in Kenya's Financial Landscape: The Rift Revealed," Centre for Development Studies, http://www.fsdkenya.org/pdf_docu ments/12-03-29_Full_FinLandcapes_report.pdf (accessed August 19, 2012), 22.

19. Jack and Suri, "Mobile Money."

20. Olga Morawczynski, "Examining the Usage and Impact of Transformational M-Banking in Kenya," in *Internationalization, Design and Global Development*, ed. N. Aykin (Berlin: Springer-Verlag, 2009).

21. Morawczynski, "Examining the Usage and Impact."

22. Jack and Suri, "Mobile Money."

23. Johnson, "The Search for Inclusion."

24. Jack and Suri, "Mobile Money."

25. Morawczynski, "Examining the Usage and Impact."

26. Jake Kendall and Bill Maurer, "Tips for 2012: Understanding Payment Behavior of African Households—A Vast and Untapped Market," http://pymnts.com, http://pymnts.com/ commentary/Tips-for-2012-Understanding-Payment-Behavior-of-African-Households-A -Vast-and-Untapped-Market (accessed September 18, 2012).

27. Maurer, "Mobile Money," 592.

28. Maurer, "Mobile Money," 601.

29. Johnson, "The Search for Inclusion," vi.

30. Sam Kitony and Leo Mutuku, *An Exploratory Study on Kenyan Consumer Ordering Habits: Final Report* (2012).

31. Bankable Frontier Associates, "'Time for Cash to Cash Out?' Scoping Kenya's Path to a Cash-Lite Society," in *FSD Insights* (FSD Kenya, 2012).

32. Ravi and Tyler, *Savings for the Poor in Kenya*, 22.

33. Ignacio Mas and Tonny Omwansa. "NexThought Monday—A Close Look at Safaricom's M-Shwari: Mobile, Yes, but How 'Cool' Is It for Customers?," last modified December 10, 2012, http://www.nextbillion.net/blogpost.aspx?blogid=3050.

34. Asli Demirguc-Kunt and Leora Klapper, *Measuring Financial Inclusion: The Global Findex Database* (Washington, DC: World Bank, 2012).

35. Ignacio Mas, "Don't Touch Our M-PESA!," last modified August 2, 2012, http:// www.ignaciomas.com/announcements/donttouchourm-pesa (accessed September 24, 2012).

36. Dalberg Global Development Advisors, *CGAP Landscape Study on International Remittances through Mobile Money: Final Report* (2012).

37. Mark Pickens, "Window on the Unbanked: Mobile Money in the Philippines," https://openknowledge.worldbank.org/bitstream/handle/10986/9488/567240BRI0CGAP11 e1Money1Philippines.pdf?sequence=1 (accessed October 4, 2012).

38. Chris Bold, "Does Branchless Banking Reach Poor People? The Evidence from India," last modified June 17, 2011, http://www.cgap.org/blog/does-branchless-banking -reach-poor-people-evidence-india (accessed 2012).

39. "For Text-Savvy Filipinos, Mobile Banking Is a Crucial Bridge," *Frontlines*, September/October 2012.

40. Demirguc-Kunt and Klapper, *Measuring Financial Inclusion*.

41. GSMA, "Money in the Philippines—The Market, the Models and Regulation," http://www.gsma.com/mobilefordevelopment/mobile-money-in-the-philippines-the-market-the-models-and-regulation (accessed August 15, 2013).

42. Pickens, "Window on the Unbanked"; Paul Leishman, "Globe Announces Big Change to Gcash Agent Network," http://www.gsma.com/mobilefordevelopment/globe-announces-big-change-to-gcash-agent-network (accessed October 4, 2012).

43. Bold, "Does Branchless Banking Reach Poor People?"

44. Ignacio Mas, "Making Mobile Money Daily Relevant."

45. Erin B. Taylor, Espelencia Baptiste, and Heather A. Horst, *Mobile Money in Haiti: Potentials and Challenges* (Institute for Money, Technology and Financial Inclusion [IMTFI], 2011).

46. Dalberg Global Development Advisors, *CGAP Landscape Study*.

47. Ann Crotty, "Analysis: UK Bank Seeks to Apply Lessons in New Continental Push," *The Star*, September 25, 2012.

48. International Finance Corporation (IFC), "Remittance Prices Worldwide: Making Markets More Transparent," http://remittanceprices.worldbank.org (accessed August 24, 2011).

49. International Finance Corporation, "Remittance Prices Worldwide."

50. Dalberg Global Development Advisors, *CGAP Landscape Study*.

51. "Remittance Corridors: New Rivers of Gold," *Economist*, April 28–May 4, 2012.

CHAPTER 8

MIGRANT MONEY

INTERTWINING THE GLOBAL
AND THE PERSONAL

When I was growing up in Delhi, my eldest sister used to send money for my school education from Mumbai where she was working. My second sister sent money home from New York. I began to send money home to my mother when I started earning in Malaysia. It was only when I started studying remittances that I realized we were unusual. In patrilineal North India, it is the sons who most often send money home. But in our family there were no sons. Moreover, the changes in gender norms because of the 1947 Partition of India meant that we did not question daughters sending money home.

The vital importance of regular remittances was also brought home to me when I interviewed a Chinese corporate executive in Malaysia in the mid-1980s as part of the history of the Central Bank of Malaysia. The conversation moved to remittances, as this was one of the important functions of Chinese banks in Malaysia in the 1930s and 1940s. During the Japanese

Occupation, communications were disrupted and remittances stopped. This is a footnote in banking history. Forty years later, this executive sobbed at his desk as he remembered that his mother and four brothers and sisters had starved to death in Canton during those war years.[1]

It was a given in my life in India and Malaysia that children helped their parents with money. Studying money in middle-income Anglo-Celtic families in Melbourne made me realize that this two-way flow of money was not universal. In Australia, money was private to the married couple. Money flowed one way from grandparents and parents to children and grandchildren. The other difference was that the parents I interviewed in Melbourne did not expect their well-off children to help them. When I asked Betsy, of whom I wrote in chapter 5, whether her children help, she said more than once, "We can manage." She said the children had their responsibilities with a growing family. This was different from my experience in India. If I sent $500 home, my mother would boast of it. It meant she had brought up filial children. This difference disturbed me. I reminded my son in Australia that when he grows up and wants to give me money, I would be delighted to accept.

It is this two-way flow of money between parents and children that is at the center of many of the remittances to developing countries when family members migrate. Family money comprises one of the largest international flows of funds. Money sent home to family and community is so steadfast and large that governments use it as security to lower the cost of loans or channel it through diaspora bonds. The personal and global are intertwined, as are family and market money. The social concept of money brings migrants and their remittances to the center of some of the most personal aspects of globalization.

MEASURING REMITTANCES

Remittances in the early 2000s were seen as small private sums that were irrelevant for development. It was an Indian migrant to the United States who sent money home who helped the World Bank to recognize that remittances are one of the largest international flows of funds. Dilip Ratha, lead economist and manager of the Migration and Remittances Development Prospects Group at the World Bank, had for many years been sending money to his family in a village in Orissa, India. The *New York Times* tells the story of how Ratha joined the bank as an economist and engaged in forensic accounting to find that in 2003, remittances to the

Philippines were fifty-one times higher than previously estimated.[2] Meeting Dilip Ratha over a latte at the World Bank, I found he smiles easily. His achievement in bringing remittances to the center of global money flows sits lightly with him. His own experience of sending money to his parents, siblings, and extended family feels like the personal core of his unveiling of the importance of remittances. It still rankles that his sister was refused a visa to study in the United States because the visa officer could not believe that a brother would fund his sister's education in the United States. Coming from a country with a remittance culture, where sons are expected to send money home and brothers are expected to help their sisters, it was easier for him to recognize the importance of remittances as an international flow of funds.

Remittances result from the mobility and migration of labor. They include three components—migrant workers' remittances, the compensation of nonresident staff such as embassy employees, and migrants' capital transfers. This three-pronged definition is important, as there is a difference in the way different countries treat these three kinds of money over time.[3]

There were an estimated 214 billion migrants worldwide in 2010. Though the relative share of migration as a proportion of total population has remained relatively stable over the last decade at around 3 percent, remittances have grown faster.[4] Remittances that go through formal money transfer channels to developing countries in 2012 were expected to reach $406 billion. Formal and informal remittances to developing countries are now three times more than official foreign assistance. For some smaller countries, formal international remittances form a large part of their GDP.[5] For individual countries, remittances can be greater than foreign direct investment.[6] Remittances have been more resilient than other private international flows when coping with economic downturns.

India and China are the two largest recipients, with India receiving an estimated $70 billion in 2012 compared with China's $66 billion.[7] Remittances, including those to high-income countries, are expected to reach $615 billion by 2014.[8] The *Economist* calls the main remittance corridors—from the United States to Mexico, China, India, the Philippines, and Vietnam, and from the Middle East and Britain to India— "new rivers of gold."[9]

The total value of remittances is even greater, as informal remittances, that is, money sent outside the formal money transfer institutions, are estimated to be at least 50 percent of recorded remittances.[10] In Asia, they could be anywhere between 15 and 80 percent of the true value of remittances.[11] The amount transferred in kind and cash given personally could be as high as 42 percent of formal remittances.[12]

Sometimes, the informal transfer is just a matter of carrying the permissible amount of cash when going back to visit. Australia permits a person to carry up to AUS$10,000 without having to report it. In other cases, it involves sending money with friends and relatives. Established informal systems include *fei-ch'ien* in China, *hundi* in Pakistan and Bangladesh, *hawala* in India and the Middle East, *padala* in the Philippines, *huikuan* in Hong Kong, and *pheikwan* in Thailand.[13] Most of them operate in similar ways.

Hawala (it means "transfer" in Arabic) serves the needs of millions of migrants. A person hands over cash to the *hawala* operator, who usually operates another business such as the corner store, a travel agency, or a delicatessen. This cash is to be delivered most often in local currency to a contact in the home country. The transfer is speedy and often offers lower fees and better exchange rates than the formal money transfer organizations. It works on established trust, and there are few instances of the customer having lost his or her money in a *hawala* deal. It operates without the formal identification requirements of the formal sector for the sender.[14] It can deliver money straight to the home. In some countries, this is essential because of the seclusion of women and the privacy of money.

The total value of remittances is even greater than formal and informal remittances, for remittances have traditionally been underreported. Ratha says the extent of underestimation of remittances can be significant, such as when the Nigerian central bank revised remittances to $17 billion from an earlier report of about $4 billion annually. At the time the World Bank estimated remittances for the whole of sub-Saharan Africa at $12 billion. Given the size of unrecorded migration flows from and within Africa, the World Bank team thinks that remittances to sub-Saharan Africa could be near $100 billion.[15]

Some categories of money flows are not counted as remittances. In many countries, money spent on gifts using foreign credit cards gets classified as "exports" or "tourism receipts." Money withdrawn by nonresidents from an ATM is also excluded from remittances. If remittances are sent to banks and kept in nonresident deposits (say by a nonresident Indian), the amount is rightly still seen as a liability, but it can and often does get withdrawn as remittances. Investments in real estate and donations to charity are also not seen as remittances. Add to this the possible

round-tripping of money sent to destination countries by *hawala* or other means to escape taxes or launder black money into white.[16]

The emphasis on measuring financial flows fails to capture the magnitude and importance of remittances in kind. When I return to India and Malaysia, I take gifts for people in twenty-one families, and not all of them are kin. "Gift remittances" with or without cash are also important gestures of recognition in Zambia that keep open the possibility of the migrant returning.[17] Among Ghanaians, imported Dutch wax prints that cost more than $100 to $150 per twelve-yard piece, have the highest prestige.[18]

REMITTANCES AND DEVELOPMENT

As the scale of remittances rises, it becomes important to ask whether remittances have reduced poverty and increased development. The literature on remittances is primarily economic. It concentrates on the impact of remittances on the household, regional, and national economy of the recipient country.[19] There has been an emphasis on remittance behavior, detailing the way remittances change with length of stay in the host country, income, age, gender, and the kind of family left behind.[20]

Household expenditure surveys, ethnographic work, and longitudinal studies in Bangladesh, Pakistan, Thailand, the Philippines, Jordan, Senegal, the Pacific, the Caribbean, and Latin America show that the receiving households spend more on food, housing, health, and children's education and reduce child labor. The severity of poverty for poor migrant households is reduced. Remittances help with the development of entrepreneurial skills that lead to small enterprises.[21] "There is now a consensus that the highest share of remittances is spent supporting households' recurrent costs, including education and health."[22]

It is more difficult to link remittances to development and the alleviation of poverty at the community level. It has been difficult to measure community remittances or diaspora philanthropy, which occupy a middle space between family remittances and foreign direct investment. Community remittances are not used to cover recurrent expenses. They resemble charitable donations rather than investments for profit.[23] The charitable impulse at the center of community remittances has meant they cannot be easily used for "productive" profit-making ventures.

At the market level, remittances can be a useful source of foreign exchange. Increased formal remittances have become an important tool for reducing national debt. They have been used to securitize loans so as to borrow at lower costs on international capital markets. Diaspora bonds are also seen as a way of channeling diaspora savings for national development.[24] Beyond this relationship with foreign exchange, securitization, and foreign direct investment, there is little "causal relationship between inflows of remittances and economic performance, although they may well be correlated."[25]

TRANSNATIONAL MONEY IS A CURRENCY OF CARE

There is a "hostile worlds" approach dividing literature that connects remittances to development and remittances as a currency of care within the transnational family. International family remittances are one of the most personal dimensions of globalization and money. Studies of family and community remittances have a wide geographic spread covering Latin America, the Caribbean, Asia, Africa, and the Pacific. These studies reveal that money is used in different ways to express ties with the transnational family and community.

I use the term "transnational family" to include the family members who have migrated across nation-states and those who have been left behind. With "twice or thrice migrants,"[26] that is, people whose family and personal histories include more than one migration, the transnational family can stretch across several national boundaries. Though these transnational families are separated by distance and national borders, they "hold together and create something that can be seen as a feeling of collective welfare and unity, namely 'familyhood,' even across national borders."[27]

Transnational families share much with families in general, and families separated by distance in particular. There is the same need for negotiation and reciprocity.[28] The transnational family, as with all other kinds of families, has a developmental cycle, which changes with life stage.[29] Family practices over life stage and generation "display" a sense of being part of the family.[30] The transnational family has to overcome distance as well as different state regimes related to passports, workforce regulations, residence, education, and health care.

Remittances become an important transnational family practice to display care. The continuing thread in the literature on remittances and the transnational family is that migrants seek to connect with the family and community they have left. This can be through remittances, regular phone calls, and periodic visits home. This search for connection is true for men and women who have migrated alone or with their nuclear families, for those who have migrated with the hope of permanent settlement or are by definition temporary workers on contract.

Male migration from Honduras to the United States illustrates how remittances become a medium of caring for the family left behind and are perceived as such. Women in a rural community who receive money to build a new home interpret this as the ultimate indicator of the success of the migrant husband or son. Receiving the extra money to buy new clothes, improve the family's diet, and pay for the children's schooling makes the costs of migration and separation feel worthwhile. Ambrosia, seventy years old, with three sons working in the United States, also sees the home repairs and extra money as an expression of "love, commitment and sacrifice."[31] Rafaela, the wife of a migrant and mother of three boys, echoes the same feelings. When she receives packages from her husband, she says, "If he sends you money or things, you know he hasn't forgotten you. You feel good."[32]

Differences in kinship obligations mean that remittances can be sent to a wide range of people, going beyond parents and siblings. A Dinka man sees himself as related and responsible for three immediate generations on his father's side and also has obligations to his wife's kin. He is expected to contribute to bride-price and any payment for bribes or fines.[33] Somali refugees send money to parents and siblings. They also send money to uncles, aunts, nephews, nieces, grandparents, cousins, and in-laws.[34] In Fiji and Tonga, nonmigrant households also receive remittances.[35]

A patrilineal kinship system in most of India translates into male migrants sending money home, as seen in chapter 4. Ghanaian women belonging to a matrilineal kinship system send money to mothers and sisters who are looking after their children. They send money to help the mother build her house and also for the migrant woman's house in the village. Ten of the fifteen Ghanaian women interviewed in Canada had built or were building a house for themselves in the village. This would lead to greater prestige in the matrilineage. In one case, the migrant woman sent money for her sister to get trained as a beautician so that she, too, could contribute money to build a house for their mother. Often the money is spent by the mother and sisters in a way that accords with the migrant's wishes.[36]

When women migrate alone, they go to work in the area of domestic work or the care and entertainment sectors. Negotiation about who the recipient should be and how the money is spent is often at the center of the discussion of remittances. As seen in chapter 4, when a woman migrates alone, she sends money to her mother or other kin who are looking after the children and/or to her spouse. A man may send remittances to his father if his wife and children are living in a joint family household.[37]

Sending money home is characteristic of the first generation. A decade-long longitudinal study of 1.5-generation (those who arrived in the United States when they were seventeen years or younger) and second-generation young adults (those born in the United States to two foreign-born parents) from Mexico, the Philippines, Vietnam, China, and a host of other Latin American and Asian countries revealed that transnational attachments are "always under 10 percent."[38] Unlike their parents, "there appears to be no 'tingling' sensation, no phantom pain, over a homeland that was never lost to them in the first place."[39]

The sending of remittances is one side of the circulation of care between transnational families. The remitting families receive valuable support from their families in the source countries. Increasingly there is support for the care of children. This care is given either in the source country or with the "flying grandmothers" taking turns helping out with their grandchildren in the country of destination. It is part of the give-and-take of transnational families.[40]

THE TENSIONS OF GLOBAL MONEY

Money changes in nature when it moves across borders and becomes global. *Transnational family money* is transformed by family negotiations and meanings over cultural and physical distance across national borders. As with other "special monies" and "social payments," remittances become a qualitatively different kind of family money. Remittances become a kind of gift money, balanced ambiguously against the financial contributions and face-to-face care given by members of the family still in the home country. The value of money is interpreted rather than calculated, as detailed in chapter 2. The dollar sent is not the dollar received.

In many ways "transnational family money" has the same characteristics as family money. When my eldest sister sent money from Mumbai or my second sister sent money from New York, both were expressing their filial care for their family in Delhi. But transnational family money differs from family money in three ways. First, senders at times feel that people at home idealize the ease with which money can be earned overseas and underestimate the costs of living. When difficult economic conditions make it hard to fulfill high family expectations, it leads to a feeling of shame and dishonor on both sides.[41]

The second difference lies with the effect of remittances on women's money management and control. This is true of women who send money and those who receive. I have written of this in detail in chapter 4. The third difference emerges from different interpretations of care. Migrants see money as a medium for "caring about" and "taking care" of their families in the home country. It is also a means of negotiating an honored place in the family. This negotiation is threatened when remittances are devalued against the day-to-day "caregiving" provided by other family members, usually siblings in the home country. When these conflicts flow into issues of inheritance, they go to the heart of being part of the transnational family and its consequent rights and responsibilities.[42]

THE MONEY TREE

Money earned overseas is seen as "easy money" and has the characteristics of "windfall income."[43] Migrants in Persian Gulf countries generally earn five to fifteen times what they would have earned locally. It is seen as money earned with less physical hardship. Each dollar, pound, or euro earned translates into large multiples of currency in the home country. Hence families who have remained behind expect more than they would if a person had moved within the country. As windfall income, they expect it to be spent in ways that differ from money earned. At times it is spent in ways that even the senders would not have contemplated for themselves. This is stressful, for often the migrant's nuclear family in the country of destination has had to do without.

This perception that migrants are a money tree is supported by migrants bringing gifts of consumer durables common in the host country but difficult to get in the source country. Villages in Kerala are dotted by showy houses built by migrants for their families. Towns in Punjab have grandiose houses that stand empty for when the migrant returns. The spending and giving bestows honor and status on the migrant. It does not reveal the difficulties of earning, the costs of settlement, and a different tax regime in a new country.

Adina, a migrant from Ghana to Canada, went back for her father's funeral even though she was unable to take the required gifts associated with funerals. At the time, she was unemployed and had had major surgery. She was able to take $500 with her, but it did not meet her mother's expectations. She was there for six weeks but was uncomfortable with her mother. She says, "I wasn't welcome in a way because I didn't go with funds."[44]

A geographic spread of research confirms that receivers often undervalue the sacrifice made by senders in sending remittances. This is true for struggling migrants and for professional middle-income migrants whose families are not in dire need. The perception that migrants have it easy and so should liberally send money home is seen in some of its starkest detail among the southern Sudanese Dinka refugees in the United States. Joseph and his family who resettled in San Diego in 1998 are a compelling illustration. Within the first two years, he "became directly responsible for 24 male and female extended family members and indirectly 62 persons displaced"[45] across Egypt, Libya, Kenya, and Uganda. Joseph also periodically helps four unrelated friends in Egypt who helped him in the past.

Six of Joseph's relatives, including two brothers, in the asylum host cities of Cairo and Tripoli require remittances of nearly $400 a month to cover their expenses for food, clothing, and medical treatment. He sends money to the others once every two months or sporadically when funds are available. Joseph also has to contribute toward bride-price, for it has to come collectively from members of the immediate three generations of one's father's lineage. Bride-price can range from cows worth $6,000 to $150,000. He also has to contribute to compensation to victims' families for crimes (e.g., adultery) committed by a member. Remittances are also expected when a relative is evicted or dies.

Joseph has had to single-handedly meet these expenses from an annual income of $28,000. He also has responsibilities for his wife's parents in Khartoum. Two of his wife's siblings stay with them, in addition to their child and another on the way. Though he has a higher income than most Dinka refugees, he has found it difficult to manage financially. At one time he disconnected the home phone because he was unable to cope with the demands. He gave his new number only to his two brothers in Cairo and Tripoli. He said, "It's very shameful, but it is the only thing I can do to stop all of those calls. People just don't understand what we are facing here."[46] There are few long-term solutions. Despite all the help Joseph gives, he faces hurtful criticism from his relatives and in-laws who have not been resettled.

In Jamaica, the more frequent communication via the mobile phone has led Jamaicans to have a more realistic image of the migration experience and the high costs of living. It has dissuaded a thirty-six-year-old man from going abroad as "every time he called his friend, he went 'on and on' about his expenses and how much he worked."[47] It convinced him that his friend who lived overseas was no better off than he was in Jamaica.

A DOLLAR SENT IS NOT THE DOLLAR RECEIVED

Another difference between family money and transnational money derives from pitting money as a medium of caring about the family against physical caregiving, usually by siblings in the home country. The different valuations between remittances and physical caring often spill into the legal arena. The conflict is not only "over who gets what but also over structure and meaning."[48]

The cultural and social framework of inheritance differs according to the system of land ownership and men's and women's rights over ancestral property. Italian migrants in Australia find their claims to inheritance are often given away to those of their siblings in Italy who stayed to look after the parents.[49] However, Hyderabadis abroad did inherit.[50] It was an incidental part of the study, and we do not know whether it was because no sibling remained behind. In the Pacific, however, "overseas migrants invariably retain land rights even after long periods of absence."[51]

In my qualitative study of eighty-six persons from the Indian diaspora in Melbourne, Australia, conducted between May 2005 and March 2010, there was a perception that the dollar sent is not the dollar received. As an Australian dollar in 2012 hovers around 50 Indian rupees, this overshadows the costs of settlement and the tax regime. The participants felt that the family in the home country did not sufficiently value the kinds of negotiations that have to take place in balancing the interests of the nuclear family in Australia and the natal family in the home country. This sense of not being valued is heightened if there is an uneven reciprocity in terms of communication and gift relationships, for it signals a lack of "caring about" the migrant offshoot of the transnational family. This gap in the valuation of transnational money can make for resentment in the remitters' nuclear family.[52]

Ishaan, age twenty-five to thirty-four, who migrated to Australia with his parents from Kenya when he was six months old, tells the story of his father sending money home. Ishaan's father is the eldest of five brothers and three sisters and the first to receive a university education. His father regularly sent money home because he thought "it was his duty." He saw himself as having financial opportunities that the rest of his family did not have. Ishaan's father sent money to his parents, brothers, and cousins. He helped educate his brothers and also helped one of his younger brothers start a business. Later in life, his father also sponsored his younger brother to move to Australia. Sometimes he had to go into debt to honor these obligations. He would take gifts and money for his family when he visited India. The finances were so tight that the family could not visit India together.[53]

At times, Ishaan says, his father tried to hide some of the money he sent home, though Ishaan's mother would find out.

> Obviously Mum was the one who'd . . . get the budget for the week and have to make the ends meet. . . . Dad was sort of cutting out a huge proportion of the family budget to send back. . . . If that does not appear to be as widely recognised or appreciated then I guess she found that frustrating as well.[54]

Physical care contributed by the son or daughter who stayed at home, against the one who left and sends money home, is often at the center of the division of property at inheritance. The conflict goes to the heart of inclusion in the transnational family and its consequent rights and responsibilities. Even when the women have ceded their claims in favor of their brothers—as in India—it is important to them that they had been left property. Hema, a direct migrant from India forty-five to fifty-four years old, laughed off the issue of inheritance after talking of the conflicts within her family in India over property. She says, "I am not even in the picture." It is not the money that matters, she says, for "there is not much I want, but it hurts emotionally in some ways when I am not taken into consideration, when things are happening there, I am completely outside." Her son Hemat says, "It definitely is a touchy issue" and has led to a family rift.[55]

Ishaan's father, for instance, did not inherit. It is not clear whether it was offered, or whether he on his own withdrew any claims he may have had. Ishaan says, "I think my Dad was largely ambivalent to an inheritance."[56] He states one reason as being that his father was not able to attend the funeral of his father in time, but he also says, "I think that he always felt, from a financial point of view, that he was not really expecting anything because he was the strongest at the time."[57]

Issues of inheritance get particularly protracted and troubled when agricultural land is involved and has passed on to the second generation of migrants. Ambika, sixty-six years old, is a multiple migrant. Her family moved from India to Malaysia, then to Singapore, and then to Australia. Ambika's husband and his father used to send money from Singapore to India. After Ambika's father-in-law died, her husband kept sending money to his father's brother. She says they would take suitcases full of gifts when they visited them. But once Ambika's husband's uncle had died, there was pressure on them from his cousins to sell. Ambika's husband finally had to sell the land. They agreed on a price—perhaps half as much as on the open market. Ambika's husband told his father's brother's sons to go to Singapore to meet with his younger brother, sign the documents, and hand over the money. His brother did not put them up in his house, "fearing they may put something in the food or water. It is not unheard of."[58] After that, Ambika and her husband had no relationship with that part of their family.

Bhagwan also realizes it is not going to be easy to keep his land in India. Bhagwan, sixty-eight years old, was born in Singapore, though his father came from India. In the 1990s, Bhagwan with his wife, Banta, migrated to Australia to be with their son and daughter. Bhagwan tells how his father in Singapore used to send money to his father in India, partly for expenses and partly for the purchase and maintenance of land. When Bhagwan's grandfather died, the land came to his three sons, including Bhagwan's father, and then to Bhagwan and his brothers. Bhagwan's sons and nephews are not interested in the land in India.[59]

As Bhagwan and Banta intend to stay in Australia, selling is the only alternative. Bhagwan balks at this because he says an important part of family history and belonging will disappear. He says, "On the deeds, there is my great-grandfather's name, my grandfather's name, my father's name. It is family history."[60] As they talk of selling the land, stories pour out of some of their friends who entrusted land to a brother-in-law or the father-in-law of one of their sons and nearly lost the land. Bhagwan and Banta talk of people from Malaysia and Singapore who are afraid to have tea in their ancestral village. "We are also afraid," says Bhagwan. Banta says she has heard "they put the pesticide used for wheat in the tea."[61] They are adamant their sons will not go with Bhagwan to India. While Bhagwan still claims to be an insider in that he knows the ways and still has contacts, he realizes that "it is a problem if you sell the land. It is a problem if you don't sell the land."[62]

DIASPORA PHILANTHROPY: MONEY IS LOCAL, TRANSNATIONAL, AND GLOBAL

Diaspora philanthropy displays how global money can be local, national, and global at the same time. In this sense it mimics participation in a transnational community, which can be multilayered without necessarily being multisited. It can be local as with hometown associations in the country or city of destination. It is transnational in the links between communities across borders and global when formed around religion and diaspora. It again becomes local when it needs hands-on implementation to ensure that the projects succeed.

The diaspora philanthropy version of global money has a long history. In China, diaspora philanthropy and global money are perhaps more continuous than elsewhere in Asia. Overseas donations in one fiscal year (July 1937–June 1938) were around $14.5 million. This large-scale giving transformed the traditional hometowns of overseas Chinese in the Pearl River Delta in Guangdong and the Xiamen region in Fujian province into modern societies. Villagers at Meixi in the late 1890s used electricity because of generators bought by Chen Fang (C. Afong), a wealthy Chinese merchant in Hawaii. Investment by overseas Chinese resulted in over 90 percent of businesses in Xiamen until 1949. "Telephone and telegraph companies, electricity, and running water, were all the result of investment by overseas Chinese."[63]

The frequency and intensity of community remittances has increased. This is because of developments in transportation and communication technologies. Receiving nations have also tried to encourage a continued connection with their migrants and thus the amount of money remitted by offering dual nationality and special programs for their welfare in their countries of destination. Federal and state governments in some source countries have also pledged to contribute to projects that are funded by diaspora philanthropy.[64]

Transnational communities come in various forms. Some are migrant extensions of villages, that is, "transnational villagers." Miraflores, a Dominican village where by 1994 over 65 percent of the households had relatives living in the greater Boston metropolitan area, is one such example.[65] Diaspora philanthropy is often channeled through hometown associations (HTAs) to finance community projects in rural localities in Mexico, Central America, and the Caribbean. HTAs raise funds for community projects via pageants, galas, festivals, and raffles. The amounts raised vary from around $2,000 to $8,000 for Guatemalan HTAs, $10,000 for Mexican HTAs, and up to $15,000 a year for El Salvadoran groups. The offer of matching funds from the federal and state governments in Mexico spurred the formation of Mexican HTAs in the United States. The average HTA lasts about ten years. Its influence is diminished with the second generation.[66]

Many of the activities of the HTAs have a religious undertone. These activities range from "repairing and embellishing the hometown church to channeling assistance through the local parish or a religious congregation after a natural disaster."[67] Colombian immigrants in the United States have funded all the equipment for learning new skills that are used in the refuge run by the Vincentine Sisters of Charity in an impoverished quarter of Bogotá to help the poor and the homeless. In the same convent, another nun operates an asylum and schools for orphaned children in the nearby city of Tunja. The money for purchasing the land for the asylum and building the school dormitories came from a New Jersey charity established by a Colombian priest, an immigrant journalist, and volunteers. The impulse to help those left behind connects with the charitable orientation of church-led activities and the needs of churches and congregations in the home countries. Giving through the local parish priest is at times a way of ensuring that the funds are used as intended rather than being eaten up by corrupt officials.[68]

Transnational communities are found across borders and within borders. People continue to be linked to their communities in the source country. Communities are also formed in the country of destination built on transnational ties of religion, language, and place. Active political participation in transnational communities across borders often translates into similarly active community participation in the country of settlement.[69]

Global giving is linked to national giving. Transnational giving in the country of destination is motivated by the same charitable impulses as giving to communities across borders. Migrants often donate to transnational communities in the destination and source countries. Bibi Balwant Kaur's (BibiJi's) story told in chapter 4 substantiates this multisited donation. A twice migrant from India to Kenya and then to the United Kingdom, BibiJi donated to projects in Kenya, India, and the United Kingdom. Kapoor Singh Siddoo's family from British Columbia funded a private hospital in a village in Punjab and also supported a Krishnamurti study center in British Columbia.[70]

While studying the Indian diaspora in Melbourne, I met Rodney, a professional over sixty-five years old. In 1977 he helped buy a building for a Syrian Orthodox Church in Melbourne. His story is one of local and transnational giving, local and global money. Rodney and his wife Rita migrated from Kerala to Melbourne in 1971. The Syrian Orthodox church in Melbourne has been an enduring commitment. It has given him a local community, a connection to the church of his country of origin, and a global link through the global hierarchy of the Syrian Orthodox Church. His wife Rita says, "I didn't think he was . . . such a religious person." Rodney demurs, saying, "It's just that for some reason as you get older you become a bit more (religious)." He adds, "I've got a . . . feeling that . . . you get it back somehow, somewhere else. . . . The blessings come in different ways."[71]

Other kinds of transnational giving may happen through visiting fund-raisers, or the money may be sent directly to the source country. This pattern is illustrated in Ashok's story. I interviewed him as part of an ongoing 2011 and 2012 study in Australia and India on migrant money. Ashok, forty-four, a thrice migrant, moved from India to the United Kingdom when he was three and then from the UK to Australia when he was twenty-six. His story of diaspora philanthropy is of semiorganized giving for education and religion in Gujarat where he was born.

When I visited Ashok and his wife in their home in Australia for the transnational study, professional cleaners were making the house ready for their religious leader and his entourage from Gujarat. As they have a long-standing relationship, Ashok prefers to channel the money from Australia to Gujarat through him via formal bank transfer, so there is accountability. He says that in 2010, AUS$100,000 would have gone from his temple in Sydney to the temples in India for their schools. Often the people who come to collect the money have no references—only fancy pictures. Ashok tells of a group who collected AUS$25,000 for a school in Gujarat. "People gave $50, $100, $500. But there were no receipts, no accountability."

Ashok has also contributed to the new Swaminarayan temple complex that opened in Bhuj, in the Kutch region of Gujarat, in May 2010. It is a temple built of marble and gold on five acres of land to replace the original temple that was destroyed in the 2001 earthquake. He was there for all seven days of the opening. "Every day six hundred thousand to seven hundred thousand people were being fed," he says. Much of the estimated Rs 150 crore (Rs 1.5 billion) came from the UK, Africa, and Australia.

Of this, six to eight crores came from Sydney, Melbourne, and Perth in Australia. At a personal level also, he donated the inheritance he received from his father and mother's side toward building a physics room and a computer lab named after his father. He did it again through the same trusted religious leader and his organization.

Successful projects need continuity of commitment from the migrant donors and on-the-ground commitment. The global and the local have to mesh together. In Punjab, India, the projects that have succeeded have often had members of the migrant family move back to the country of origin and sustainable organizations in the home country that can maintain and expand the project. This is why large projects based on community remittances are initiated by migrants after middle age, and more likely when they are near retirement. The Siddoo story of the hospital in a village in Punjab meant that the Siddoo daughters spent several months a year at the hospital attending to about one hundred patients a day. When they went back to Canada, the hospital's year-round doctor managed the hospital. The sisters are now in their eighties and have had to cut back their activities in the last two or three years. They stay in their separate homes in West Vancouver and continue to support the hospital in Aur, India, and the Krishnamurti Centre near Victoria, Canada.[72]

MIGRANT MONEY MELDS FAMILY MONEY AND MARKET MONEY

The nature of global money as seen in one-way remittances to the source country has changed in the last two decades. Money now flows two ways between middle-income source countries to countries of destination. This two-way flow more closely represents the circulation of care in transnational families. At different life stages as needs and capacities change on both sides, money for family and community is replaced or supplemented by money for business and investment. Remittances which were family and community money at one life stage become market money at another.

Money flowed one way for the Malaysian executive who sobbed at his desk. My family in India also did not have the money to send to me when I migrated to Malaysia in the late 1960s. Even if they could, the 1960s to 1980s in India were years of foreign exchange control. The change in the pattern of migration and remittances struck me when I studied Indian international students and skilled migrants in Melbourne. The students told how the family raised money for their education in India. At times it meant the parents emptied out their retirement fund or sold property. Families also borrowed from relatives and the bank. At first the money flowed from India to Australia. When it was possible, students sent money from Australia to India to help family and to pay off the loan. Family help did not stop at the initial tuition payments. Once the student gained permanent residence, some families helped with the deposit or even the full payment for a house. They helped with setting up a business. Sometimes sizeable amounts of money were transferred when the parents joined their children in Australia and liquidated some property in India. The concept of *migrant money* brings this flow of money from India for education, housing, and business together with the more traditional idea of sending money home. Global money now flows two ways.

The melding together of family and investment money at different life stages from the source and destination countries is illustrated in Charandeep and Girish's stories. I interviewed them as part of the ongoing migrant money study in India and Australia in 2012.

Charandeep's story is one where the parents paid for education. Then Charandeep was able to send money home. And now that his parents have decided to settle in Australia, the plan is to sell property in India to buy a home and investment property in Australia. Charandeep, thirty-three, came to study in Australia in 2005 and is now a permanent resident. He is the only living child of a retired policeman in a regional city in Punjab, India. His parents have a home in the city and agricultural land. They see themselves as a middle-income family. Charandeep's father used the remaining AUS\$15,000 from his provident fund and borrowed AUS\$35,000 from the bank to pay for Charandeep's Australian education.

Charandeep doesn't know the details of the loan but says the interest rate was very high. He arrived with AUS\$4,000 in hand. He knew his father was willing to send him more money if he needed it. Charandeep says, "I remember, exactly after forty days, I found a job." He worked as a kitchen hand in a chocolate factory. His shifts sometimes finished after 1 a.m. and he would miss the last train. He then had to stay overnight with friends. When his mother heard that on those nights he would go to sleep with just a glass of milk, she asked her husband to send him money for a car. Charandeep's father sent him AUS\$4,000.

Charandeep says his father told him he was

even willing to pay me whatever were the living and lodging expenses. . . . I asked him, "Where would you get the money from?" He said, "You don't need to worry. I'll arrange it." I understood he would sell some part of the property to do that.

Charandeep began paying off the loan when he started working. He hopes to pay the last Rs 3.5 lakhs or so (about AUS$6,500) in one go. He bought a car for his father—a Suzuki Alto—on installments. He remembered his mother wore no jewelry. She had sold it forty years earlier to buy the house in which they live in India. He asked his mother, "Do you want to buy any jewelry now?" She said no. But she is very fond of buying [*salwar kameez*] suits and shawls. So now whenever I go back, I buy her five, six shawls." He also gives her AUS$1,000 separately from his father. When he goes to visit, he gives about AUS$200 in money and gifts to the old and needy women in his village. He takes gifts for his extended kin. He also takes AUS$4,000 in cash or sends money through friends who are going to India.

Charandeep's parents have decided to settle in Australia. When I met his father in his home in India, he said, "Our only child is there. It is difficult and expensive to come and go. . . . Yes, in time we will sell our property here."

With this AUS$500,000 or so, the family will buy one house outright in an outer suburb and perhaps an investment property in Australia. In four to five years they might sell their city house in India and buy a flat to have the option of coming and going.

Girish's story illustrates migrant money at a later life stage. He has used his migrant links to get involved in business, philanthropy, and investment in India. Girish and his wife Gori migrated to Australia in 1994 as skilled migrants. Girish was turning fifty when he changed his life and that of his family to work on a project in India in the philanthropic health sector. In order to work there over the medium term, he and Gori have built a three-story house by the beach. It gives the family a long-term option of being in India and Australia. At present the children are not enamored with this possibility. Gori says the children asked her, "Why did you spend so much money on the house in India? You could have bought . . . a flat in the city that we could have used."

Why India? I ask. Gori says, "That's where we were born." Girish says, "I know India, and I think I can probably be the bridge between here and there." Girish says he was at a life stage when he was financially secure in Australia. They have a home in Australia. Their son is in university. The daughter is thirteen so still has a way to go. But his family is not doing without, while he follows his dream. He has been planning such a move for sixteen years, building his networks and working on projects in India. With the current project, he is in India three weeks out of four. His mother and sister in India see more of him. Back in Australia, his wife Gori looks after their daughter and son.

It is difficult to quantify migrant money. It includes two-way remittances, migrant-related trade, investment in business and real estate, and foreign direct investment (FDI). World Bank data on remittances only focus on the money going from the country of destination to the source country. National data on trade and business often do not allow the separation of migrant from non-migrant-related trade and investment. The literatures on trade, FDI, and remittances continue to be separate, though there is an emerging literature that links migrants to direct foreign investment.[73] There is evidence that migrants can stimulate FDI to their countries of origin.[74] About two-thirds of China's cumulative FDI is migrant related, originating from Hong Kong, Taiwan, Macau, and Singapore.[75] The Indian diaspora, on the other hand, has contributed only 1.3 percent of FDI.[76]

In Australia the data are limited on two-way remittances that flow from the education of Indian international students and the greater numbers of skilled migrants. More money flows from India to Australia than the other way around. We are unable as yet to quantify investment in migrant-related business, housing, and FDI. Thinking in terms of migrant money can potentially change the narrative of migration. Migrants can produce "rivers of gold" for the country of destination as well as the source country.

The second Longitudinal Survey of Immigrants to Australia (LSIA), managed by the Department of Immigration and Multicultural and Indigenous Affairs (DIMIA) provides the only available data on money and financial assets brought, received, and sent overseas by new offshore migrants in their first two years. LSIA2 covers 3,124 principal applicants (PAs) who arrived between September 1999 and August 2000. The main finding from LSIA2 is that the Indian-born migrants who arrived between 1999 and 2000 brought and received eighteen times as much as they sent to India in the first two years.[77]

Migrant money, like remittances, can be classified as family money or market money. When Indian families remit family money for international education, these remittances are classified under the export of services from Australia to India. The families of 72,801 Indian international students remitted an estimated AUS$2.1 billion to the Australian economy and generated 21,112 full-time equivalent jobs in 2011. This was money that came from India for the welfare of international students, most of whom saw themselves as potential migrants.[78]

Migrant money and remittances bring together some of the important themes of this book. Placing the social concept of money at the center of the study of globalization enables us to expand the reach of globalization to include the study of global flows of labor, families, and money. Migration, one of the most momentous decisions in the life of individuals and families, becomes a major player in the story of money and globalization. It is the most personal dimension of globalization. Those in the transnational family who have moved and those who have stayed behind cope with new ways of being and seeing. The money they send and receive is family money that on some occasions is seen as trade in services, is invested in businesses or housing, or is part of FDI. These family monies are part of one of the largest international flows of funds to developing countries. Migrant money remains to be quantified on a comparative basis to reveal its importance to the destination countries.

Migrant money is also a case study of the characteristics of global money as it intersects the local, national, and global dimensions of relationships. Senders and recipients at times value family remittances differently, revealing the role of interpretation in the value of money. With diaspora philanthropy, local giving can have a global aim, whereas global giving at times requires local care.

NOTES

1. Supriya Singh, *Bank Negara Malaysia: The First 25 Years, 1959–1984* (Kuala Lumpur: Bank Negara Malaysia, 1984).

2. Jason DeParle, "World Banker and His Cash Return Home," *New York Times*, March 17, 2008.

3. Dilip Ratha, "Workers' Remittances: An Important and Stable Source of External Development Finance," in *Global Development Finance 2003* (Washington, DC: World Bank, 2003).

4. International Organization for Migration, "Facts and Figures," http://www.iom.int/cms/en/sites/iom/home/about-migration/facts--figures-1.html (accessed January 20, 2013).

5. Dilip Ratha, Gemechu Ayana Aga, and Ani Silwal, "Remittances to Developing Countries Will Surpass $400 Billion in 2012," in *Migration and Development Brief* (Washington, DC: Migration and Remittances Unit, Development Prospects Group, World Bank, 2012).

6. Sanket Mohapatra, Dilip Ratha, and Ani Silwa, "Migration and Development Brief 13," World Bank, http://siteresources.worldbank.org/INTPROSPECTS/Resources/334934-1110315015165/MigrationAndDevelopmentBrief13.pdf (accessed May 23, 2011).

7. Ratha, Aga, and Silwal, "Remittances to Developing Countries."

8. Dilip Ratha and Ani Silwal, "Migration and Development Brief 18: Remittance Flows in 2011—an Update," Migration and Remittances Unit, Development Economics (DEC) and Poverty Reduction and Economic Management (PREM) network, World Bank, http://siteresources.worldbank.org/INTPROSPECTS/Resources/334934-1110315015165/MigrationandDevelopmentBrief18.pdf (accessed May 8, 2012).

9. "Remittance Corridors: New Rivers of Gold," *Economist*, April 28–May 4, 2012.

10. Development Prospects Group, "Migration and Development Brief 2," Migration and Remittances Team, World Bank, http://web.worldbank.org/WBSITE/EXTERNAL/NEWS/0,,contentMDK:21124587~pagePK:64257043~piPK:437376~theSitePK:4607,00.html (accessed August 21, 2007).

11. Leonides Buencamino and Sergei Gorbunov, "Informal Money Transfer Systems: Opportunities and Challenges for Development Finance," United Nations, http://www.un.org/esa/esa02dp26.pdf (accessed May 5, 2005).

12. Bimal Ghosh, *Migrants' Remittances and Development: Myths, Rhetoric, and Realities* (Geneva: International Organization for Migration [IOM], 2006).

13. W. L. Cassidy, *Fei-Chien, or Flying Money: A Study of Chinese Underground Banking* (1990).

14. Nikos Passas, "Formalizing the Informal? Problems in the National and International Regulation of Hawala," in *Regulatory Frameworks for Hawala and Other Remittance Systems* (Washington, DC: International Monetary Fund, Monetary and Financial Systems Department, 2005).

15. Personal communication, Dilip Ratha, October 20, 2011.

16. Personal communication, Dilip Ratha, October 20, 2011.

17. Lisa Cliggett, "Remitting the Gift: Zambian Mobility and Anthropological Insights for Migration Studies," *Population, Space and Place* 11 (2005).

18. Madeleine Wong, "The Gendered Politics of Remittances in Ghanaian Transnational Families," *Economic Geography* 82, no. 4 (2006).

19. Arthur W. Helweg, "Emigrant Remittances: Their Nature and Impact on a Punjabi Village," *New Community* 10, no. 3 (1983); A. S. Oberai and H. K. Manmohan Singh, "Migration, Remittances and Rural Development: Findings of a Case Study in the Indian Punjab," *International Labour Review* 119, no. 2 (1980); Christiane Kuptsch and Philip Martin, "Migration and Development: Remittances and Cooperation with the Diaspora," International Institute for Labour Studies (IILS), http://www.gtz.de/migration-and-development/download/dokumentation-plenum2.pdf (accessed August 25, 2004).

20. Roger Ballard, "The South Asian Presence in Britain and Its Transnational Connections," in *Culture and Economy in the Indian Diaspora*, ed. Bhikhu Parekh, Gurharpal Singh, and Steven Vertovec (London: Routledge, 2003); Global Development Finance, "Global Development Finance: Harnessing Cyclical Gains for Development 2004," World Bank, http://siteresources.worldbank.org/GDFINT2004/Home/20177154/GDF_2004%20pdf.pdf (accessed August 25, 2004); World Bank, "Global Development Finance: 2004," http://siteresources.worldbank.org/GDFINT2004/Home/20175281/gdf_appendix%20A

.pdf (accessed August 6, 2004); "Global Economic Prospects 2006: Economic Implications of Remittances and Migration," World Bank, http://econ.worldbank.org/external/default/main?pagePK=64165259&theSitePK=469372&piPK=64165421&menuPK=6416 6322&entityID=000112742_20051114174928 (accessed August 23, 2007); Manuel Orozco, "Transnationalism and Development: Trends and Opportunities In: Latin America," in *Remittances: Development Impact and Future Prospects*, ed. S. M. Maimbo and Dilip Ratha (Washington, DC: World Bank, 2005); Tolu Muliaina, "Mismatched Perceptions: Views on Remittance Obligations among Remittance Senders and Recipients," in *Remittances, Microfinance and Development: Building the Links*, ed. Judith Shaw (Brisbane: Foundation for Development Cooperation, 2006); R. P. C. Brown and B. Poirine, "Weak vs. Strong Altruism: A Model of Migrants' Remittances with Human Capital Investment and Intrafamilial Transfers," *International Migration Review* 39, no. 2 (2005); Louis DeSipio, *Sending Money Home . . . for Now: Remittances and Immigrant Adaptation in the United States* (Tomas Rivera Policy Institute, 2000), 30.

21. Catalina Amuedo-Dorantes and Susan Pozo, "Remittances, Health Insurance, and Healthcare Use of Populations in Origin Communities: Evidence from Mexico," PAA 2005 Submission (n.d.), http://paa2005.princeton.edu/download.aspx?submissionId=51499 (accessed April 27, 2009); Ghosh, *Migrants' Remittances and Development: Myths, Rhetoric, and Realities*; DeSipio, *Sending Money Home . . . for Now*; A. Quisumbing and S. McNiven, "Moving Forward, Looking Back: The Impact of Migration and Remittances on Assets, Consumption, and Credit Constraints in the Rural Philippines," *Journal of Development Studies* 46, no. 1 (2010); M. Gabbarot and C. Clarke, "Social Capital, Migration and Development in the Valles Centrales of Oaxaca, Mexico: Non-Migrants and Communities of Origin Matter," *Bulletin of Latin American Research* 29, no. 2 (2010); Prema A. Kurien, *Kaleidoscopic Ethnicity: International Migration and the Reconstruction of Community Identities in India* (New Delhi: Oxford University Press, 2002).

22. Luin Goldring, "Family and Collective Remittances to Mexico: A Multi-Dimensional Typology," *Development and Change* 35, no. 4 (2004): 807.

23. Goldring, "Family and Collective Remittances to Mexico."

24. Dilip Ratha, Sanket Mohapatra, and Ani Silwal, "Migration and Development Brief 12: Outlook for Remittance Flows 2010–11," Migration and Remittances Team, Development Prospects Group, World Bank, http://siteresources.worldbank.org/INTPROSPECTS/Resources/334934-1110315015165/MigrationAndDevelopmentBrief12.pdf (accessed July 28, 2010); Dilip Ratha and Sanket Mohapatra, "Preliminary Estimates of Diaspora Savings," Migration and Remittances Unit, World Bank, http://siteresources.worldbank.org/TOPICS/Resources/214970-1288877981391/MigrationAndDevelopmentBrief14_DiasporaSavings.pdf (accessed February 5, 2011).

25. Ghosh, *Migrants' Remittances and Development*, 96.

26. Parminder Bhachu, "New Cultural Forms and Transnational South Asian Women: Culture, Class, and Consumption among British South Asian Women in the Diaspora," in *Nation and Migration: The Politics of Space in the South Asian Diaspora*, ed. Peter Van der Veer (Philadelphia: University of Pennsylvania Press, 1995).

27. Deborah F. Bryceson and Ulla Vuorela, "Transnational Families in the Twenty-First Century," in *The Transnational Family: New European Frontiers and Global Networks*, ed. Deborah Bryceson and Ulla Vuorela (New York: Berg, 2002), 3.

28. Janet Finch, "Displaying Families," *Sociology* 41, no. 1 (2007).

29. Brenda S. A. Yeoh, Shirlena Huang, and Theodora Lam, "Transnationalizing the 'Asian' Family: Imaginaries, Intimacies and Strategic Intents," *Global Networks* 5, no. 4 (2005).

30. Finch, "Displaying Families."

31. Sean McKenzie and Cecilia Menjívar, "The Meanings of Migration, Remittances and Gifts: Views of Honduran Women Who Stay," *Global Networks* 11, no. 1 (2010): 69.

32. McKenzie and Menjívar, "The Meanings of Migration," 70.

33. Stephanie Riak Akuei, "Remittances as Unforeseen Burdens: The Livelihoods and Social Obligations of Sudanese Refugees," in *Global Migration Perspectives* (Geneva: Global Commission on International Migration, 2005).

34. Anna Lindley, "The Early-Morning Phonecall: Remittances from a Refugee Diaspora Perspective," *Journal of Ethnic and Migration Studies* 35, no. 8 (2009).

35. World Bank, *At Home and Away: Expanding Job Opportunities for Pacific Islanders through Labor Mobility* (Washington, DC: World Bank, 2006).

36. Wong, "The Gendered Politics of Remittances."

37. Kurien, *Kaleidoscopic Ethnicity*.

38. Rubén G. Rumbaut, "Severed or Sustained Attachments? Language, Identity, and Imagined Communities in the Post-Immigrant Generation," in *The Changing Face of Home: The Transnational Lives of the Second Generation*, ed. Peggy Levitt and Mary C. Waters (New York: Sage, 2002), 89.

39. Rumbaut, "Severed or Sustained Attachments?," 91.

40. Loretta Baldassar and Laura Merla, eds., *Transnational Families, Migration and Kin-Work: From Care Chains to Care Circulation* (Routledge, forthcoming).

41. Supriya Singh, Shanthi Robertson, and Anuja Cabraal, "Transnational Family Money: Remittances, Gifts and Inheritance," *Journal of Intercultural Studies* 33, no. 5 (2012).

42. Singh, Robertson, and Cabraal, "Transnational Family Money."

43. Kurien, *Kaleidoscopic Ethnicity*; Wong, "The Gendered Politics of Remittances."

44. Wong, "The Gendered Politics of Remittances," 368.

45. Akuei, "Remittances as Unforeseen Burdens," 7.

46. Akuei, "Remittances as Unforeseen Burdens," 10.

47. Heather A. Horst, "The Blessings and Burdens of Communication: Cell Phones in Jamaican Transnational Social Fields," *Global Networks* 6, no. 2 (2006): 156.

48. Viviana A. Zelizer, *The Purchase of Intimacy* (Princeton, NJ: Princeton University Press, 2005), 225.

49. Loretta Baldassar, Cora Vellekoop Baldock, and Raelene Wilding, *Families Caring across Borders: Migration, Ageing and Transnational Caregiving* (New York: Palgrave Macmillan, 2007).

50. Karen Isaksen Leonard, *Locating Home: India's Hyderabadis Abroad* (Stanford, CA: Stanford University Press, 2007).

51. John Connell and Richard P. C. Brown, "Remittances in the Pacific: An Overview," Asian Development Bank, http://www.adb.org/Documents/Reports/Remittances-Pacific/default.asp (accessed October 8, 2007).

52. Singh, Robertson, and Cabraal, "Transnational Family Money"; Supriya Singh, Anuja Cabraal, and Shanthi Robertson, "Remittances as a Currency of Care: A Focus on 'Twice Migrants' among the Indian Diaspora in Australia," *Journal of Comparative Family Studies* 41, no. 2 (2010).

53. Singh, Robertson, and Cabraal, "Transnational Family Money."

54. Singh, Robertson, and Cabraal, "Transnational Family Money," 485.

55. Singh, Robertson, and Cabraal, "Transnational Family Money," 486.

56. Singh, Robertson, and Cabraal, "Transnational Family Money," 486.

57. Singh, Robertson, and Cabraal, "Transnational Family Money," 486.

58. Singh, Cabraal, and Robertson, "Remittances as a Currency of Care," 255.

59. Singh, Cabraal, and Robertson, "Remittances as a Currency of Care," 255.

60. Singh, Cabraal, and Robertson, "Remittances as a Currency of Care," 256.

61. Singh, Cabraal, and Robertson, "Remittances as a Currency of Care," 256.

62. Singh, Cabraal, and Robertson, "Remittances as a Currency of Care," 256.

63. Xiao-huang Yin and Zhiyong Lan, "Why Do They Give? Chinese American Transnational Philanthropy since the 1970s," in *Diaspora Philanthropy and Equitable Development in China and India*, ed. Peter F. Geithner, Paula D. Johnson, and Lincoln C. Chen (Cambridge, MA: Global Equity Initiative, Asia Center, Harvard University, 2004), 79.

64. Alejandro Portes and Rubén G. Rumbaut, *Immigrant America: A Portrait* (Berkeley: University of California Press, 2006); Peggy Levitt, "Transnational Migration: Taking Stock and Future Directions," *Global Networks* 1, no. 3 (2001).

65. Levitt, "Transnational Migration: Taking Stock and Future Directions."

66. Paula Doherty Johnson, *Diaspora Philanthropy: Influences, Initiatives, and Issues* (Philanthropic Initiative Inc. and Global Equity Initiative, Harvard University, 2007).

67. Portes and Rumbaut, *Immigrant America*, 312.

68. Portes and Rumbaut, *Immigrant America*, 311–12.

69. Portes and Rumbaut, *Immigrant America*, 312.

70. Hugh Johnston, "The Sikhs of British Columbia and Their Philanthropy in Punjab," in *Sikh Diaspora Philanthropy in Punjab: Global Giving for Local Good*, ed. Verne A. Dusenbery and Darshan S. Tatla (New Delhi: Oxford University Press, 2009).

71. Supriya Singh, "Transnational Community and Money in the Indian Diaspora in Melbourne" (paper presented at the City, Community and Globalisation Roundtable, Melbourne, Australia, June 9–10, 2011).

72. Hugh J. M. Johnston, *Jewels of the Qila: The Remarkable Story of an Indo-Canadian Family* (Vancouver: University of British Columbia Press, 2011).

73. Jen Dickinson and Adrian J. Bailey, "(Re)Membering Diaspora: Uneven Geographies of Indian Dual Citizenship," *Political Geography* 26 (2007); R. Chami, C. Fullenkamp, and S. Jahjah, "Are Immigrant Remittance Flows a Source of Capital for Development?," *IMF Staff Papers* 52, no. 1 (2005); Kellee S. Tsai, "Friends, Family or Foreigners? The Political Economy of Diasporic FDI and Remittances in China and India," *China Report* 46, no. 4 (2010).

74. Beata S. Javorcik et al., "Migrant Networks and Foreign Direct Investment," *Journal of Development Economics* 94, no. 2 (2011).

75. Tsai, "Friends, Family or Foreigners?"

76. PTI, "India Not after NRIs' Money, Montek Tells Diaspora," *Economic Times*, January 9, 2011.

77. Supriya Singh and Liliya Gatina, "Migrant Money: Two-Way Flows between Australia and India" (unpublished, RMIT University, 2012).

78. Singh and Gatina, "Migrant Money: Two-Way Flows."

CHAPTER 9

RETHINKING MONEY, TECHNOLOGY, AND GLOBALIZATION

Thinking of globalization and money has taken me from shell money in Kiribati to M-PESA in Kenya, GCash in the Philippines, and the QQ coin in China. This journey has covered new and old ways of banking and payments, cash and electronic money, the *shagun* and the *ang-pow*, Dinka remittances from the United States, money among the unbanked and women, and money in markets and households. So what has changed and what has remained constant about money, banking, and payments in a global world?

CHANGE AND CONSTANCY OF MONEY

Seeing Kiribati shell money in the Australian Museum in Sydney, I became conscious of my own use of money. I receive my pay and dividends by direct credit. I use BPay and direct debit to pay my bills online, Internet bank transfers for donations, the stored-value Myki card for public transport, PayPal for Skype, and a credit card for groceries online. I can pay and receive money across distance, though I still give cash for a latte at the train platform. I pay the cleaning lady and the gardener in cash. I also place AUS$50 in a colored envelope as a ritual gift for a wedding in the Sikh community in Melbourne. I pay the plumber and handyman by check, though the electrician prefers direct credit. The last check I received was nearly a year ago, and it was from overseas. I continue to use a mix of forms and channels of money. The mix has changed with the smaller use of checks and cash.

Like the shell money and pigs in Vanuatu or cattle and *tugudu* cloth among the Tiv of Nigeria for ceremonial payments, I give gold jewelry at the marriages of very close kin or friends who are like family. My sister in New York most often gives me a gift of gold when I visit. Gold is the medium of remembering—not just the person but a generational history of relationship.

The biggest change is being able to send money online across borders and using it anywhere in the world. I transfer money from my bank account in Melbourne to my account in Delhi. I can now withdraw this money by ATM in Dharamshala. Bank drafts to correspondent banks and interstate checks belong to a past era. My friends discuss which credit card will minimize fees for overseas cash withdrawals. Money was always global following routes of trade and empire. But now money has become global because I can transmit it across borders to family, community, or investment. It is not as instantaneous as M-PESA, but two days is better than it used to be.

The use of digital channels to pay and receive money has become traditional in high-income countries, particularly for the young. The mobile phone is transforming money in low-income countries where most of the people are unbanked. It was unthinkable a decade ago that a person in Africa could send money instantaneously via a mobile phone to his mother in a village two hundred kilometers away.

These changes are not universal. I think of Irene in Papua New Guinea and Khadeja in Bangladesh who do not have a bank account. Irene also does not have a mobile phone, though she is able to use her husband's phone. Nomsa in South Africa does have a bank account because her government benefits are directly credited to her account. But most of her transactions continue to be in cash and face to face. For them the biggest change would be to have a savings bank account that is affordable and accessible; a hassle-free loan to deal with emergencies and to build up health, education, and wealth; and insurance to protect goods that cannot be easily replaced. For Amar and Amrit in Dharamshala, the important change would be to know how much money they have, preferably in a bank account, and the power to use it as they wish.

Despite these changes in the technology of the transfer of money, there is a constancy about money. This is true for shell money in the Pacific, Pay-Pal, Ithaca HOURS, bitcoin, the QQ coin in China, and the US dollar. Trust remains at the center of what defines money. Money is valued only when it is used in networks of trust and common systems of meaning. In Kiribati, people believed in shell money as money. I also believe the same thing with today's electronic money. So do the people with whom I transact.

Multiple monies continue to be important. I use different kinds of money to fit the social meanings of activities and relationships. Just as the precolonial Tiv would not use a brass rod to buy food, I will not give a gift of gold to an acquaintance. I will pay cash for my coffee but not to my plumber. I receive and pay money online for an increasing range of activities and relationships, but the *shagun* is always handed over in cash that is suitably packaged.

Money remains personal in intimate relationships. Money is impersonal in some market relationships and personal in others. Choosing the appropriate form and channel of money means connecting it with the social meanings of activities and relationships. I do not have a personal relationship with a bank. I never did. Perhaps it was because I was a woman and most bankers used to be male. Perhaps it was that I neither deposited nor borrowed enough to be of interest to the branch manager. Multiple bank accounts to separate different kinds of money also dilute the relationship with one particular bank or banker. The bank is important, for as yet it is the main way I manage money in the market and in my personal life.

Buying a house is personal, but choosing the mortgage is a matter of price and accompanying conditions. Donating for an important cause is personal. The reason and choice of an investment may be personal and connect to developing freedoms and capabilities. But the process of transmitting money and negotiating contracts and guarantees is impersonal.

The household continues to be an important focus for the management and control of money. It is a way of negotiating power and displaying trust and commitment. Having money, as opposed to being poor, remains an enabler of choice, independence, and interdependence. Women all over the world feel responsible for the welfare of the household and children. But with all other aspects of money, there are important cultural differences in the meanings and uses of money.

Money continues to be a medium of relationships. The emotional content of money has remained important across countries. In every culture and society there are stories of families torn apart because of disputes over inheritance or trust funds. These are issues about money. But deeper still, the hurt is about love and trust and a person's belonging to the family.

RETHINKING GLOBALIZATION

Placing the social and cultural concept of money at the center leads to a more inclusive and personal picture of globalization. Globalization focuses rightly on the greater interconnectedness of financial markets and international financial organizations. But it also needs to include half the world that is unbanked. An emphasis on money in the market has to connect with women's and men's roles in money management and control in the household.

This inclusive approach brings issues of gender and social exclusion to the fore. It includes women who work at the bottom of global supply chains distant from the regulations ensuring "decent work." It links concerns about equity and fairness to economic globalization. Some of the most important global initiatives relating to money and the economy address financial exclusion and poverty in developing countries. So the most vigorous conversations regarding globalization and some of the most important exchanges of ideas are happening between countries of the global South.

As money is shaped by social relationships and cultural values, cultural differences become an important focus for the study of globalization. This is a useful corrective, for money can be global, national, and local at the same time. Banks are part of global exchanges, but they are subject to national regulation. Their products and services are influenced by cultural variations in family forms and practices.

Cultural and national differences limit generalizations about economic globalization and the use of ICTs. We need to ask, do the broad contours of globalization and technology apply to the unbanked, the poor, and women? Would it work for Irene in Papua New Guinea or for Khadeja in Bangladesh? Is financial inclusion served by a focus on households if Amar in Dharamshala did not know she had a joint account until her husband died?

The social and cultural concept of money personalizes the story of globalization. Reading of financial markets, of the global financial crisis, and of trade and investment most often leaves us in the world of numbers, abstraction, and negotiations of national economic policy and international standards. But globalization deeply affects the lives and worldviews of migrants and those they leave behind. Mobility and migration can change deeply held notions of what a family is, of the "proper" roles of men and women as they relate to money, and of the intimacy involved in communication across distance. Mobility changes ideas of belonging and often fosters a comfort with multiple national identities. A person's friendship networks change. Families move not only between one country and another but are dispersed globally so that visits to multiple countries are family visits and another version of going home.

THE TRANSFORMATIVE ROLE OF ICTs

The new information and communication technologies have made globalization more connected and money more mobile and electronic. At the same time, socioeconomic factors, cultural differences, and social relationships continue to shape access, use, and design of ICTs.

M-PESA was introduced in Kenya in 2007. In five years it has changed the money landscape and the payments ecosystem. The M-PESA model has gone global across the South. Success has varied depending on how well the success factors have come together in different countries. The success of M-PESA resulted from a coming together of Vodafone, a global mobile telephone operator; a national regulator who was focused on enlarging the reach of formal payments and addressing financial inclusion; and a local subsidiary, Safaricom, who had a business model that could tap into the needs of Kenyans to more easily send money home and deliver profits to the agents, Safaricom, and Vodafone.

M-PESA also signals that the center of innovation relating to money and payments has moved to the South. People interested in financial inclusion and mobile money congregate around iHub on Ngong Road, Nairobi. Regulators interested in spreading the reach of banks visit Brazil. Microfinance, one of the most important global initiatives for addressing poverty and particularly women's marginalization, originated in Bangladesh. It is these innovations that address the most pressing global problems of financial exclusion and poverty.

There are exciting developments in new methods of payment and banking, particularly in the United States. The excitement lies in their attempts at placing user needs at the center of their design. These are still too new to judge them by their use. For the most part, they are confined to the United States, addressing a young, professional, and technically adept user group. They are yet to be tested in a global framework.

Some of the far-reaching innovations in the United States, Kenya, and India focus on new ways of using old technologies, like prepaid cards and the branch. They use modern technologies to provide behind-the-scenes support. The transformative aspects of the ICTs lie in mixing new and old technologies in different ways. Green Dot in the United States combines the prepaid card with the possibility of online deposits in return for a lower fee.

M-PESA uses the mobile phone as a channel for the transfer of cash through a face-to-face agent network that provides an accessible point of personal interaction. Kshetriya Gramin Financial Services (KGFS) in India revolves around the physical branch in areas that are inadequately served by other financial institutions. Branch staff visit a customer's home to ask about the family's wealth management goals. KGFS connects with banks and insurance companies via new technologies to provide a complete portfolio of financial services.

Some of the steps ahead could involve further mixes of the old and the new. Mobile money has exciting possibilities for people who are banked and unbanked. It is moving in the direction of offering better tools for savings toward one's goals. Microfinance that deals effectively with small loans is also becoming more flexible and is incorporating savings. But none of them as yet offer a combination of day-to-day management of money, the ability to build medium- and long-term savings, and flexible credit. It is as if we need to take a dash of what Simple is doing in the United States regarding money management, add the social network and comfort of RoSCAs in South Africa, connect to a bank for credit, and access an insurance company for protection. Solutions that address the needs of the banked and the unbanked, men and women, and the poor and the not so poor will be centered on people and their activities in different cultural contexts. It will also mean ensuring that the providers are able to get a suitable market return.

It is difficult to predict whether banks on their own or in combination with MNOs or aggregators of financial services will take the global lead. It is also not possible to detail the future mix of cash, checks, and online forms of money. The important question is not whether cash will continue or not, but how people in a global world, in different cultural contexts, can use money in ways that empower them.

REFERENCES

"Aadhar-Linked Norm May Be Relaxed." *The Pioneer*, December 11, 2012.

Adam, Karla. "Occupy Wall Street Protests Go Global." *Washington Post*, October 15, 2011. http://articles.washingtonpost.com/2011-10-15/world/35277659_1_police-officers-protesters-debt-crisis.

Agarwal, Bina. *A Field of One's Own: Gender and Land Rights in South Asia*. 2nd ed. Cambridge: Cambridge University Press, 1996.

Akin, David. "Cash and Shell Money in Kwaio, Solomon Islands." In *Money and Modernity: State and Local Currencies in Melanesia*, ed. David Akin and Joel Robbins, 103–30. Pittsburgh: University of Pittsburgh Press, 1999.

Akuei, Stephanie Riak. "Remittances as Unforeseen Burdens: The Livelihoods and Social Obligations of Sudanese Refugees." In *Global Migration Perspectives*. Geneva: Global Commission on International Migration, 2005.

Amuedo-Dorantes, Catalina, and Susan Pozo. "Remittances, Health Insurance, and Healthcare Use of Populations in Origin Communities: Evidence from Mexico." PAA 2005 Submission, n.d. http://paa2005.princeton.edu/download.aspx?submissionId=51499 (accessed April 27, 2009).

Ananth, Bindu, Greg Chen, and Stephen Rasmussen. *The Pursuit of Complete Financial Inclusion: The KGFS Model in India*. Washington, DC: CGAP and IFMR Trust, 2012.

Australian Securities and Investments Commission (ASIC). "Electronic Funds Transfer Code of Conduct: As Revised by the Australian Securities and Investments Commission's EFT Working Group." http://www.asic.gov.au/asic/pdflib.nsf/LookupByFileName/EFT-Code-as-amended-from-1-July-2012.pdf/$file/EFT-Code-as-amended-from-1-July-2012.pdf (accessed October 27, 2012).

Bagnall, John, Sophia Chong, and Kylie Smith. *Strategic Review of Innovation in the Payments System: Results of the Reserve Bank of Australia's 2010 Consumer Payments Use Study*. Reserve Bank of Australia, 2011.

Bagnall, John, and Darren Flood. "Cash Use in Australia: New Survey Evidence." *Reserve Bank of Australia Bulletin*, September 2011, 55–62.

Bakardjieva, Maria, and Richard Smith. "The Internet in Everyday Life." *New Media and Society* 3, no. 1 (2001): 67–83.

Baldassar, Loretta, Cora Vellekoop Baldock, and Raelene Wilding. *Families Caring across Borders: Migration, Ageing and Transnational Caregiving*. New York: Palgrave Macmillan, 2007.

Baldassar, Loretta, and Laura Merla, eds. *Transnational Families, Migration and Kin-Work: From Care Chains to Care Circulation*. Routledge, forthcoming.

Ballard, Roger. "The South Asian Presence in Britain and Its Transnational Connections." In *Culture and Economy in the Indian Diaspora*, ed. Bhikhu Parekh, Gurharpal Singh, and Steven Vertovec, 197–222. London: Routledge, 2003.

Banerjee, Abhijit, Pranab Bardhan, Esther Duflo, Erica Field, Dean Karlan, Asim Khwaja, Dilip Mookherjee, Rohini Pande, and Raghuram Rajan. "Help Microfinance, Don't Kill It." *Indian Express*, November 26, 2010. http://www.indianexpress.com/news/help -microfinance-dont-kill-it/716105/0.

Banerjee, Abhijit V., and Esther Duflo. *Poor Economics: A Radical Rethinking of the Way to Fight Global Poverty*. New York: PublicAffairs, 2011.

Banerjee, Shweta S. "Building India's Model of Agent Banking." http://www.cgap.org/blog/ building-india%E2%80%99s-model-agent-banking (accessed September 27, 2012).

Bank for International Settlements. *Detailed Tables on Preliminary Locational and Consolidated Banking Statistics at End-June 2012*. Basel: Monetary and Economic Department, Bank for International Settlements, 2012.

———. *Securities Statistics and Syndicated Loans*. Basel: Bank for International Settlements, 2012.

———. *Semiannual OTC Derivatives Statistics at End-June 2012*. 2012.

Bank Negara Malaysia. "Policymakers Concur on Need to Harness Technological Advancements to Widen Access to Financial Services." http://www.bnm.gov.my/index .php?ch=8&pg=14&ac=1958 (accessed December 8, 2009).

"The Bank That Likes to Say Less." *Economist*, September 22, 2012. http://www.economist .com/node/21563302.

Bankable Frontier Associates. "'Time for Cash to Cash Out?' Scoping Kenya's Path to a Cash-Lite Society." In *FSD Insights*. FSD Kenya, 2012.

Banking Codes and Standards Board of India. "Code of Bank's Commitments to Customers." http://www.bcsbi.org.in/Code_of_Banks.html (accessed May 7, 2008).

Banyan. "On the Prowl." *Economist*, December 1, 2012. http://www.economist.com/ news/asia/21567363-unexpected-figure-emerging-most-powerful-politician-indias -government-prowl.

Basham, A. L. *The Wonder That Was India*. New York: Grove Press, 1954.

Basu, Srimati. "*Haklenewali*: Indian Women's Negotiations of Discourses of Inheritance." In *Dowry & Inheritance*, ed. Srimati Basu, 151–70. New Delhi: Women Unlimited, 2005.

———. "The Politics of Giving: Dowry and Inheritance as Feminist Issues." In *Dowry & Inheritance*, ed. Srimati Basu, i–liv. New Delhi: Women Unlimited, 2005.

Bauman, Z. *Liquid Love: On the Frailty of Human Bonds*. Cambridge, UK: Polity Press, 2003.

Beck-Gernsheim, Elisabeth. *Reinventing the Family: In Search of New Lifestyles*. Cambridge, UK: Polity Press, 2002.

"Berlin Becomes Latest 'Bitcoin Hotspot.'" http://www.bitcoinmoney.com/post/35733263353/ bitcoin-clusters (accessed November 25, 2012).

Bertrand, Marianne, Sendhil Mullainathan, and Eldar Shafir. "Behavioral Economics and Marketing in Aid of Decision Making among the Poor." *Journal of Public Policy and Marketing* 25, no. 1 (2006): 8–23.

Bhachu, Parminder. "New Cultural Forms and Transnational South Asian Women: Culture, Class, and Consumption among British South Asian Women in the Diaspora." In *Nation and Migration: The Politics of Space in the South Asian Diaspora*, ed. Peter Van der Veer, 222–44. Philadelphia: University of Pennsylvania Press, 1995.

Bhagwati, Jagdish. *In Defense of Globalization*. Oxford: Oxford University Press, 2004, 2007.

Bijker, Wiebe E., and John Law. "General Introduction." In *Shaping Technology/Building Society: Studies in Sociotechnical Change*, ed. Wiebe E. Bijker and John Law, 1–14. Cambridge, MA: MIT Press, 1992.

BIS Committee on Payment and Settlement Systems. *Innovations in Retail Payments*. Basle: Bank for International Settlements (BIS), 2012.

———. *Statistics on Payment, Clearing and Settlement Systems in the CPSS Countries—Figures for 2011—Preliminary Release*. Basle: Bank for International Settlements (BIS), 2012.

Bloch, Maurice. "The Symbolism of Money in Imerina." In *Money and the Morality of Exchange*, ed. J. Parry and M. Bloch, 165–90. Cambridge: Cambridge University Press, 1989.

Bohannan, Paul. "The Impact of Money on an African Subsistence Economy." *Journal of Economic History* 19, no. 4 (1959): 491–503.

Bold, Chris. "Does Branchless Banking Reach Poor People? The Evidence from India." http://www.cgap.org/blog/does-branchless-banking-reach-poor-people-evidence-india (accessed 2012).

Brown, John Seely, and Paul Duguid. *The Social Life of Information*. Boston: Harvard Business School Press, 2000.

Brown, Richard P. C., and Bernard Poirine. "A Model of Migrants' Remittances with Human Capital Investment and Intrafamilial Transfers." *International Migration Review* 39, no. 2 (2005): 407–38.

———. "Weak vs. Strong Altruism: A Model of Migrants' Remittances with Human Capital Investment and Intrafamilial Transfers." *International Migration Review* 39, no. 2 (2005).

Bryceson, Deborah F., and Ulla Vuorela. "Transnational Families in the Twenty-First Century." In *The Transnational Family: New European Frontiers and Global Networks*, ed. Deborah Bryceson and Ulla Vuorela, 3–30. New York: Berg, 2002.

Buencamino, Leonides, and Sergei Gorbunov. "Informal Money Transfer Systems: Opportunities and Challenges for Development Finance." United Nations. http://www.un.org/esa/esa02dp26.pdf (accessed May 5, 2005).

Bullock, Michele. "A Guide to the Card Payments System Reforms." *Reserve Bank of Australia Bulletin*, September 2010, 51–59.

Bustillos, Maria. "The Bitcoin Boom." *New Yorker*, April 2, 2013. http://www.newyorker.com/online/blogs/elements/2013/04/the-future-of-bitcoin.html.

Cabraal, Anuja. "The Impact of Microfinance on the Capabilities of Participants." PhD dissertation, RMIT University, 2011.

Cassidy, W. L. *Fei-Chien, or Flying Money: A Study of Chinese Underground Banking.* 1990.

Cetina, Karin Knorr, and Alex Preda. Introduction to *The Sociology of Financial Markets*, ed. Karin Knorr Cetina and Alex Preda, 1–14. Oxford: Oxford University Press, 2005.

CGAP. "India Banking Agents Survey 2012." http://www.cgap.org/data/india-banking -agents-survey-2012 (accessed November 23, 2012).

———. *Update on Regulation of Branchless Banking in India.* CGAP, 2010.

CGAP and DFID. "Scenarios for Branchless Banking in 2020." www.cgap.org/gm/docu ment-1.9.40599/FN57.pdf (accessed December 6, 2009).

Chami, R., C. Fullenkamp, and S. Jahjah. "Are Immigrant Remittance Flows a Source of Capital for Development?" *IMF Staff Papers* 52, no. 1 (2005): 55–81.

Chang, Mariko Lin. *Shortchanged: Why Women Have Less Wealth and What Can Be Done about It.* Oxford: Oxford University Press, 2010.

Chaves, Eric. "Simple's Pitch: A No-Fee, No Hassle Bank Account." CNN Money. http:// money.cnn.com/2011/12/20/technology/simple_bank/index.htm (accessed November 26, 2012).

Cheal, David. *The Gift Economy.* London: Routledge, 1988.

Chen, Adrian. "The Underground Website Where You Can Buy Any Drug Imaginable." http://gawker.com/5805928/the-underground-website-where-you-can-buy-any-drug -imaginable (accessed January 16, 2013).

Chen, Greg. "Eko's Mobile Banking: Demonstrating the Power of a Basic Payments Product." CGAP, 2012. http://www.cgap.org/blog/eko%E2%80%99s-mobile-banking -demonstrating-power-basic-payments-product.

Chesler, P., and E. J. Goodman. *Women, Money and Power.* New York: William Morrow, 1976.

Cliggett, Lisa. "Remitting the Gift: Zambian Mobility and Anthropological Insights for Migration Studies." *Population, Space and Place* 11 (2005): 35–48.

Cohan, William D. *Money and Power: How Goldman Sachs Came to Rule the World.* London: Allen Lane, 2011.

"Coinbase, First Crowd Funded Bitcoin Company, Raises over $600k." Asian Development Bank. https://www.privateinternetaccess.com/blog/tag/crowd-funding (accessed November 25, 2012).

Collins, Daryl, Jonathan Morduch, Stuart Rutherford, and Orlanda Ruthven. *Portfolios of the Poor: How the World's Poor Live on $2 a Day.* Princeton, NJ: Princeton University Press, 2009.

Connell, John, and Richard P. C. Brown. "Remittances in the Pacific: An Overview." Asian Development Bank. http://www.adb.org/Documents/Reports/Remittances-Pacific/ default.asp (accessed October 8, 2007).

Connolly, Chris, M. Georgouras, L. Hems, and L. Wolfson. *Measuring Financial Exclusion in Australia.* Centre for Social Impact (CSI)—University of New South Wales, 2011.

Cook, Nancy. "Deploying Electrons to Battle . . . the Biggest and Baddest Banks." *National Journal*, June 7, 2012.

Crandall, Angela, Albert Otieno, Leonida Mutuku, Jessica Colaço, Jasper Grosskurth, and Peter Otieno. *Mobile Phone Usage at the Kenyan Base of the Pyramid: Final Report.* Nairobi: iHub Research and Research Solutions Africa, 2012.

Crotty, Ann. "Analysis: UK Bank Seeks to Apply Lessons in New Continental Push." *The Star*, September 25, 2012.

Dalberg Global Development Advisors. *CGAP Landscape Study on International Remittances through Mobile Money: Final Report.* 2012.

Davies, Glyn. *A History of Money: From Ancient Times to the Present Day.* Cardiff: University of Wales Press, 1994.

Dejardin, Amelita King. *Gender Dimensions of Globalization.* International Labour Organization, 2008.

Demirguc-Kunt, Asli, and Leora Klapper. *Measuring Financial Inclusion: The Global Findex Database.* Washington, DC: World Bank, 2012.

DeParle, Jason. "World Banker and His Cash Return Home." *New York Times,* March 17, 2008. http://www.nytimes.com/2008/03/17/world/asia/17remit.html.

Dertouzos, Michael L. *The Unfinished Revolution: Human-Centered Computers and What They Can Do for Us.* New York: HarperCollins, 2001.

DeSipio, Louis. *Sending Money Home . . . for Now: Remittances and Immigrant Adaptation in the United States.* Tomas Rivera Policy Institute, 2000.

Development Prospects Group. "Migration and Development Brief 2." Migration and Remittances Team. World Bank. http://web.worldbank.org/WBSITE/EXTERNAL/NEWS/0,,contentMDK:21124587~pagePK:64257043~piPK:437376~theSitePK:4607,00.html (accessed August 21, 2007).

Dickinson, Jen, and Adrian J. Bailey. "(Re)Membering Diaspora: Uneven Geographies of Indian Dual Citizenship." *Political Geography* 26 (2007): 757–74.

"The Digital Age: Reaching Out." *Economist,* January 12–18, 2013.

Dodd, Nigel. *The Sociology of Money: Economics, Reason and Contemporary Society.* Cambridge, UK: Polity Press, 1994.

Donovan, Kevin. "Mobile Money for Financial Inclusion." In *Information and Communications for Development 2012: Maximizing Mobile,* ed. World Bank Group, 61–73. Washington, DC: World Bank and Infodev, 2012.

———. "What's Next for Mobile Money?" World Bank. https://blogs.worldbank.org/psd/team/kevin-donovan (accessed September 24, 2012).

Dutton, William H., ed. *Information and Communication Technologies: Visions and Realities.* Oxford: Oxford University Press, 1996.

Eagleton, Catherine, and Jonathan Williams. *Money: A History.* London: British Museum Press, 2007.

Ewen, E. *Immigrant Women in the Land of Dollars: Life and Culture on the Lower East Side, 1890–1925.* New York: Monthly Review Press, 1985.

Federal Deposit Insurance Corporation. *2011 FDIC National Survey of Unbanked and Underbanked Households: Executive Summary.* Federal Deposit Insurance Corporation, 2012.

Ferguson, Niall. *The Ascent of Money: A Financial History of the World.* Camberwell, Victoria: Allen Lane, 2008.

Financial Sector Deepening (FSD) Kenya. *Financial Access in Kenya: Results of the 2005 National Survey.* 2007.

Finch, Janet. "Displaying Families." *Sociology* 41, no. 1 (2007): 65–81.

"FM Says Some New Bank Licences Expected before March 2014." *The Hindu,* June 6, 2013.

Foner, Nancy. "Transnationalism Then and Now: New York Immigrants Today and at the Turn of the Twentieth Century." In *Migration, Transnationalization, and Race in a Changing New York*, ed. Héctor R. Cordero-Guzmán, Robert C. Smith, and Ramón Grosfoguel, 35–57. Philadelphia: Temple University Press, 2001.

"For Text-Savvy Filipinos, Mobile Banking Is a Crucial Bridge." *Frontlines*, September/October 2012. http://transition.usaid.gov/press/frontlines/fl_sep12/FL_sep12_PHILIP PINES.html.

Freeman, Carla. "Is Local: Global as Feminine: Masculine? Rethinking the Gender of Globalization." *Signs* 26, no. 4 (2001): 1007–37.

Gabbarot, M., and C. Clarke. "Social Capital, Migration and Development in the Valles Centrales of Oaxaca, Mexico: Non-Migrants and Communities of Origin Matter." *Bulletin of Latin American Research* 29, no. 2 (2010): 187–207.

Gamburd, Michele Ruth. "Absent Women and Their Extended Families." In *Negotiation and Social Space: A Gendered Analysis of Changing Kin and Security Networks in South Asia and Sub-Saharan Africa*, ed. Carla Risseeuw and Kamala Ganesh, 276–91. Walnut Creek, CA: AltaMira Press, 1998.

Garcia-Rey, Nilsa. "Ithaca Hours: An Interview with Paul Glover." *Reality Sandwich*, March 22, 2011.

Geertz, Clifford. *Works and Lives: The Anthropologist as Author*. Stanford, CA: Stanford University Press, 1988.

George, Sheba Mariam. *When Women Come First: Gender and Class in Transnational Migration*. Berkeley: University of California Press, 2005.

Gerber, Paula. "Making Indigenous Australians 'Disappear': Problems Arising from Our Birth Registration Systems." *Alternative Law Journal* 34, no. 3 (2009): 158–67.

Ghosh, Bimal. *Migrants' Remittances and Development: Myths, Rhetoric, and Realities*. Geneva: International Organization for Migration (IOM), 2006.

Ghosh, Jayati. "Migration and Gender Empowerment: Recent Trends and Emerging Issues." In *Human Development Research Paper*. United Nations Development Programme, 2009.

Giddens, Anthony. *The Transformation of Intimacy: Sexuality, Love and Eroticism in Modern Societies*. Stanford, CA: Stanford University Press, 1992.

Gillwald, Alison, Anne Milek, and Christoph Stork. *Gender Assessment of ICT Access and Usage in Africa*. Research ICTafrica.net, 2010.

Global Development Finance. "Global Development Finance: Harnessing Cyclical Gains for Development 2004." World Bank. http://siteresources.worldbank.org/GDFINT2004/Home/20177154/GDF_2004%20pdf.pdf (accessed August 25, 2004).

Godinho, Vinita, and Supriya Singh. "Indigenous Money Is a 'Special Money.'" 2012. Unpublished work.

Goldring, Luin. "Family and Collective Remittances to Mexico: A Multi-Dimensional Typology." *Development and Change* 35, no. 4 (2004): 799–840.

Gomes, Lee. "Money for the Masses." *The Future of Money*. MIT Technology Review, 2012. http://www.technologyreview.com/news/427333/money-for-the-masses.

Graham, Judy F., Edward J. Stendardi Jr., Joan K. Myers, and Mark J. Graham. "Gender Differences in Investment Strategies: An Information Processing Perspective." *International Journal of Bank Marketing* 20, no. 1 (2002): 17–26.

GSMA. "Mobile Money in the Philippines—The Market, the Models and Regulation." http://www.gsma.com/mobilefordevelopment/mobile-money-in-the-philippines-the-market-the-models-and-regulation (accessed August 15, 2013).

——. *Striving and Surviving: Exploring the Lives of Women at the Base of the Pyramid.* 2012.

Guyer, Jane I. *Marginal Gains: Monetary Transactions in Atlantic Africa.* 2004.

——. "Soft Currencies, Cash Economies, New Monies: Past and Present." *Proceedings of the National Academy of Sciences of the United States of America* 109, no. 7 (2012): 2214–21.

Hagger, Andrew. "Money Insider: Peer-to-Peer Lending Gathers Pace as Faith in Banks Falters." *The Independent,* September 22, 2012. http://www.independent.co.uk/money/spend-save/money-insider-peertopeer-lending-gathers-pace-as-faith-in-banks-falters-8163841.html.

Han, Clara. *Life in Debt: Times of Care and Violence in Neoliberal Chile.* Berkeley: University of California Press, 2012. http://RMIT.eblib.com.au/patron/FullRecord.aspx?p=896312.

Hansen, Annegrethe, and Christian Clausen. "Social Shaping Perspectives in Danish Technology Assessment." *Technology in Society* 25, no. 3 (2003): 431–51.

Hart, Keith. "Money Is Always Personal and Impersonal." *Anthropology Today* 23, no. 5 (October 2007): 12–16.

Helweg, Arthur W. "Emigrant Remittances: Their Nature and Impact on a Punjabi Village." *New Community* 10, no. 3 (1983): 435–43.

Hidayati, Siti. "Cash-in and Cash-out Agents for Mobile Money in Indonesia." In *The Fletcher School: Leadership Program for Financial Inclusion—Policy Memoranda.* Fletcher School, Tufts University, 2011.

"High-Tech Cleaning in Japan." http://factsanddetails.com/japan.php?itemid=666&catid=19&subcatid=126#03 (accessed November 12, 2012).

Holton, Robert J. *Global Finance.* New York: Routledge, 2012.

——. *Globalization and the Nation-State.* New York: St. Martin's, 1998.

——. *Making Globalization.* New York: Palgrave Macmillan, 2005.

Holton, Sandra Stanley. *Quaker Women: Personal Life, Memory and Radicalism in the Lives of Women Friends, 1780–1930.* Abingdon, UK: Routledge, 2007.

Horst, Heather A. "The Blessings and Burdens of Communication: Cell Phones in Jamaican Transnational Social Fields." *Global Networks* 6, no. 2 (2006): 143–59.

Huffman, Kirk. "Making Real Money in the Solomons." *Explore* 32, no. 2 (2010): 2–4.

——. "Pigs, Prestige and Copyright in the Western Pacific." *Explore* 29, no. 6 (2007): 22–25.

"ILO Declaration on Social Justice for a Fair Globalization." http://www.ilo.org/public/english/bureau/dgo/download/dg_announce_en.pdf (accessed November 4, 2012).

International Finance Corporation (IFC). "Remittance Prices Worldwide: Making Markets More Transparent." http://remittanceprices.worldbank.org (accessed August 24, 2011).

International Labour Office. *Bolsa Família in Brazil: Context, Concept and Impacts.* Geneva: International Labour Office, Social Security Department, 2009.

International Organization for Migration. "Facts and Figures." http://www.iom.int/cms/en/sites/iom/home/about-migration/facts--figures-1.html (accessed January 20, 2013).

"Is It a Phone, Is It a Bank? Mobile Banking." *Economist,* March 30, 2013.

Islamic Microfinance: An Emerging Market Niche. CGAP, 2008.

Jack, William, and Tavneet Suri. "Mobile Money: The Economics of M-PESA." NBER Working Paper No. 16721, 2011.

Jackson, Benjamin. "First Look: Simple Reimagines Banking." http://thenextweb.com/insider/2012/08/01/first-look-simple-reimagines-banking (accessed November 26, 2012).

Javorcik, Beata S., Çağlar Özden, Mariana Spatareanu, and Cristina Neagu. "Migrant Networks and Foreign Direct Investment." *Journal of Development Economics* 94, no. 2 (2011): 231–41.

Johnson, Paula Doherty. *Diaspora Philanthropy: Influences, Initiatives, and Issues.* Philanthropic Initiative Inc. and Global Equity Initiative, Harvard University, 2007.

Johnson, Susan. "Gender Norms in Financial Markets: Evidence from Kenya." *World Development* 32, no. 8 (2004): 1355–74.

———. "The Search for Inclusion in Kenya's Financial Landscape: The Rift Revealed." Centre for Development Studies. http://www.fsdkenya.org/pdf_documents/12-03-29_Full_FinLandcapes_report.pdf (accessed August 19, 2012).

Johnston, Hugh. "The Sikhs of British Columbia and Their Philanthropy in Punjab." In *Sikh Diaspora Philanthropy in Punjab: Global Giving for Local Good*, ed. Verne A. Dusenbery and Darshan S. Tatla, 169–83. New Delhi: Oxford University Press, 2009.

Johnston, Hugh J. M. *Jewels of the Qila: The Remarkable Story of an Indo-Canadian Family.* Vancouver: University of British Columbia Press, 2011.

Kahneman, Daniel. *Thinking, Fast and Slow.* New York: Farrar, Straus & Giroux, 2011.

Karnani, Aneel G. "Mirage at the Bottom of the Pyramid." In William Davidson Institute Working Paper No. 835. University of Michigan, 2006.

Kendall, Jake, and Bill Maurer. "Tips for 2012: Understanding Payment Behavior of African Households—a Vast and Untapped Market." http://pymnts.com/commentary/Tips-for-2012-Understanding-Payment-Behavior-of-African-Households-A-Vast-and-Untapped-Market (accessed September 8, 2012).

Khaled, Mohammed. "Why Has Islamic Microfinance Not Reached Scale Yet?" http://www.cgap.org/blog/why-has-islamic-microfinance-not-reached-scale-yet (accessed 2012).

Khera, Reetika. "Long Road Ahead for Cash Transfers." *Financial Express*, December 4, 2012.

King, Brett. *Bank 2.0: How Customer Behavior and Technology Will Change the Future of Financial Services.* Singapore: Marshall Cavendish Business, 2010.

———. "Bye-bye Checking and Current Account." http://www.finextra.com/community/fullblog.aspx?blogid=6586 (accessed 2012).

King, Douglas A. "The Debate on Credit Card Surcharges." Retail Payments Risk Forum. http://portalsandrails.frbatlanta.org/2012/07/debate-on-credit-card-surcharges.html (accessed January 17, 2013).

Kishwar, Madhu. "Dowry and Inheritance Rights." In *Dowry & Inheritance*, ed. Srimati Basu, 298–303. New Delhi: Women Unlimited, 2005.

Kitony, Sam, and Leo Mutuku. *An Exploratory Study on Kenyan Consumer Ordering Habits: Final Report.* 2012.

Klebanow, Sheila. "Power, Gender and Money." In *Money and Mind*, ed. Sheila Klebanow and Eugene L. Lowenkopf, 51–59. New York: Plenum, 1991.

Kose, M. A., E. Prasad, K. Rogoff, and S. J. Wei. "Financial Globalization: A Reappraisal." *IMF Staff Papers* 56, no. 1 (2009): 8–62.

Kuptsch, Christiane, and Philip Martin. "Migration and Development: Remittances and Cooperation with the Diaspora." International Institute for Labour Studies. http://www.gtz.de/migration-and-development/download/dokumentation-plenum2.pdf (accessed August 25, 2004).

Kurien, Prema A. *Kaleidoscopic Ethnicity: International Migration and the Reconstruction of Community Identities in India*. New Delhi: Oxford University Press, 2002.

Lagan, Bernard. "The Smartest Girls in the Room." *Global Mail*, December 3, 2012. http://www.theglobalmail.org/feature/the-smartest-girls-in-the-room/503.

Landrum, Nancy E. "Advancing the 'Base of the Pyramid' Debate." *Strategic Management Review* 1, no. 1 (2007).

Lawton, Jenny. "What Is Sexually Transmitted Debt?" In *Women and Credit: A Forum on Sexually Transmitted Debt*, ed. R. Meikle, 7–10. Melbourne: Ministry of Consumer Affairs, 1991.

Leishman, Paul. "Globe Announces Big Change to GCash Agent Network." http://www.gsma.com/mobilefordevelopment/globe-announces-big-change-to-gcash-agent-network (accessed October 4, 2012).

Leonard, Karen Isaksen. *Locating Home: India's Hyderabadis Abroad*. Stanford, CA: Stanford University Press, 2007.

———. *Making Ethnic Choices: California's Punjabi Mexican Americans*. Philadelphia: Temple University Press, 1992.

Levitin, A. "Priceless? The Economic Costs of Credit Card Merchant Restraints." *UCLA Law Review* 55 (2008): 1321–1406.

Levitt, Peggy. "Transnational Migration: Taking Stock and Future Directions." *Global Networks* 1, no. 3 (2001): 195–216.

Light, Joe. "Would You Lend Money to These People?" *Wall Street Journal*, April 13, 2012. http://online.wsj.com/article/SB10001424052702304587704577333801201736034.html.

Lindley, Anna. "The Early-Morning Phonecall: Remittances from a Refugee Diaspora Perspective." *Journal of Ethnic and Migration Studies* 35, no. 8 (2009): 1315–34.

LiPuma, Edward, and Benjamin Lee. *Financial Derivatives and the Globalization of Risk*. Durham, NC: Duke University Press, 2004.

Livingstone, Sonia. "New Media, New Audiences?" *New Media & Society* 1, no. 1 (1999): 59–66.

———. *Young People and New Media*. London: Sage, 2002.

Ludw, Sean. "Bank of America Who? Square Now Processing $10b in Payments Annually." *Venture Beat*. http://venturebeat.com/company/square (accessed November 27, 2012).

Lukes, S. *Power: A Radical View*. London: Macmillan, 1974.

"M-Banking Resilient to Tax Increase." *BMI Middle East and Africa Telecommunications Insights*, April 1, 2013.

MacKenzie, Donald, and Judy Wajcman, eds. *The Social Shaping of Technology*. Buckingham: Open University Press, 1999.

Makanjee, Maya. "Access to Financial Services in Africa: Gender Analysis." Paper presented at the African Women's Economic Summit, Nairobi, March 19, 2010.

Manji, Ambreena. "Eliminating Poverty? 'Financial Inclusion,' Access to Land, and Gender Equality in International Development." *Modern Law Review* 73, no. 6 (2010): 985–1025.

Markowitz, Eric. "30 under 30: America's Coolest Young Entrepreneurs 2012." *Inc.*, 2012.

Marx, K. "Economic and Philosophical Manuscripts." In *Karl Marx: Early Texts*, ed. D. McLellan, 130–83. Oxford: Basil Blackwell, 1971.

Mas, Ignacio. "Don't Touch Our M-PESA!" http://www.ignaciomas.com/announcements/donttouchourm-pesa (accessed September 24, 2012).

———. "Making Mobile Money Daily Relevant." http://papers.ssrn.com/sol3/papers.cfm?abstract_id=2018807 (accessed September 13, 2012).

Mas, Ignacio, and Tonny Omwansa. "NexThought Monday—A Close Look at Safaricom's M-Shwari: Mobile, Yes, but How 'Cool' Is It for Customers?" Last modified December 10, 2012. http://www.nextbillion.net/blogpost.aspx?blogid=3050.

Maurer, Bill. "Incalculable Payments: Money, Scale, and the South African Offshore Grey Money Amnesty." *African Studies Review* 50, no. 2 (2007): 125–38.

———. "Mobile Money: Communication, Consumption and Change in the Payments Space." *Journal of Development Studies* 48, no. 5 (2012): 589–604.

———. "Money Nutters." *Economic Sociology: The European Electronic Newsletter* 12, no. 3 (2011): 5–11.

———. *Mutual Life, Limited: Islamic Banking, Alternative Currencies, Lateral Reason.* Princeton, NJ: Princeton University Press, 2005.

———. "Note from IMTFI: Mobile Money Regulation—a Story Arc of Best Practices and Emerging Realizations." Microlinks. http://microlinks.kdid.org/learning-marketplace/notes/note-imtfi-mobile-money-regulation-story-arc-best-practices-and-emerging (September 29, 2012).

———. "Payment: Forms and Functions of Value Transfer in Contemporary Society." *Cambridge Anthropology* 30, no. 2 (2012): 15–35.

McAuslan, Patrick. "Personal Reflections on Drafting Laws to Improve Women's Access to Land: Is There a Magic Wand?" *Journal of Eastern African Studies* 4, no. 1 (2010): 114–30.

McGirt, Ellen. "For Making Magic out of the Mercantile." *Fast Company.* http://www.fastcompany.com/most-innovative-companies/2012/square (accessed November 27, 2012).

McKenzie, Sean, and Cecilia Menjívar. "The Meanings of Migration, Remittances and Gifts: Views of Honduran Women Who Stay." *Global Networks* 11, no. 1 (2010): 63–81.

Menon, Aditya. "UPA to Milk Cash Cow for Elections: Game Changing Direct Cash Transfer Scheme for Poor to Boost Prospects in Next Elections." *Mail Online*, November 26, 2012.

"Microfinance in India: Road to Redemption." *Economist*, January 12, 2013.

Miller, Claire Cain. "Starbucks and Square to Team Up." *New York Times*, August 8, 2012. http://www.nytimes.com/2012/08/08/technology/starbucks-and-square-to-team-up.html?_r=0.

Ministry of Commerce, People's Republic of China. "China Bars Use of Virtual Money for Trading in Real Goods." http://english.mofcom.gov.cn/aarticle/newsrelease/commonnews/200906/20090606364208.html (accessed November 26, 2012).

Misra, Seema, and Enakshi Ganguly Thukral. "A Study of Two Villages in Bihar." In *Dowry & Inheritance*, ed. Srimati Basu, 138–50. New Delhi: Women Unlimited, 2005.

Moghadam, V. M. "Gender and Globalization: Representations, Realities, Resistances." SHS/GED Seminar Series. http://www.unesco.org/new/fileadmin/MULTIMEDIA/HQ/SHS/pdf/Gender-Globalization.pdf (accessed November 4, 2012).

Mohapatra, Sanket, Dilip Ratha, and Ani Silwa. "Migration and Development Brief 13." World Bank. http://siteresources.worldbank.org/INTPROSPECTS/Resources/334934-1110315015165/MigrationAndDevelopmentBrief13.pdf (accessed May 23, 2011).

Morawczynski, Olga. "Examining the Usage and Impact of Transformational M-Banking in Kenya." In *Internationalization, Design and Global Development*, ed. N. Aykin, 495–504. Berlin: Springer-Verlag, 2009.

Mozur, Paul, and Juro Osawa. "Internet Breadth Helps Buoy Tencent." *Wall Street Journal*, August 14, 2012. http://online.wsj.com/article/SB1000087239639044477240457758880418418326.html.

Mugo, Matu. "Regulation of Banking and Payment Agents in Kenya." In *The Fletcher School: Leadership Program for Financial Inclusion—Policy Memoranda*, 47–52. Fletcher School, Tufts University, 2011.

Muliaina, Tolu. "Mismatched Perceptions: Views on Remittance Obligations among Remittance Senders and Recipients." In *Remittances, Microfinance and Development: Building the Links*, ed. Judith Shaw, 26–32. Brisbane: Foundation for Development Co-operation, 2006.

Nandhi, Mani A. *Effects of Mobile Banking on the Savings Practices of Low Income Users—The Indian Experience*. Irvine, CA: Institute for Money, Technology and Financial Inclusion, 2012.

Nduati, Stephen Mwaura. "Challenges and Opportunities to Promote Financial Inclusion." Paper presented at the International Forum for Central Banks: Payment Systems and Financial Inclusion, Quito, Ecuador, August 2, 2012.

———. "Enhancing Financial Inclusion through Technological Innovations." In *The Fletcher School: Leadership Program for Financial Inclusion—Policy Memoranda*. Fletcher School, Tufts University, 2011.

Nussbaum, Martha C. *Creating Capabilities: The Human Development Approach*. Cambridge, MA: Belknap Press of Harvard University Press, 2011.

Nyamu-Musembi, Celestine. "Breathing Life into Dead Theories about Property Rights: De Soto and Land Relations in Rural Africa." In IDS Working Paper 272. Brighton: Institute of Development Studies, 2006.

Oberai, A. S., and H. K. Manmohan Singh. "Migration, Remittances and Rural Development: Findings of a Case Study in the Indian Punjab." *International Labour Review* 119, no. 2 (1980): 229–41.

Omwansa, Tonny K., and Nicholas P. Sullivan. *Money, Real Quick: The Story of M-PESA*. London: Guardian Books, 2012.

Orozco, Manuel. "Transnationalism and Development: Trends and Opportunities in: Latin America." In *Remittances: Development Impact and Future Prospects*, ed. S. M. Maimbo and Dilip Ratha, 308–28. Washington, DC: World Bank, 2005.

Ossandón, José. "The Economy of the Quota: The Financial Ecologies and Commercial Circuits of Retail Credit Cards in Santiago, Chile." Institute for Money, Technology and Financial Inclusion. http://blog.imtfi.uci.edu/2012/11/the-economy-of-quota-financial.html (accessed April 1, 2013).

Ostry, Jonathan D., Atish R. Ghosh, Karl Habermeier, Marcos Chamon, Mahvash S. Qureshi, and Dennis B. S. Reinhardt. "Capital Inflows: The Role of Controls." In *IMF Staff Position Note*. International Monetary Fund, 2010.

Pahl, Jan. *Money and Marriage*. London: Macmillan, 1989.

Panda, Pradeep, and Bina Agarwal. "Marital Violence, Human Development and Women's Property Status in India." *World Development* 33, no. 5 (2005): 823–50.

Papanek, H., and L. Schwede. "Women Are Good with Money: Earning and Managing in an Indonesian City." In *A Home Divided: Women and Income in the Third World*, ed. D. Dwyer and J. Bruce, 71–98. Stanford, CA: Stanford University Press, 1988.

Parreñas, Rhacel Salazar. *Children of Global Migration: Transnational Families and Gendered Woes*. Stanford, CA: Stanford University Press, 2005.

Passas, Nikos. "Formalizing the Informal? Problems in the National and International Regulation of Hawala." In *Regulatory Frameworks for Hawala and Other Remittance Systems*, 7–16. Washington, DC: International Monetary Fund, Monetary and Financial Systems Department, 2005.

PayPal. "Get the Latest on Paypal." https://www.paypal-media.com/about (accessed November 26, 2012).

Pearce, Rohan. "Money Laundering Using Virtual Worlds, Bitcoin on Watchdog's Radar." *Computerworld*, August 15, 2012.

Pessar, Patricia R. "Engendering Migration Studies." *American Behavioral Scientist* 42, no. 4 (1999): 577–600.

Pickens, Mark. "Window on the Unbanked: Mobile Money in the Philippines." https://openknowledge.worldbank.org/bitstream/handle/10986/9488/567240BRI0CGAP1le1Money1Philippines.pdf?sequence=1 (accessed October 4, 2012).

"PM Initiates Direct Cash Transfer Scheme." *Hindustan Times*, November 26, 2012.

Porteous, David. *The Enabling Environment for Mobile Banking in Africa*. 2006. http://www.bankablefrontier.com/assets/ee.mobil.banking.report.v3.1.pdf.

Portes, Alejandro, and Rubén G. Rumbaut. *Immigrant America: A Portrait*. Berkeley: University of California Press, 2006.

Prahalad, C. K. *The Fortune at the Bottom of the Pyramid*. Delhi: Pearson Education (Singapore), 2005.

PTI. "India Not after NRIs' Money, Montek Tells Diaspora." *Economic Times*, January 9, 2011. http://bx.businessweek.com/foreign-direct-investment/view?url=http%3A%2F%2Fc.moreover.com%2Fclick%2Fhere.pl%3Fr3915209860%26f%3D9791.

Purewal, Navtej K. "Gender, Seva, and Social Institutions: A Case Study of the Bebe Nanaki Gurdwara and Charitable Trust, Birmingham, UK." In *Sikh Diaspora Philanthropy in Punjab: Global Giving for Local Good*, ed. Verne A. Dusenbery and Darshan S. Tatla, 205–15. New Delhi: Oxford University Press, 2009.

Quisumbing, A., and S. McNiven. "Moving Forward, Looking Back: The Impact of Migration and Remittances on Assets, Consumption, and Credit Constraints in the Rural Philippines." *Journal of Development Studies* 46, no. 1 (2010): 91–113.

Rabow, Jerome, Michelle Charness, Arlene E. Aguilar, and Jeanne Toomajian. "Women and Money: Cultural Contrasts." In *Sociological Studies of Child Development*, ed. Patricia A. Adler and Peter Adler, 191–219. Greenwich, CT: JAI Press, 1992.

Rajan, Raghuram. *Fault Lines: How Hidden Fractures Still Threaten the World Economy*. Princeton, NJ: Princeton University Press, 2010.

Ratha, Dilip. "Workers' Remittances: An Important and Stable Source of External Development Finance." In *Global Development Finance 2003*. Washington, DC: World Bank, 2003.

Ratha, Dilip, Gemechu Ayana Aga, and Ani Silwal. "Remittances to Developing Countries Will Surpass $400 Billion in 2012." In *Migration and Development Brief*. Washington, DC: Migration and Remittances Unit, Development Prospects Group, World Bank, 2012.

Ratha, Dilip, and Sanket Mohapatra. "Preliminary Estimates of Diaspora Savings." World Bank. http://siteresources.worldbank.org/TOPICS/Resources/214970-1288877981391/MigrationAndDevelopmentBrief14_DiasporaSavings.pdf (accessed February 5, 2011).

Ratha, Dilip, Sanket Mohapatra, and Ani Silwal. "Migration and Development Brief 12: Outlook for Remittance Flows 2010–11." World Bank. http://siteresources.worldbank.org/INTPROSPECTS/Resources/334934-1110315015165/MigrationAndDevelopmentBrief12.pdf (accessed May 23, 2011).

Ratha, Dilip, and Ani Silwal. "Migration and Development Brief 18: Remittance Flows in 2011—an Update." World Bank. http://siteresources.worldbank.org/INTPROSPECTS/Resources/334934-1110315015165/MigrationandDevelopmentBrief18.pdf (accessed June 14, 2013).

Ravi, Anjana, and Eric Tyler. *Savings for the Poor in Kenya*. New America Foundation, 2012.

"Remittance Corridors: New Rivers of Gold." *Economist*, April 28–May 4, 2012, 64–64.

Reskin, Barbara F., and Patricia A. Roos. *Job Queues, Gender Queues: Explaining Women's Inroads into Male Occupations*. Philadelphia: Temple University Press, 1990.

Roth, Daniel. "The Future of Money: It's Flexible, Frictionless and (Almost) Free." *Wired*, February 22, 2010.

Rumbaut, Rubén G. "Severed or Sustained Attachments? Language, Identity, and Imagined Communities in the Post-Immigrant Generation." In *The Changing Face of Home: The Transnational Lives of the Second Generation*, ed. Peggy Levitt and Mary C. Waters, 43–95. New York: Sage, 2002.

Samarajiva, Rohan. "Mobile at the Bottom of the Pyramid: Informing Policy from the Demand Side." Special issue, *Mobile Telephony* 7, no. 3 (2011): iii–vii.

Sambasivan, Nithya, Ed Cutrell, Kentaro Toyama, and Bonnie Nardi, "Intermediated Technology Use in Developing Communities." Paper presented at the CHI 2010: HCI and the Developing World, Atlanta, Georgia, April 10–15, 2010.

Sanyal, Paromita. "From Credit to Collective Action: The Role of Microfinance in Promoting Women's Social Capital and Normative Influence." *American Sociological Review* 74 (August 2009): 529–50.

Sassen, Saskia. "The Embeddedness of Electronic Markets: The Case of Global Capital Markets." In *The Sociology of Financial Markets*, ed. Karin Knorr Cetina and Alex Preda, 17–37. Oxford: Oxford University Press, 2005.

———. *A Sociology of Globalization*. New York: Norton, 2007.

Sathye, Milind. "Could Peer-to-Peer Lending Challenge Our Banks?" *The Conversation*, June 28, 2012.

Sawhney, H., and K. Jayakar, "Universal Service: Migration of Metaphors." Paper presented at the Telecommunications Policy Research Conference, Solomons Island, Maryland, October 5–7, 1996.

Schrage, Michael. "The Debriefing: John Seely Brown." *Wired*. http://www.wired.com/wired/archive/8.08/brown.html?pg=2&topic=&topic_set= (accessed October 6, 2005).

Schwartz, Carl, Justin Fabo, Owen Bailey, and Louise Carter. "Payment Costs in Australia." Paper presented at the Payments System Review Conference, Sydney, Australia, November 29, 2007.

Sen, Amartya. *Development as Freedom*. Oxford: Oxford University Press, 1999.

———. "Ruinous Policy Stymies Europe's Grand Vision." *The Age*, July 5, 2012. http://www
.theage.com.au/business/ruinous-policy-stymies-europes-grand-vision-20120704-21hi5
.html#ixzz1zoZy4Sk8.

Senior, Kate, David Perkins, and John Bern. "Variation in Material Wellbeing in a Welfare
Based Economy." Wollongong: South East Arnhem Land Collaborative Research Project, University of Wollongong, 2002.

Sheng, Andrew. *From Asian to Global Financial Crisis: An Asian Regulator's View of Unfettered Finance in the 1990s and 2000s*. Cambridge: Cambridge University Press, 2009.

Shetty, Mayur. "Soon, Dial *99# to Access Your Bank Account." *Economic Times*, November 27, 2012.

Shiller, Robert J. *The Subprime Solution: How Today's Financial Crisis Happened, and What
to Do about It*. Princeton, NJ: Princeton University Press, 2008.

Silverstone, Roger, and Leslie Haddon. "Design and Domestication of Information and
Communication Technologies: Technical Change and Everyday Life." In *Communica-
tion by Design: The Politics of Information and Communication Technologies*, ed. Robin
Mansell and Roger Silverstone, 44–74. Oxford: Oxford University Press, 1996.

Simmel, Georg. *The Philosophy of Money*. London: Routledge & Kegan Paul, 1990.

Singh, Supriya. "Balancing Separateness and Jointness of Money in Relationships: The
Design of Bank Accounts in Australia and India." In *Human Computer Interaction International*, 505–14. San Diego, CA, 2009.

———. *Bank Negara Malaysia: The First 25 Years, 1959–1984*. Kuala Lumpur: Bank Negara
Malaysia, 1984.

———. *The Bankers: Australia's Leading Bankers Talk about Banking Today*. North Sydney:
Allen & Unwin Australia, 1991.

———. "The Digital Packaging of Electronic Money." In *Usability and Internationalization:
Global and Local User Interfaces*, ed. Nuray Aykin, 469–75. Berlin: Springer, 2007.

———. "Electronic Money: Understanding Its Use to Increase the Effectiveness of Policy."
Telecommunications Policy 23, no. 10–11 (1999): 753–73.

———. "Marriage, Money and Information: Australian Consumers' Use of Banks." PhD
dissertation, La Trobe, 1994.

———. *Marriage Money: The Social Shaping of Money in Marriage and Banking*. St. Leonards,
NSW: Allen & Unwin, 1997.

———. *On the Sulu Sea*. Kuala Lumpur: Angsana Publications, 1984.

———. "Secure Shared Passwords: The Social and Cultural Centered Design of Banking."
Journal of Financial Transformation 23(2008): 110–14.

———. "Studying the User: A Matter of Perspective." *Media International Australia* 98
(February 2001): 113–27.

———. "Transnational Community and Money in the Indian Diaspora in Melbourne."
Paper presented at the City, Community and Globalisation Roundtable, Melbourne,
Australia, June 9–10, 2011.

———. *The Use of Electronic Money in the Home*. Melbourne: Centre for International Research on Communication and Information Technologies, 1996.

Singh, Supriya, and Mala Bhandari. "Money Management and Control in the Indian Joint
Family across Generations." *Sociological Review* 60, no. 1 (2012): 46–67.

Singh, Supriya, and Anuja Cabraal. "Women, Money and the Bank." Paper presented at the Financial Literacy, Banking and Identity Conference, Melbourne, Australia, October 25–26, 2006.

Singh, Supriya, Anuja Cabraal, Catherine Demosthenous, Gunela Astbrink, and Michele Furlong. "Password Sharing: Implications for Security Design Based on Social Practice." Paper presented at the SIGCHI Conference on Human Factors in Computing Systems CHI '07, San Jose, California, 2007.

Singh, Supriya, Anuja Cabraal, and Shanthi Robertson. "Remittances as a Currency of Care: A Focus on 'Twice Migrants' among the Indian Diaspora in Australia." *Journal of Comparative Family Studies* 41, no. 2 (2010): 245–63.

Singh, Supriya, and Liliya Gatina. "Migrant Money: Two-Way Flows between Australia and India." Unpublished, RMIT University, 2012.

Singh, Supriya, and Clive Morley. "Gender and Financial Accounts in Marriage." *Journal of Sociology* 47, no. 1 (2011): 3–16.

Singh, Supriya, and Yaso Nadarajah. "School Fees, Beer and 'Meri': Gender, Cash and the Mobile in the Morobe Province of Papua New Guinea." Institute for Money, Technology and Financial Inclusion. http://www.imtfi.uci.edu/files/imtfi/blog_working_papers/working_paper_singh.pdf (accessed September 20, 2012).

Singh, Supriya, Shanthi Robertson, and Anuja Cabraal. "Transnational Family Money: Remittances, Gifts and Inheritance." *Journal of Intercultural Studies* 33, no. 5 (2012): 475–92.

Smith, Aaron, Janna Anderson, and Lee Rainie. "The Future of Money in a Mobile Age." In *Imagining the Internet*. Pew Research Center, 2012.

Steger, Manfred B. *Globalization: A Very Short Introduction*. Oxford: Oxford University Press, 2009.

———. *The Rise of the Global Imaginary: Political Ideologies from the French Revolution to the Global War on Terror*. Oxford: Oxford University Press, 2008.

Steger, Manfred B., and Ravi K. Roy. *Neoliberalism: A Very Short Introduction*. Oxford: Oxford University Press, 2010.

Stephens, Maria C. "Promoting Responsible Financial Inclusion: A Risk-Based Approach to Supporting Mobile Financial Services Expansion." *Banking and Finance Law Review* 27, no. 2 (2012): 329–43.

Stiglitz, Joseph. *Freefall: Free Markets and the Sinking of the Global Economy*. London: Penguin, 2010.

Summers, A. *Damned Whores and God's Police*. Ringwood, Victoria: Penguin, 1994.

Taiapa, Julia TeUrikore Turupa. *"Ta Te Whanau Ohanga": The Economics of the Whanau— the Maori Component of the Intra Family Income Study*. Palmerston North: Department of Maori Studies, Massey University, 1994.

Taylor, Erin B., Espelencia Baptiste, and Heather A. Horst. *Mobile Money in Haiti: Potentials and Challenges*. Institute for Money, Technology and Financial Inclusion (IMTFI), 2011.

Tett, Gillian. *Fool's Gold: How the Bold Dream of a Small Tribe at J. P. Morgan Was Corrupted by Wall Street Greed and Unleashed a Catastrophe*. New York: Free Press, 2009.

Thomas, Owen. "Simple Is Ramping up Its Revolution in Banking—Square's Cofounder Just Got His Card." *Business Insider*, June 16, 2012.

"38 Cr Aadhaar Numbers Issued So Far; 60 Cr by 2014: Nilekani." Nextbigwhat.com, April 30, 2013.

Tsai, Kellee S. "Friends, Family or Foreigners? The Political Economy of Diasporic FDI and Remittances in China and India." *China Report* 46, no. 4 (2010): 387–429.

Vogler, Carolyn. "Money in the Household: Some Underlying Issues of Power." *Sociological Review* 46, no. 4 (1998): 687–713.

Vogler, Carolyn, Clare Lyonette, and Richard D. Wiggins. "Money, Power and Spending Decisions in Intimate Relationships." *Sociological Review* 56, no. 1 (2008): 117–43.

Vogler, Carolyn, and Jan Pahl. "Social and Economic Change and the Organisation of Money within Marriage." *Work, Employment and Society* 7, no. 1 (1993): 71–95.

Wajcman, Judy. "Addressing Technological Change: The Challenge to Social Theory." *Current Sociology* 50, no. 3 (2002): 347–63.

Wallace, Benjamin. "The Rise and Fall of Bitcoin." *Wired*, November 23, 2011.

Wallman, Sandra. "Introduction: Contemporary Futures." In *Contemporary Futures: Perspectives from Social Anthropology*, ed. Sandra Wallman, 1–20. London: Routledge, 1992.

Wang, Yang, and Scott D. Mainwaring. "'Human-Currency Interaction': Learning from Virtual Currency Use in China." Paper presented at the CHI 2008, Florence, Italy, April 5–8, 2008.

Waring, M. *Counting for Nothing: What Men Value and What Women Are Worth.* Wellington, NZ: Allen & Unwin and Port Nicholson Press, 1988.

Weber, Max. *Economy and Society.* Berkeley: University of California Press, 1978.

———. *The Theory of Social and Economic Organization.* New York: Free Press, 1947.

"Why Is India's UID Aadhar a Big Data Challenge and Opportunity?" *Information Week India*, February 7, 2013.

Wilkis, Ariel. "Morality and Popular Finance: Moral Capital as a Kind of Guarantee." *Estudios de la Economía.* http://estudiosdelaeconomia.wordpress.com/2012/10/23/morality -and-popular-finance-moral-capital-as-a-kind-of-guarantee (accessed April 1, 2013).

Williams, Margery. *The Velveteen Rabbit or How Toys Become Real.* New York: Fremont & Green, 1995.

Wolf, Naomi. *Fire with Fire.* New York: Random House, 1993.

Wolman, David. *The End of Money: Counterfeiters, Preachers, Techies, Dreamers—and the Coming Cashless Society.* Cambridge, MA: Da Capo Press, 2012.

Wong, Madeleine. "The Gendered Politics of Remittances in Ghanaian Transnational Families." *Economic Geography* 82, no. 4 (2006): 355–81.

World Bank. *At Home and Away: Expanding Job Opportunities for Pacific Islanders through Labor Mobility.* Washington, DC: World Bank, 2006.

———. "Global Development Finance: 2004." http://siteresources.worldbank.org/ GDFINT2004/Home/20175281/gdf_appendix%20A.pdf (accessed August 6, 2004).

———. "Global Economic Prospects 2006: Economic Implications of Remittances and Migration." http://econ.worldbank.org/external/default/main?pagePK=64165259&theSitePK=4 69372&piPK=64165421&menuPK=64166322&entityID=000112742_20051114174928 (accessed August 23, 2007).

———. *Remittance Prices Worldwide: Making Markets More Transparent.* Washington, DC: World Bank, 2012.

———. *Removing Barriers to Economic Inclusion: Measuring Gender Parity in 141 Economies.* Washington, DC: World Bank, 2012.

———. *World Development Report 2012.* Washington, DC: World Bank, 2012.

Yeoh, Brenda S. A., Shirlena Huang, and Theodora Lam. "Transnationalizing the 'Asian' Family: Imaginaries, Intimacies and Strategic Intents." *Global Networks* 5, no. 4 (2005): 307–15.

Yin, Xiao-huang, and Zhiyong Lan. "Why Do They Give? Chinese American Transnational Philanthropy since the 1970s." In *Diaspora Philanthropy and Equitable Development in China and India,* ed. Peter F. Geithner, Paula D. Johnson, and Lincoln C. Chen, 79–127. Cambridge, MA: Global Equity Initiative, Asia Center, Harvard University, 2004.

Zainudeen, Ayesha, Tahani Iqbal, and Rohan Samarajiva. "Who's Got the Phone? Gender and the Use of the Telephone at the Bottom of the Pyramid." *New Media & Society* 12, no. 4 (2010): 549–66.

Zainudeen, Ayesha, and Dimuthu Ratnadiwakara. "Are the Poor Stuck in Voice? Conditions for Adoption of More-Than-Voice Mobile Services." Special issue, *Mobile Telephony* 7, no. 3 (2011): 45–59.

Zaloom, Caitlin. "Ambiguous Numbers: Trading Technologies and Interpretation in Financial Markets." *American Ethnologist* 30 (2003): 258–72.

Zelizer, Viviana A. *Economic Lives: How Culture Shapes the Economy.* Princeton, NJ: Princeton University Press, 2011.

———. "The Gender of Money." *Wall Street Journal,* January 27, 2011. http://blogs.wsj .com/ideas-market/2011/01/27/the-gender-of-money.

———. *Morals and Markets: The Development of Life Insurance in the United States.* New York: Columbia University Press, 1979.

———. *Pricing the Priceless Child: The Changing Social Value of Children.* New York: Basic Books, 1985.

———. *The Purchase of Intimacy.* Princeton, NJ: Princeton University Press, 2005.

———. *The Social Meaning of Money.* New York: Basic Books, 1994.

———. "The Social Meaning of Money: 'Special Monies.'" *American Journal of Sociology* 95, no. 2 (1989): 342–77.

INDEX

ABOUT THE AUTHOR

Supriya Singh is a professor of the sociology of communications at the Graduate School of Business and Law, RMIT University, in Melbourne, Australia. Her research in Australia, Malaysia, India, and the Pacific has focused on the sociology of money and banking; migration, remittances and the transnational family; the user-centered design of information and communication technologies; and methodological issues relating to qualitative research. Her previous books are *Marriage Money: The Social Shaping of Money in Marriage and Banking* (1997), *The Bankers: Australia's Leading Bankers Talk about Banking Today* (1991), *Bank Negara Malaysia: The First 25 Years, 1959–1984* (1984), and *On the Sulu Sea* (1984).